# Lapland

## the Bradt Travel Guide

## James Proctor

edition

I

www.bradtguides.com

Bradt Travel Guides Ltd, UK
The Globe Pequot Press Inc, USA

Prehistoric rock carvings
at Alta
page 140

North Cape
page 149

North Cape

Honningsvåg

Mehamn

Berlevåg

Båtsfjord

Havøysund

Hammerfest

Vardø

*Barents
Sea*

Tana

Vadsø

▲1067m

Lakselv

Kirkenes

Utsjoki

Bjøonevatn

Nikel

MURMANSK

Karasjok

▲
641m

Kaamanen

R   U   S   S   I   A

tedu

Inari

utokeino

Ivalo

*Kola  Peninsula*

▲
629m

▲
599m

Saariselkä
599m

Monchegorsk

Harriniva Dog
Sledding Centre
page 94

Muonio

▲
581m

Kittila

F   I   N   L   A   N   D

Kandalaksha

Sodankylä

Kolari

Pajala

▲
540m

Kuolayarvi

Salla

*Arctic Circle*

Kemijärvi

Vikajärvi

Rovaniemi

Santa Claus and
the Arctic Circle
page 106

rtorneå

Kuusamo

verkalix

Ranua

Haparanda

Tornio

Kemi

▲
432m

Taivalkoski

Simo

Voynitsa

*Gulf of
Bothnia*

Pudasjärvi

Haukipudas

# Lapland
# Don't
# miss...

### Lofoten Islands
The most dramatic scenery
in Lapland
(Arctic) page 71

### North Cape
The top of Europe,
Norwegian Lapland
(Arctic) page 149

**Gammelstad**
Nederluleå church,
Gammelstad,
Swedish Lapland
(JF) page 41

**Icehotel**
A suite in
the Icehotel,
Jukkasjärvi, Sweden
(Arctic) page 58

**Santa Claus**
Rovaniemi, Finland
(Arctic) page 106

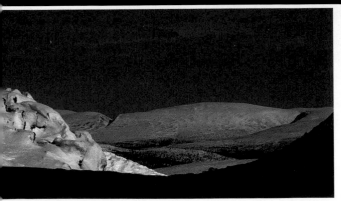

*top*   **Pine forest and bog,**
**Finnish Lapland**
(DT) page 99

*above*   **River near Rovaneimi**
(DT) page 100

*left*   **Pallastunturi, Finland**
(LM) page 111

*top* **Hiking near Rovaniemi, Finland**
(LM)

*above* **A village at the North Cape, Norway**
(LM) page 149

*right* **Traditional Sami *lávvu* (tent), North Norway**
(LM)

# AUTHOR

James Proctor first visited Lapland in 1983 on board the legendary *Lapland Arrow* train from Stockholm. The thrill of crossing the Arctic Circle proved irresistible and James has been back and forth ever since. While working as the BBC's Scandinavia correspondent, he produced reports on everything from the reindeer races at the Jokkmokk winter market to the effects of the Chernobyl nuclear disaster on the Sámi community. James now divides his time as a travel writer between the south of France and his forest retreat in Sweden. A self-appointed Nanook of the North, he has also written *Faroe Islands: the Bradt Travel Guide* and co-written *The Rough Guide to Sweden*, *The Rough Guide to Iceland* and contributed to *The Rough Guide to Scandinavia*.

## AUTHOR STORY

Ever since mistakenly studying Swedish at university (I actually signed up to do Spanish but went to the wrong lecture room), I have been fascinated by Scandinavia. It's still an area of Europe which is little known and little discovered. Yet, that is precisely its charm. In today's world there are few places where you can travel for hours through vast areas of untouched nature without seeing a soul. When I lived in Sweden during the mid-1990s, I travelled frequently to Lapland, in both winter and summer, and soon understood that this was a very special part of Scandinavia. Lapland remains, however, a vague concept to most people. In compiling this guide, it has been my aim to lift the lid off this remote Arctic region and to bring its attractions to a wider audience.

The book you have in your hands is the only English-language guide to Lapland, and also the first guide to Scandinavia that is not country-specific. Lapland is a region that spreads across three, arguably four, countries and travel here is determined more by routes than by national borders. Hence, I have organised the chapters of this guide by route, rather than country, to save you constantly flicking backwards and forwards when you cross a border to find the next town account. In *Lapland: the Bradt Travel Guide*, one town account follows another, irrespective of whether you are in Norwegian, Swedish or Finnish Lapland. When researching this guide, I clocked up a dizzying 6,000km: Lapland is truly huge and, accordingly, there's plenty to fill a holiday of two weeks or more – after all, Lapland has much more to offer than being the home of Santa Claus.

The range of landscapes you'll encounter is enormous, everything from barren treeless upland plateaux, to densely forested river valleys, to jagged mountain peaks and sea cliffs. As a Scandinavian specialist, it is with great pride that I recommend a visit to Lapland – it's a chance to experience nature in the raw like nowhere else in Europe. Listen to the whisper of the wind through the birch trees and breathe the crisp air heavy with the scent of pine, and you're well on your way to understanding what Lapland is all about.

## PUBLISHER'S FOREWORD
*Hilary Bradt*

The first Bradt travel guide was written in 1974 by George and Hilary Bradt on a river barge floating down a tributary of the Amazon. In the 1980s and '90s the focus shifted away from hiking to broader-based guides covering new destinations – usually the first to be published about these places. In the 21st century Bradt continues to publish such ground-breaking guides, as well as others to established holiday destinations, incorporating in-depth information on culture and natural history with the nuts and bolts of where to stay and what to see.

Bradt authors support responsible travel, and provide advice not only on minimum impact but also on how to give something back through local charities. In this way a true synergy is achieved between the traveller and local communities.

\* \* \*

It's always fun to publish guides to places that don't officially exist. Lapland, spanning four countries, is one of them. The home of Santa Claus, of reindeer, and the famous Icehotel, this is also a region of great cultural interest and glorious wintry landscapes. James Proctor is accustomed to wrapping up warm (he wrote our *Faroes* guide) and has done a sterling job at presenting the attractions in a manner that gets you looking out your longjohns prior to a trip.

**First edition November 2007**
Bradt Travel Guides Ltd
23 High Street, Chalfont St Peter, Bucks SL9 9QE, England; www.bradtguides.com
Published in the USA by The Globe Pequot Press Inc, 246 Goose Lane,
PO Box 480, Guilford, Connecticut 06437-0480

Text copyright © 2007 James Proctor
Maps copyright © 2007 Bradt Travel Guides Ltd
Illustrations copyright © 2007 individual photographers and artists
For Bradt: Editorial Project Manager Anna Moores
Project Management: Navigator Guides, www.navigatorguides.com

British Library Cataloguing in Publication Data
A catalogue record for this book is available from the British Library
ISBN-10: 1 84162 235 4
ISBN-13: 978184162 235 4

**Photographs**
Arcticphoto.co.uk (Arctic), Juliet Ferguson/Alamy (JF), Lapland Marketing Ltd/www.lapland finland.com (LM), James Proctor (JP), Peter Rosén/RosénMedia (PR), David Tipling (DT)
*Front cover* Reindeer, Norwegian Lapland (Arco Images/Alamy)
*Title page* Sámi girl, Sweden (Arctic), Canoeing, Ylläs, Finland (LM) and Husky, Rovaniemi, Finland (DT)
*Back cover* Aurora Borealis, Abisko, Swedish Lapland (PR) and Santa Claus (Arctic)
**Illustrations** Carole Vincer
**Maps** Alan Whitaker with regional maps compiled from Philip's Europe Mapping (www.philips-maps.co.uk), Dave Priestley

Typeset from the author's disk by Dorchester Typesetting Group
Printed and bound in Italy by Legoprint SpA, Trento

# Acknowledgements

Some 6,000km later, I would like to extend heartfelt thanks to Georgina Hancock at Discover the World, whose last-minute organisational skills are second to none. Her patience and good humour were much appreciated. Thanks are due also to my friends and contacts at tourist offices across Lapland who have helped me piece this book together, in particular, Hege in Honningsvåg, Knut in Tromsø, Ritva in Tornio, Lena in Luleå, Peter in Arvidsjaur, Birgitta in Jokkmokk and Anne-Marie in Kiruna. Mikael in Junosuando deserves special thanks for his patience in dealing with me on skis, and Maja for her truly exceptional bread-making skills – and gorgeous orange cake. Thanks also to Chris White at North Trek for checking the Natural History section. Lance, the man who wishes I would write about the Seychelles instead of Scandinavia, is, as ever, my rock.

## FEEDBACK REQUEST

Although I am a regular visitor to Scandinavia, prices and places change frequently and I would be delighted to hear your experiences of travel in Lapland. Did you discover a new spot for dinner, a thrilling adventure tour or a cosy new guesthouse or hotel? Has this guide been useful? What would you like to see changed? Your information will help make future editions of this guide even better. Please send your comments to Bradt Travel Guides, 23 High Street, Chalfont St Peter, Bucks SL9 9LE, England; e info@bradtguides.com.

# Contents

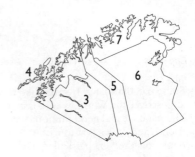

## LIST OF MAPS

# Introduction

*Jođi lea buoret go oru*
'Better to keep moving than to stay in one place'

Sámi proverb

For a place that doesn't officially exist, Lapland is famous the world over. Children know this snowy winter wonderland as the home of Santa Claus and his illustrious red-nosed reindeer, Rudolph, who take to the starry skies over Lapland every Christmas Eve to deliver presents and goodies to homes across the globe, a truly remarkable feat of aviation, timetabling and largesse that leaves even the world's favourite airlines lost for words. However, beyond the popular image of Lapland, little is known about this mysterious region lost somewhere on the very fringes of Europe. It's the aim of this guidebook, the only one in English dedicated solely to Lapland, to unlock some of the secrets of this vast, forgotten corner of the continent, larger in size than the entire United Kingdom.

First-time visitors are often astonished at the sheer variety of Lapland's landscapes: classic Norwegian fjords amid some of the most awe-inspiring mountain scenery anywhere in Europe; sweeping forests of pine and spruce that cloak the great inland plateaux of Swedish Lapland; and austere, treeless fells surrounded by steely grey lakes and unforgiving marshes give Finnish Lapland its very individual character. This is Scandinavia at its most elemental. Thanks to good road, rail and air links, travel between the different regions of Lapland is straightforward making it perfectly possible to visit Santa Claus in Finland, spend a night at the Icehotel in Sweden and go whale-watching in Norway all on the same trip. True, winter temperatures can plummet to −30°C and below, but public transport in Lapland is reliable, accommodation is warm and snug and eating out throws up a variety of options; reindeer, a local source of fat-free nutrition that's been consumed by generations of Laplanders, could even be on the menu.

Inevitably, the indigenous inhabitants of Lapland, the Sámi (who dislike the name 'Lapps', which was imposed on them by insensitive southerners) are today a minority in their own land and make up barely 7% of the total population. The promotion of Sámi culture is widespread and efforts to save the nine different dialects of the Sámi tongue from extinction have (so far) been successful. Travel across Lapland and sooner or later you'll see Sámi in their brightly coloured traditional dress – this is sometimes put on for tourists, but at key festivals in the Sámi calendar, wearing these clothes is a sign of pride and fraternity. The nomadic lifestyle may have all but disappeared but there's still a strong sense of community, which reaches across national borders.

Inextricably drawn to lost places, I first travelled to Lapland in 1983 and have been a regular visitor ever since. There's quite simply something about the sheer austerity of the nature – and, at times, the gruffness of the people who choose to live inside the Arctic Circle – that fascinates me. Lapland may be at its most magical during the long winter months when daylight is in short supply and snow lies thick on the ground – it's certainly the perfect time to head out on a snowmobile tour or a dog sled safari, or, indeed, to curl up with a good book beside a wood-burning stove inside a log cabin – but it's equally alluring in summer when the Midnight Sun and the quality of the light in the northern sky are perhaps two of the most difficult things about Lapland to qualify on paper. Visit Norwegian, Swedish or Finnish Lapland and you'll take away much more than Santa Claus could ever give you.

## THE BRADT DEFINITION OF LAPLAND

Spanning no fewer than four countries, Lapland is different things to different people. For the sake of this guidebook, we have determined Lapland to be roughly contained by the Arctic Circle in the south, the Arctic Ocean in the north and the Russian-Finnish border in the east. Strictly speaking, Lapland is found in Norway, Sweden, Finland *and* Russia. However, due to tiresome visa restrictions and a lack of tourist facilities in Russian Lapland (effectively, the Kola peninsula west of Murmansk), we have limited our coverage of Lapland to those areas that lie within the aforementioned Nordic countries. Travel across borders here is easy and troublefree and a visit to Lapland, therefore, can feature anything up to three countries.

**FCO TRAVEL ADVICE**
know before you go
fco.gov.uk/travel

Bradt Travel Guides is a partner to the 'know before you go' campaign, masterminded by the UK Foreign and Commonwealth Office to promote the importance of finding out about a destination before you travel. By combining the up-to-date advice of the FCO with the in-depth knowledge of Bradt authors, you'll ensure that your trip will be as trouble-free as possible.

## www.fco.gov.uk/travel

# Part One

## GENERAL INFORMATION

**Location** Lapland is in the northernmost part of Scandinavia. The region spreads across Norway, Sweden, Finland (and the Kola peninsula in Russia not covered in this book) and is generally considered to lie between the Arctic Circle at 66°N and the North Cape at 71°N. The homeland of Lapland's indigenous population, the Sámi, stretches as far south as central Sweden and Norway, an area they call Sápmi.

**Size/area** Lapland covers approximately 300,000 km$^2$ (115,000 square miles), an area bigger than the whole of the United Kingdom.

**Climate** Subarctic with sparse vegetation. See pages 3–4 for more information.

**Status** Lapland is composed of Finnish, Norwegian and Swedish provinces, which answer to national governments in Helsinki, Oslo and Stockholm. The Sámi parliaments in Finland, Norway and Sweden aim to promote Sámi culture though they have limited political power.

**Population** Approximately 900,000 people live in Lapland of whom around 66,000 are indigenous Sámi (40,000 in Norway, 20,000 in Sweden and 6,000 in Finland).

**Main towns** Finnish Lapland: Ivalo, Rovaniemi, Tornio; Norwegian Lapland: Hammerfest, Narvik, Tromsø; Swedish Lapland: Luleå, Gällivare, Kiruna

**Language** Finnish, Norwegian, Sámi and Swedish

**Religion** The Sámi believe in animism whereby everything in nature from animals to minerals has a soul; otherwise Evangelical-Lutheran.

**Currency/exchange rate** Finnish Lapland: euro (£1 = €1.44, US$1 = €0.71); Norwegian Lapland: Norwegian krone (£1 = 10.98kr; US$1 = 5.38kr); Swedish Lapland: Swedish krona (£1 = 13.13kr; US$1 = 6.43kr) (Oct 2007).

**International telephone codes** Finland +358, Norway +47, Sweden +46

**Time** Winter: Norwegian and Swedish Lapland GMT + 1hr, Finnish Lapland GMT + 2hr; summer Norwegian and Swedish Lapland GMT + 2hr, Finnish Lapland GMT + 3hr

**Electrical voltage** 220V; European two-pin plugs

**Weights and measures** Metric

**Flag** The Sámi flag is based on the motifs of a shaman's drum and the sun. It features a yellow and green stripe crossed by red and blue circle, all overlaid against a blue and red background.

**Public holidays** Finnish Lapland: 1, 6 January, Good Friday, Easter Sunday, Easter Monday, 17 May, Whit Sunday, 23 June, 3 November, 6, 25, 26 December; Norwegian Lapland: 1 January, Maundy Thursday, Good Friday, Easter Sunday, Easter Monday, 1, 17 May, Whit Sunday, Whit Monday, 25, 26 December; Swedish Lapland: 1, 6 January, Good Friday, Easter Sunday, Easter Monday, 1, 17 May, Whit Sunday, 6, 23 June, 3 November, 25, 26 December

# Background Information

**GEOGRAPHY** Western and northern areas of Lapland, predominantly in Norway, comprise fjords, deep valleys and mountains, whereas further south and east, in Swedish and Finnish Lapland, the land is flatter and made up of countless marshes and lakes, the largest of which is Inarijärvi in Finland. The highest mountain is Kebnekaise (2,111m), near Kiruna in Swedish Lapland.The geography of Lapland falls roughly into three main categories. The **coastal fringe** of Norwegian Lapland and its immediate hinterland is characterised by countless rocky islands and skerries, deep fjords that penetrate considerable distances inland and a chain of mountain and lesser peaks, predominantly found in northwestern areas between Narvik and Tromsø. Moving east and south away from the coast, the terrain of Swedish and Finnish Lapland is characterised by low mountains and **sweeping plains** blanketed with boreal coniferous forest, subduing its irregularities and eliminating colour variation through the constancy of its greenery. The mountains here, unlike those in Norwegian Lapland, are widely dispersed and rise sharply above the surrounding country. Several of the north's great rivers, such as the Luleälv, Tornionjoki and Kemijoki, drain these vast areas and empty into the upper reaches of the Gulf of Bothnia. Between these two main zones lies Lapland's third geographic category: the Finnmarksvidda or **Finnmark plateau**. Stretching south of the Norwegian town of Alta for around two hundred kilometres to beyond the Finnish border, this barren upland plateau is virtually treeless; its main features are rivers and lakes, which criss-cross the *vidda* on their way to the sea.

**CLIMATE** Although Lapland's climate is **subarctic**, there are considerable variations between milder maritime regions and those further inland, which suffer the full brunt of the Arctic winter chill. The coastal areas of Norwegian Lapland are considerably milder and wetter than the inland plateaux of Swedish and Finnish Lapland, where, for example, January mean temperatures are commonly below –15°C, and in some areas as low as –30°C. Large parts of Lapland receive less than 500mm of precipitation per year.

The flow of the warm North Atlantic drift is the factor of greatest importance in modifying the climate of coastal stretches of Norwegian Lapland. Here there is no great excess of either cold or heat; winter temperatures fluctuate a couple of degrees either side of freezing, and in summer they reach 10–12°C. As distance from the sea increases, so, in general, winter temperatures decrease and summer temperatures increase; maritime influences seldom find their way over the mountain chain dividing Norway from Sweden and the Finnmarksvidda from Finland.

During the **winter** months, most precipitation falls as **snow**, often resulting in considerable depths. In Sodankylä, for example, just inside the Arctic Circle in Finnish Lapland, snow can lie at depths of at least 60cm from October to

3

| | Tromsø (Norway) | Sodankylä (Finland) | Jokkmokk (Sweden) |
|---|---|---|---|
| January | –6°C/104mm | –14°C/33mm | –14°C/30mm |
| February | –6°C/87mm | –13°C/28mm | –14°C/27mm |
| March | –4°C/82mm | –8°C/26mm | –9°C/24mm |
| April | –1°C/64mm | –2°C/29mm | –2°C/30mm |
| May | 4°C/49mm | 5°C/35mm | 4°C/35mm |
| June | 8°C/58mm | 12°C/61mm | 11°C/48mm |
| July | 12°C/68mm | 14°C/70mm | 14°C/78mm |
| August | 11°C/79mm | 11°C/63mm | 11°C/74mm |
| September | 6°C/102mm | 6°C/57mm | 6°C/55mm |
| October | 1°C/133mm | –1°C/48mm | –1°C/41mm |
| November | –3°C/100mm | –8°C/41mm | –8°C/36mm |
| December | –5°C/101mm | –12°C/33mm | –14°C/32mm |

mid-March. The annual duration of snow cover is determined by air temperature and precipitation. Much of Lapland is covered with snow for more than 200 days per year; in the mountains of Swedish Lapland this figure rises to 220 days per year whereas the Lofoten islands have only 120 days with snow.

The long winters naturally have an impact on the growing season in Lapland, which lasts less than 130 days on average, extending roughly from mid-May to mid-September, a full two months shorter than that of southern Sweden and western Norway. During the short **summer** months, Finnish Lapland, far away from the cloud-producing mountains of the coastal fringes, is one of the sunniest regions in the whole of Scandinavia, whereas rain clouds crossing the mountain range make Riksgränsen in Swedish Lapland one of the wettest spots in the entire country. Conversely, Abisko, barely 35km to the east, lies in a rain shadow and is the driest place in Sweden.

**The Arctic Circle: polar night and midnight sun** The imaginary line drawn around the earth at roughly 66°N, known as the **Arctic Circle**, marks the southernmost extent of the polar night in winter and the midnight sun in summer. At the circle, there is one day of total darkness each winter on the **winter solstice** (albeit the period around midday is edged with blue or grey since the sun is only just below the horizon) and, conversely, one day of 24-hour daylight at the **summer solstice**. As you travel north, so the length of the polar night and period of midnight sun increases.

| Location | Polar night | Midnight sun |
|---|---|---|
| Kilpisjärvi | 25 Nov–17 Jan | 22 May–25 Jul |
| North Cape | 18 Nov–24 Jan | 11 May–31 Jul |
| Sodankylä | 18 Dec–24 Dec | 29 May–14 Jul |
| Utsjoki | 25 Nov–17 Jan | 16 May–27 Jul |

Incidentally, the Arctic Circle is actually moving north by 14–15 metres every year due to the earth's uneven orbit. In ten to twenty thousand years time this northward drift will stop, when the Arctic Circle will be roughly at 68°N, and it will start to drift southwards again.

**Northern lights: aurora borealis** One of the most spectacular sights in Lapland is the aurora borealis, as they are known in Latin, or the northern lights. During the darkest months of winter, the sky is often lit up by these shimmering arcs of green, blue and yellowish light, which can disappear as fast as they appear. The science behind their existence is complex but essentially the displays are caused by solar wind or particles charged by the sun, which light up as they reach the earth's atmosphere: blue is nitrogen and yellowy-green is oxygen. In order to see the northern lights, the night sky must be clear of cloud. It is said that the colder and stiller the conditions the better the chances of a display, and the further north you travel the more impressive the lights will be. If you're flying to Lapland during the hours of darkness, be alert as you look out of the plane windows because the aurora borealis can also be seen clearly when you are in the air above the cloud.

## HISTORY

Over the centuries the history of Lapland has been characterised by countless struggles by greater powers, notably Denmark-Norway and Sweden-Finland, for domination. Lapland's rich natural resources proved alluring as early as the Viking period. However, it is perhaps in more modern times – particularly during and after World War II, when large tracts of Lapland were destroyed and seemingly every building burnt to the ground as occupying Nazi forces implemented their scorched earth policy as they retreated south – that the world became aware of Lapland and its fate. The resettling of refugees who had fled the fighting only to return to discover their homes reduced to piles of rubble and the rebuilding of an entire region's infrastructure after the war proved some of the toughest challenges Lapland has ever faced. This, and the repeated abuse of the rights of an indigenous people, the Sámi, has greatly influenced the face of today's Lapland.

**EARLY SETTLERS** The first real signs of life in what we now call Lapland can be traced back around 7,000 years when the ice cap that once covered Scandinavia slowly began to melt and retreat. Primitive signs of human habitation have been found around Alta in Norwegian Lapland dating back to this period, though it is not clear whether these first Laplanders were Sámi or not. Prehistoric **rock carvings** here, created between 2,500 and 6,000 years ago, clearly show how people hunted reindeer and other beasts for survival. Their tools and jewellery show influences from other peoples living further south, providing proof that they didn't exist in a cultural void.

The first written accounts of life in the far north date from the late 9th century. Ottar of Hålogaland, a chieftain and farmer from central Norway, not only told the English king, Alfred the Great, about his expeditions along the Arctic Ocean coast and around the Kola peninsula, but he also gave details of his trade with the Sámi from whom he collected taxes in the form of skins, feathers and whales' teeth. According to Ottar, other merchants settled around the head of the Gulf of Bothnia were also journeying north to trade and collect taxes from the Sámi at this time.

Another source of detail from this period is contained in the **Icelandic saga** of Egill Skallagrímsson, which recounts events during the reign of the Norwegian king Harald Fairhair. The king's representative in what is now Swedish Lapland, Torolv Kveldúlfsson, conducted trade with the Sámi, collected taxes and plundered and killed anyone who crossed his path. According to the saga, he accepted an invitation to fight on behalf of King Faravid who presided over an area of land at the head of the Gulf of Bothnia under siege from harrying tribes from what is now central and southern Finland. If the saga is accurate, King Faravid is the first leader from Finnish Lapland to be mentioned in any written account of Lapland's history.

**THE GREAT POWERS** During the Middle Ages, Lapland's rich natural resources, in particular skins, furs and fish, led to rivalries between the great powers of the time, Denmark-Norway, Sweden-Finland and Russia. The Sámi were often subject to taxes from all three countries as a result of the lack of national borders in the north. In an attempt to control the valuable fur trade with Lapland, the Swedish king, Magnus Eriksson, passed a law in the mid-14th century which ensured that all goods for export had to be handled by either Stockholm or Turku in Finland. A similar law followed in Denmark-Norway giving Copenhagen and Bergen sole export and import rights. As a direct result of both laws, trade and development in Lapland stagnated.

During the 16th century Sweden cranked up its attempts to control Lapland – not just fiscally but now politically, too. Following victory over the Russians at Narva in 1584, which effectively ended Russia's maritime access to the Baltic Sea, Sweden was keen to squeeze its enemy further by taking control of Lapland, which lay along Russia's only other sea route to the west from Arkangelsk.

It was around this time, too, that missionaries were dispatched to Lapland in an attempt to strengthen the position of the Swedish crown in the far north. Churches were built across the region and trade became centred on these new places of worship attracting inhabitants from regions further south. However, further conflict between Sweden and Denmark, which culminated in the peace agreement of Knäred in 1613, led to an agreement by Sweden to relinquish control over Lapland. A visit to northern Norway and the Kola peninsula by the Danish king, Christian IV, in the 1790s was a clear sign to Sweden and the rest of Europe that Denmark-Norway considered itself to have won control over Lapland.

**THE RUSSIAN INVASION** In February 1808 Russian troops loyal to Tsar Alexander I attacked Swedish positions in Finland as part of a secret pact between the tsar and the French emperor, Napoleon. The Swedish king, Gustav VI Adolf, fell foul of the plot by refusing to assist the French in blockading England's seaports. Poorly equipped and badly trained Swedish troops retreated to Umeå and Tornio as the Russians advanced leaving Finland undefended. In March 1809 the Russians pushed forward again towards Tornio driving the Swedish forces to withdraw westwards. Finland's fate was sealed and as part of the peace agreement of Fredrikshamn of September 1809 Sweden was forced to cede Finland to Russia. A new border was drawn from the head of the Gulf of Bothnia along the rivers Tornio, Muonio and Könkämä towards Kilpisjärvi (the current border between Sweden and Finland) splitting former villages and parishes in two and setting Finnish Lapland firmly within the Russian sphere of influence.

Although large numbers of Finns had begun leaving their homeland for neighbouring Norwegian Lapland in the 1700s, this migration continued and intensified after the Russian takeover; in all it is estimated that 10,000 people fled to escape the harsh economic conditions that prevailed in Finland at this time and to look for prosperity across the border. Indeed, the rich fishing grounds of the Arctic Ocean attracted many Finns who chose to settle in Vadsø on the Varangerfjord, a town which became more Finnish than Norwegian and even today carries its own Finnish name, Vesisaari.

As so often in Lapland's history, the Sámi bore the brunt of this new colonisation and as the Finns moved north they took land which had previously been used for reindeer herding. Over the centuries it has been a common Finnish agricultural practice to clear large areas of forestland for farming by burning down the trees and then planting crops such as rye in the rich ashes that then cover the ground. This practice destroys the land and forests which the Sámi need to tend their reindeer.

During the **Crimean War** in the mid-1850s a wind of change began to blow through the Swedish capital, Stockholm, where the king became suspicious of Russia's expansionist intentions in Finland (until 1809 Finland had been part of Sweden). He turned to England and France for support should Russia lay claim to yet more Swedish or Norwegian territory (after centuries of Danish domination, Norway entered a union with Sweden in 1814).

The newly created border between Sweden and Russia-Finland was closed and Sweden refused to grant Russia grazing and fishing rights on Swedish territory. This agreement, contained in the November Treaty of 1855 of the Crimean War, remained in force until 1908. The Russians retaliated in 1855 and made it illegal for Norwegian Sámi to drive their reindeer across the border into Finland. Norway followed suit in 1889, closing its border with Finland. The border closures hit the Sámi hard and effectively made it impossible for their reindeer to follow their traditional patterns of migration. As a direct result, many families abandoned their homes and sought new pastures, notably in Swedish Lapland. Meanwhile, across the border in Norway, the fear of Russian aggression was deemed so real that farmers from the south of Norway were encouraged to move north to foster a greater sense of Norwegian nationalism in these remote northern outposts. The Finnish migrants felt the full brunt of this Norwegianisation policy and were openly regarded by the authorities in Oslo as a danger to the state.

**INTO THE 20TH CENTURY** At the turn of the last century, Lapland was on its knees economically. **Poverty** was widespead in all parts of the region and a shortage of food was a fact of life for most families. In Norwegian Lapland, although ever decreasing fish catches and the falling price of fish on world markets were the key causes of the problem, the fishing community's total dependency on middlemen who set unrealistic terms for loans and debt collection only served to compound matters. In Swedish and Finnish Lapland things were little better. A series of failed harvests due to drought and severe winters meant that many families were on the brink of starvation during the winter of 1902–03.

However, some of the greatest geopolitical changes ever to affect Lapland were now only a matter of years away. In 1905, the union between Sweden and Norway, which lasted just short of a century, was peacefully dissolved and Norway came of age taking on all the trappings of a modern independent state for the first time in its history.

Although Lapland wasn't directly involved in **World War I** (Norway and Sweden had declared themselves neutral states), the Russians made Finnish Tornio, on the Gulf of Bothnia, their main port to the west since the Germans controlled the entrance to the Baltic Sea, the Öresund strait. Between 1914 and 1917 the population of Finnish Lapland benefited financially from Tornio's new prominence and many people became involved in the transport of goods and refugees in and out of Russia. One person who transited through Tornio at this time was none other than Vladimir Ilich Lenin who returned to Russia from exile in April 1917 ahead of the **Russian revolution**. Profiting from the general confusion in St Petersburg, Finland lost no time in declaring its independence from Russia on 6 December the same year, bringing an end to its existence as a **Grand Duchy** under the Tsar. With the outbreak of the revolution, Russia withdrew from World War I and Finnish Lapland was, for the first time in its history, under direct rule from Helsinki.

However, between late January and mid-May 1918 **civil war** raged in Finland between the Social Democrat-led Red Guard and the White Guard, a right-wing private army, over the future direction of the newly independent country. Finnish Lapland came under the control of the Whites whereas the Reds dominated in

Helsinki and the industrial cities of the south. The victorious Whites regarded the civil war as one of (Russian) liberation, something that set the tone for the policy of Finnish nationalism which later followed. The Russian-Finnish border was not fixed until the **Treaty of Tartu** of October 1920 when, in return for the areas of Repola and Porajärvi, north of Lake Ladoga, Russia ceded a strategic arm of land to Finland, which gave the Finns ice-free access to the Barents Sea at Petsamo (Pechenga in Russian).

Following the discovery of nickel in the area, mining began a year later and a road linking Sodankylä via Ivalo to the Petsamo fjord was completed in 1931 making Petsamo an unlikely Lapland tourist destination; it was the only port on the Barents Sea that could be reached by car. The Petsamo strip remained Finnish territory until 1944 when it was ceded to the Soviets as part of the armistice agreement.

**WORLD WAR II** Three months after the start of World War II, Stalin's troops attacked Finland on 30 November 1939 after Helsinki refused to accept Soviet demands to cede Finnish territory on the Karelian isthmus in order to protect Leningrad; Moscow wanted the Finns to move the border 25km to the west. At this time the Soviet-Finnish border was just 32km from Leningrad and Stalin feared Germany, despite having signed a non-aggression pact with the Soviet Union just three months earlier, would use Finland as a bridgehead from which to invade. Outnumbered four to one, the Finns initially had the upper hand in the campaign which became known as the **Winter War**. They moved adeptly on skis and dressed in white camouflage against the snow, and the harsh winter conditions with temperatures down to −40°C coupled with local knowledge played to their advantage – they managed to hold out against the superior enemy until March 1940.

Under German representation the Finns agreed to negotiate the terms of a peace agreement with the Soviet Union. The **Moscow Peace Treaty** inflicted a grievous wound on Finland: the loss of around 10% of its pre-war territory. In the south, the Karelian isthmus, including the country's second city, Viipuri (Vyborg in Russian), a large part of Karelia and the whole of Lake Ladoga were handed over to protect Leningrad. In the north, large parts of the Salla area of Lapland (now referred to as Old Salla) were given to the Soviets in order to move the Finnish border away from the sensitive Leningrad–Murmansk rail line; at one point the frontier came within 80km of the Soviet rail network.

The Finns also agreed to construct a new rail route on their own territory from Kemijärvi, northeast of Rovaniemi, to the new border. The aim of this was to provide the Soviet Union with a direct route between the port of Kandalaksha (Kantalahti in Finnish), on the White Sea, and the head of the Gulf of Bothnia at Kemi. Finland ceded part of the recently acquired Petsamo area of Lapland, four islands in the Gulf of Finland and agreed to lease the Hanko peninsula, in the far southwest of the country, to the Soviets for 30 years so they could establish a naval base there to control the sea approaches to Leningrad.

On 9 April 1940, Germany attacked and invaded Norway in order to take advantage of the country's strategically important Atlantic coastline, thwarting the British, who had the same plan. Although the Norwegians were unprepared for the surprise attack, resistance lasted for two months, and the month-long **Battle of Narvik** became one of the first major confrontations between Britain's Royal Navy and the German Kriegsmarine of the war. Narvik provided an ice-free harbour for the export of valuable iron ore from the mines at Kiruna and Gällivare in Swedish Lapland and was therefore a prize possession for both sides. Following the fall of France, the Norwegians surrendered on 8 June 1940.

During the five years of Nazi occupation, the Norwegians mounted a campaign of civil disobedience and resistance. It became common practice, for example, to pretend not to understand German when addressed by a soldier and not to sit next to German troops when travelling on public transport; the Germans retaliated by making it illegal to stand on a bus if seats were available.

During World War II, Sweden followed a policy of questionable **neutrality**. Surrounded by German forces all around, the Stockholm government agreed to German requests to transit troops and war equipment through neutral Sweden to occupied Norway – something the Norwegians still to this day find hard to accept. Firmly in control of the port of Narvik, the Nazis bought Swedish iron ore from the mines in Kiruna and Gällivare and transported it to Norway for export to steel plants in Germany where it was critical to war production.

Following Germany's attack on the Soviet Union under Operation Barbarossa, Finland joined World War II on 25 June 1941 against the Soviets, provoked by bombing raids by Moscow on several Finnish cities including Helsinki and Turku. Finland had previously given Germany permission to move troops across its territory and to use Finnish air bases to launch attacks on the Soviet Union. Although the Finnish leadership and people never shared the Nazis' ideology, they did subscribe to the common goal of defeating the Soviet Union – an attempt to rectify the injustice, as they saw it, done to them in the Moscow Peace Treaty and to regain what the Soviets had taken from them.

In late July 1941 the British bombed the ports of Petsamo and Kirkenes, which were being used by the Germans as supply bases from which to attack Murmansk; damage was limited, however, since the harbour in Petsamo was almost empty of ships, though 15 British aircraft were shot down. On Finnish independence day, 6 December 1941, Britain declared war on Finland. Despite this, the Finns succeeded in retaking Karelia though they refused requests by the Germans to continue eastwards and attack Leningrad, just as they objected to their involvement in blowing up the Murmansk railway line.

By early 1943, Finland began actively to seek a way out of the war following the disastrous German defeat at Stalingrad. Intermittent negotiations stalled and Stalin opted to force Finland's hand bombing Helsinki in February 1944. The Continuation War came to an end with the signing of the **Moscow Armistice** on 19 September 1944; the conditions for peace similar to those laid down by the **Moscow Peace Treaty** of 1940, namely, that Finland had to cede parts of Karelia, Salla and islands in the Gulf of Finland. However, Finland lost Petsamo and was forced to lease Porkkala (west of Helsinki) to the Soviets for 50 years, though this was returned in 1956. **War reparations** totalling US$300 million were payable to the Soviet Union and Finland was bound to drive German troops out of its territory, which led to the Lapland war.

**THE LAPLAND WAR** Since summer 1943, the German command had been making preparations for the eventuality that Finland might sign a separate peace accord with the Soviet Union. Plans were laid to withdraw forces northwards to protect the nickel mines of Petsamo and, accordingly, roads between Finnish and Norwegian Lapland were greatly improved by the use of prisoner of war labour. In late 1944 there were still around 200,000 German troops in Finnish Lapland who, despite years of fighting and fatigue, had no intention of capitulating before their former allies. Caught in a pincer movement between advancing Soviet troops pushing west and Finnish forces moving north, the **Germans retreated** and destroyed everything in their path. Particularly fierce battles were fought at Tankavaara and Kaunispää, south of Ivalo, as the Germans headed for Norway. As they retreated the Germans employed a **scorched earth policy** in retaliation for the betrayal by their former colleagues, the Finns. The order was given directly by the German commander in Lapland, General Lothar Rendulic, who was convicted of war crimes by the Allies after the war and sentenced to 20 years' imprisonment though his sentence was later reduced to ten years. The Germans burnt the provincial capital, Rovaniemi, to the ground leaving just 13% of the town's buildings remaining. It is estimated that around half of all structures in Finnish Lapland were destroyed; all but two bridges in the region were blown up and roads were mined. From the other side of the border in Sweden, relatives watched helplessly as one village after another went up in flames; the smoke could be seen for miles around. Indeed, north of the Arctic Circle, nine out of every ten buildings were burnt.

In response to a request by the Helsinki government in September 1944, Sweden opened its border to 50,000 Finnish **refugees** who crossed the frontier at several points between Karesuando in the north and Haparanda in the south, bringing with them everything they could carry. In total, around 100,000 refugees fled Finnish Lapland at this time.

Nor was Norwegian Lapland spared: between the Varangerfjord in the east and Skibotn, southeast of Tromsø, everything from hospitals to telegraph poles was destroyed. Hitler himself ordered the evacuation of the region's population ahead of the approaching Soviet troops from the east. Some 45,000 people were forced out of their homes, which were then systematically destroyed, but it is estimated that one in three inhabitants of Finnmark, the northernmost province in Norwegian Lapland, escaped the evacuation by hiding in caves and tents in the countryside. In Kirkenes, for example, many people sought refuge in a bomb shelter under the town.

The scale of the reconstruction required after World War II, particularly in Finnish Lapland, was immense. Not only did Finland have to pay US$300 million to the Soviet Union in war reparations but it had lost roughly 10% of its land area, including important industrial centres such as Viipuri, and the northern third of the country had been laid to waste. Despite investment in new industries in the south of Finland, which attracted new workers from across the country, Finnish Lapland's economy remained essentially agricultural. Between 1950 and 1980, around 55,000 people left the region in search of a better life abroad, predominantly in Sweden, where they sought work in the iron ore industries in Kiruna and Luleå.

The problems facing Norwegian Laplanders on their return to their former homes were no different from those that people in northern Finland were dealing with; over the decades thousands of people, here too, decided to leave the area to find work in southern Norway. It is estimated that about 170,000 people emigrated from Lapland in the 30-year period to 1980.

**THE CHERNOBYL DISASTER AND ITS AFTERMATH** In the early hours of 26 April 1986 the most far-reaching disaster ever to hit Lapland occurred a thousand miles away at the Chernobyl nuclear plant in Ukraine (then part of the Soviet Union). Regarded as the worst accident ever in the history of **nuclear power** generation, a plume of radioactive fallout, carried by winds and rain, fell over large parts of eastern Europe and, in particular, northern areas of Scandinavia.

The radioactivity was first detected by Swedish scientists two days after the accident, forcing tons of fresh produce to be destroyed. Lichen, the reindeer's main food source, acted like a sponge and absorbed large amounts of **radiation**, which, in turn, was consumed by reindeer grazing in Lapland's forests. At the time of the explosion, it was estimated that reindeer meat could not be safely consumed for at least 40 years.

However, since Chernobyl, radiation levels have fallen and original estimates have been downsized, though soil across Lapland remains contaminated. The Swedish Food Administration authority declared that reindeer meat with a high bequerel per kilogram level was unfit for human consumption. In the 1986 slaughter, 80% of Sweden's **reindeer population** was slaughtered, a move that devastated the Sámi community since their livelihood depends, to a large extent, on the production of reindeer meat for the domestic market. Amid continuing uncertainty over the effects of consuming infected meat, bequerel levels were later lowered in Norway and Sweden, and compensation payments were made by central governments to Sámi who slaughtered their animals.

It is still too early to accurately state what the true health consequences of Chernobyl have been on the Sámi and other inhabitants of Lapland since the incubation periods for cancer following exposure to radiation can vary from five to 30 years. The accident has forced the Sámi to adapt their herding practices and their uses for the reindeer's carcass – the Sámi have traditionally used every part of the deer from its hooves and blood to its entrails. Radiation-free lichen is now imported and mixed to reindeers' feed to avoid further contamination and several weeks before slaughter animals are fed special pellets, which prevent radioactive caesium from entering the bloodstream and can reduce radiation levels in slaughtered meat by 50–75% and in milk by 80%. Despite these measures, average contamination rates in Lapland's reindeer are expected to remain high for the next 20 years.

**LAPLAND TODAY** Through the founding of the three **Sámi parliaments** in Lapland, the voice of the region's indigenous population has become louder. First Norway in 1989, then Sweden in 1993 and finally Finland in 1996 passed legislation to set up these elected bodies whose task it is to maintain and develop Sámi language and culture. Although real political power is limited, the existence of the parliaments is a sign by national governments in the south that the Sámi have a right to be heard in matters that directly affect them.

Attempts have been made in recent years to increase cross-border **economic cooperation** in Lapland – not only between the different Nordic countries, but also with neighbouring Russia. Local politicians are backing efforts to create a Barents Sea trading region, and, with that in mind, direct flights have been established with Murmansk and bus links with Kandalaksha to facilitate contact; several companies now even offer short tourist trips into Russian Lapland. The idea of developing an economic base in Lapland, independent of that in southern Scandinavia, is perfectly sensible when you consider distances: the southern Swedish city of Gothenburg, for example, is closer to Venice in Italy than it is to Kiruna in Swedish Lapland.

Perhaps the greatest challenge facing Lapland today, though, is how to stem the increasing numbers of people who are choosing to leave the region to find better job prospects in the south of their respective countries. The lure of bigger salaries and urban sophistication available in the south is too strong for many to resist. The result is that Lapland is haemorrhaging valuable expertise and talent which it sorely needs to keep: the **population density** in Finnish Lapland, for example, is just two people per km$^2$, compared with the national average of 17 people per km$^2$.

## GOVERNMENT AND POLITICS

The three parts of Lapland covered in this book, Norwegian, Swedish and Finnish, come under direct rule from Oslo, Stockholm and Helsinki respectively. All areas send MPs to their national parliaments. Finland is a republic, but Norway and Sweden are constitutional monarchies, which have a king as the head of state.

Finland and Sweden are members of the European Union, both joining on 1 January 1995, whereas Norway, despite holding a public referendum on EU membership at the same time as its Nordic neighbours, elected to stay outside the Union. However, in order to maintain the long-standing Nordic passport union, whereby Nordic citizens enjoyed the right of travel across the region without passports, Norway was allowed to join the EU's Schengen zone (a group of countries that allow passport-free travel) alongside Sweden and Finland despite its non-membership of the European Union. As a result there is free movement of people, goods and services between the different parts of Lapland and it is extremely unusual to be asked to show your passport when crossing national borders, even on entering and leaving the EU.

Although there is no political body that wields power over Lapland as a whole, the three Sámi parliaments located in Kiruna (Sweden), Karasjok (Norway) and Inari (Finland) are all charged with protecting the rights, culture and language of northern Scandinavia's indigenous population and often work together on cross-border issues which affect the entire Sámi community.

## SÁMI ECONOMY

**REINDEER HUSBANDRY** The reindeer has been at the centre of Sámi life and culture for thousands of years. Despite the devastating effects of the Chernobyl nuclear disaster in 1986, which contaminated vast tracts of key grazing land, many Sámi still follow a semi-nomadic lifestyle determined by their deer, but the days when entire families followed the seasonal movement of the animals across the plains are long gone. Instead, reindeer husbandry today is subject to advances in modern technology just like any other industry; herders travel by snowmobile in winter rather than by sled, live in modern houses rather than traditional *kåtor* (round wooden huts that resemble teepees) and communicate by mobile phone.

Since their access to food varies from season to season, the mountain and forest reindeer are migratory animals. Mountain reindeer are especially susceptible to irritating insects, such as mosquitoes, and move up onto the mountain tops during summer days where there are cool patches of snow and fewer insects. The **Mountain Sámi** follow their animals from the forest up to the treeline by the time spring comes, then on into the mountains for summer; in August they start making their way down.

Forest reindeer, on the other hand, prefer open, more marshy areas when there is no snow on the ground, moving deep into the forest when tormented by insects; the **Forest Sámi** consequently move with their herds within the forests. Come September, many animals are slaughtered in corrals dotted across the region. Then, following the mating season in late September and October, both species are to be found in the forests during the long winter months where it is easier to dig for lichen in the snow. The reindeer's gestation period lasts for around 225 days; calves are born in May and suckle throughout the summer months.

Reindeer husbandry requires vast tracts of lands as a result of its migratory nature and sparse food resources. Over the centuries, the reindeer industry in all three countries has had to learn to co-exist with other forms of industry and land use, which has naturally led to a number of conflicts between the Sámi and non-indigenous groups in Lapland. For example, Sámi have accused Swedes of stealing their land; Swedes have accused Sámi of scrounging off the state. Sweden didn't officially recognise the Sámi as an indigenous group (and consequently acknowledge their rights) until 1977. In 1988, the Minister for Agriculture and Sámi Affairs asked the Sámi, on behalf of her government, to forgive the way the Swedish state had treated them throughout history.

**FISHING** Fishing is the oldest, though now smallest, branch of Sámi industry and has long traditions in Lapland culture. In Norway, the Sámi carry out sea and inland fishing, whereas in Sweden and Finland the Sámi only fish inland, in lakes and rivers. Lawyers and the Norwegian Sámi parliament have asserted that Sámi who live along the coastline have age-old rights to exploit the coastal waters, though this has yet to be laid down in national legislation. When reindeer herders tend their animals from remote highland settlements during the summer months, their diet consists mainly of fish. The right to fish in many mountain lakes has been asserted by many Sámi with the result that some have been set aside for the sole use of reindeer herding Sámi. This decision has given rise to envy not only among the non-indigenous population, but also among non-reindeer-herding Sámi.

## PEOPLE

As the definition of 'Sámi' is ambiguous and varies from one country to another, population experts have found it difficult to quantify exactly how many Sámi live in Lapland. However, generally accepted figures show that there are around 70,000 Sámi living across the region: 40,000 in Norway, 20,000 in Sweden, 6,000 in Finland and a further 4,000 in Russia. The total population of Lapland, when we apply this book's definition, is around 900,000, making the Sámi about 7% of the total. The overwhelming 93% is made up of non-indigenous Norwegians, Swedes and Finns. Although there is a high degree of co-operation between the two communities, there still remains a great deal of mistrust and misunderstanding; indigenous Sámi culture is strikingly different from that of mainstream Scandinavia. Consequently, we have given information about the minority Sámi people and their culture.

## LANGUAGE

Norwegian, Swedish and Finnish are the majority languages in Lapland, but the Sámi also speak their own language known as **Sámegiella** (Sámi). It belongs to the Finno-Ugric family and its closest relatives are Finnish and Estonian, and, much more distantly, Hungarian. The distance between Sámi and Hungarian, though, is as great as that between English and Persian, which are languages of the same family. Having said that, Sámi is not a single language. Instead, **nine varieties** of Sámi are recognised, which fall into three main groups: Eastern Sámi, Central Sámi and Southern Sámi.

Within the Central Sámi division, the dialect known as **Northern Sámi** is spoken by around 15,000–17,000 people across the provinces of Finnmark and Troms in Norwegian Lapland and northern areas of Swedish and Finnish Lapland. It is the largest of all nine dialects and is regarded as the standard Sámi language; it is therefore the variant we use in this guide. Its core area, both with regard to number and concentration of speakers, as well as cultural and linguistic vitality, is found around Karasjok and Kautokeino in Norwegian Lapland.

The other two main groups, **Eastern Sámi** and **Southern Sámi**, comprise four dialects each. The eastern branch is composed of two dialects, which are only spoken on the Kola peninsula in Russian Lapland, as well as Inari Sámi and Skolt Sámi, spoken in northeastern Finland. Southern Sámi is made up of Lule Sámi (centred on the Swedish city of Luleå), Pite Sámi (in and around Piteå), Ume Sámi (Umeå) and South Sámi, which stretches all the way down to the province of Dalarna in central Sweden.

With a few exceptions, neighbouring varieties of Sámi are mutually intelligible, though the linguistic and orthographical (not to mention geographical) distance between Southern Sámi and Northern Sámi is so great that many experts argue they should be considered as different languages rather than dialects of the same tongue. The second largest dialect is Lule Sámi with around 1,500 speakers; other dialects such as Inari and Skolt Sámi have barely 500 speakers each.

Today Sámi is a legally recognised language in the northern and eastern municipalities of Finnish and Norwegian Lapland respectively, and was granted the status of one of Sweden's five minority languages in 2002.

It is thought that Sámi and Finnish originate from the same proto-language but became separated around 1000 BC. At this time it is unlikely that there were any notable differences in pronunciation or grammar between speakers in different areas. However, by the 9th century AD, linguists believe that the major subdivisions that now exist between the various Sámi dialects had taken shape. The differences between the various dialects spoken in the areas covered by this guide developed due to the nomadic nature of the speakers' lives and the intermittent contact they had with people from other areas.

Sámi first appeared as a written language in the 17th century in Sweden since missionaries dispatched to Lapland by the crown required information to be written in the local language; spelling was based on the southern dialects. North of the border in Norway emphasis was given to Northern Sámi and the first Sámi grammar appeared in 1748. The clergyman Nils Vibe Stockfleth produced another grammar almost a hundred years later in which he employed artificial orthographic characters to portray Sámi sounds that were not present in Norwegian. Although a unified spelling system was in place for Northern Sámi by 1951, the Finnish Sámi continued to use a different system based on their own conventions. It wasn't until the 1970s that all three countries managed to agree on a single orthography, which was a compromise between all those in use; spelling in Northern Sámi was finally standardised in 1978 and is based largely on Stockfleth's system, which has contributed some unusual consonants to the Sámi alphabet of today.

Only one in three Sámi people can actually speak their native tongue and all Sámi speakers are bilingual. This is because the language was harshly suppressed until recent years, so many parents failed to speak Sámi to their children and thus transmit it to the next generation as they regarded knowing the language to be a social handicap.

In Norway, for example, from the second part of the 19th century, the authorities carried out a policy of assimilation, depriving Sámi of its function in primary education. The reason was partly nationalistic: Norway was newly independent and the idea of 'one nation – one language' played a prominent role in the philosophy of some nationalists in Oslo. The fear of Finland, too (see *History*, page 6), helped to create a unified purely Norwegian front in these northern frontier areas. In addition, a law existed in Norway from 1902 to 1963 forbidding the sale of state-owned land in the province of Finnmark to anyone who couldn't write, speak or read Norwegian. Although this law was aimed primarily at immigrating Finns, it had a negative effect on the development of Sámi in Norwegian Lapland. Only in 1959 did the Norwegians reintroduce Sámi as the language of instruction in schools.

In Sweden, Sámi was never forbidden in school as it was in Norway, though Swedish also took a dominant role. Things began to change in the late 1970s, when parliament passed a law allowing linguistic minorities the right to instruction in their home language. The situation was largely similar in Finland, where Sámi has only recently been given an equal status with Finnish in areas where most Sámi live.

For a glossary of Sámi reindeer terms see *Appendix 2*, pages 166–7.

In common with many other indigenous peoples, living in harmony with nature is key to the Sámi's existence. Their view of the world was **animistic** by nature, with some shamanistic features, and there's evidence that elements of these ancient beliefs were practised until the late 1940s. Animism holds that every element in nature, be it a stone, the wind or an animal, has a soul and, accordingly, the Sámi still believe today that human beings should move through the countryside without making a noise or disturbance.

Alongside the material world was an underworld where everything was more defined than in the material world and where the dead continued their lives. A *noaidi* or **shaman** was the link between the underworld and the present. A shaman was generally a young man who received a calling from the spirits to enter a period of learning in order to move between the two worlds. On particularly demanding trips into the underworld, the shaman would use a *goavddis* or **drum** and would probably also perform a *joik*, a form of throat singing (also known in Mongolia), to help him achieve a state of ecstasy and reach out to the spirits. Outsiders considered the *goavddis* to be charged with magic and therefore a satanic instrument of evil; owners of drums were paraded before the courts and fined, flogged or killed and their drums burnt.

Perhaps the element of Sámi belief most tangible today is the practice of leaving an offering at a *sieidi*, or sacred image, such as a tree, rock, mountain, lake or even waterfall situated at strategic points for the reindeer herder or hunter. It was common practice, particularly at the beginning of the hunting season, to leave a coin or some other object of value. Indeed, as recently as 1994, coins and reindeer antler were found at a *sieidi* in the province of Finnmark. It is not known whether this represents an offering or simply a continuing tradition.

Although the animistic elements of the ancient beliefs live on, today's Sámi are Christian. Many adhere to the conservative religious movement known as **Laestadianism**, which is known across the north of Scandinavia. The Swedish revivalist preacher Lars Levi Laestadius (1800–61) saw it as his mission to rid Lapland of the scourge of alcohol. Posted to the parish of Karesuando in Swedish Lapland in 1826, he saw the effects of alcohol abuse at first hand; not only was most of the congregation drunk during his church services, but children were left to fend for themselves and reindeer were allowed to drift aimlessly, risking attack by wolves and other predators, as the herders lay drunk in their huts. When he met a young Sámi girl, Mary of Lapland, in 1844 Laestadius was inspired to renew his efforts to steer the Sámi towards a life of total purity and teetotalism.

After Laestadius died, the movement split into opposing factions: a conservative western group in Sweden and Norway, and a more liberal eastern one in Finland. Today, followers lead their lives according to a strict set of rules: contraception, make-up and hair dye are forbidden, so too are dancing, watching television, wearing a tie and playing rhythmic music; drinking, of course, is totally out of the question.

## CULTURE

Today, one of the best known features of Sámi culture is the **joik**, or chanting, akin to that of some North American Indian cultures which, until 30 years ago, was outlawed because of its alleged association with paganism. Sung acappella or occasionally accompanied by a drum, the *joik* is not a song about a person or a place, rather an attempt to transfer the essence of someone or something into song; the Sámi, therefore, *joik* their friends, rather than *joik* about them. A *joik* is often personal and may even be composed for an individual at the time of birth. In recent years, the *joik* has found an appreciative audience outside Lapland thanks, in part, to the group *Enigma*, which had a hit with the *joik*-influenced 'Return to Innocence' in 1994; the Norwegian jazz saxophonist, Jan Garbarek, who has used Sámi rhythms in his music; and the Sámi singer Mari Boine, who hails from the Finnmark province of Norwegian Lapland, and enjoyed international recognition with her début album, *Gula Gula*.

Until the early part of the 20th century, there was precious little written cultural material available to the Sámi; for generations, people had relied on the **oral tradition** of story telling, and tended to write in Norwegian, Swedish or Finnish, if at all. Only at the beginning of the 20th century did Sámi authors begin to compose literature in their mother tongue. Writing in Northern Sámi, Johan Turi (1854–1936) is regarded as the first modern Sámi author. His *Muittalus sámiid birra*, which appeared in 1910, dealt with everyday life in Lapland, language and beliefs, and was translated into several languages including English. Probably the best known of Lapland's contemporary authors is Nils-Aslak Valkeapää (1943–2001), from Enontekiö in Finnish Lapland, who also worked as a singer; he won the Nordic Council's prize for literature in 1991.

One of the most tangible elements of Sámi culture is **handicrafts**. As you travel around Lapland, you will see examples of Sámi handicrafts seemingly everywhere you turn: everything from cups made of hollowed-out birchwood, which were traditionally used for drinking from rivers and lakes while reindeer herding, to exquisite wallets and purses made of reindeer hide. Although targeted at the modern tourist trade, most elements of Sámi handicraft have a long tradition of fabrication. Their shapes have been honed over centuries: there are no sharp edges, for example, to Sámi knives or other similar tools to avoid getting caught in knapsacks or trouser pockets while out on the fells.

## NATURAL HISTORY

Lapland's unique geographical position has produced a highly distinctive natural history. The range of flora and fauna is not huge but it is certainly impressive. Whether it is whales or reindeer, eagles or the three-toed woodpecker, you are likely to encounter some unusual wildlife as befits the unusual terrain. The landscape varies from tundra to lush river valleys with heavily forested hills, fells and swamps in between. Despite – or perhaps because of – the fact that much of it is still a virtual wilderness, it is little surprise that Lapland has always been a favourite destination for nature lovers.

**FLORA** The main dividing line in terms of what vegetation to expect is the treeline. Above it is mostly tundra, literally 'treeless plains' where all plants struggle to survive. Below it there is much greater variety and, at certain times of the year, a colourful display of plant life, most spectacularly in the early autumn as leaves turn red and gold on the trees.

**Tundra** The principal feature of tundra is the absence of any trees, but otherwise it can be very varied. Although based on permafrost, depending on the natural drainage available the terrain can be wet, in the form of peatland, or dry. The bogs tend to be characterised by many tall hummocks encrusted with a wide variety of lichens; some of them have been living for more than a hundred years, as well as plants like **crowberry** and **cloudberry**. **Cotton grass** and **sedge marshes** cover large areas and there are huge varieties of moss, but in some parts of Finnmark in Norwegian Lapland the terrain is so rocky that plant life is minimal.

Where moisture seeps down into hollows and depressions you will find willow scrub, which can grow to impressive heights of two metres or more in places. **Northern willow** is the most common, followed by **downy willow** and, where there's a lot of chalk or lime in the soil, **woolly willow**. The amount of snow and the rate of thawing make a big difference to plant life. Where the snow lingers long into spring and even summer, the wetness encourages **liverworts** and small herbs as well as **bilberry** and **mat grass**. Certain varieties of **buttercup** grow among the snow beds and **dwarf azalea** can provide some additional colour, too.

**Forests** Lapland's coniferous forests are known as 'taiga' and have very few tree types. The principal ones are the **Scots pine** and the **Norway spruce**. At higher altitudes the tougher **downy birch** often provides a border strip to the forests that can go on for many kilometres. In places you will find a lot of aspen, alder and rowan, but these tend to be in more isolated patches. When the deciduous trees change colour in September to October the displays of reds, golds and yellows are awe inspiring.

Under the tree cover **juniper** is the most common shrub, although even this can be quite sparse. The generally poor, acidic soil in much of the region means that at the forest-floor level plants struggle to survive. You are most likely to see crowberry, cowberry, and bilberry, while certain heathers reach well into the north of Lapland, even as far as the North Cape. **Ferns** do well in some forest areas, along with the inevitable **lichens**, mosses and liverworts. This is especially true where there is a lot of fallen, dead wood, which breaks down into forest floor humus. Thistles grow in patches.

Watch out for the spectacular large **monkshood**, with large leaves and tall purple spikes. It looks impressive where in grows, mainly in southern Lapland, but it is highly poisonous. **Forget-me-nots**, **sorrel**, **cow parsley** and various worts are among the herbs that are commonly found. Surprisingly several types of **orchids** also do well, including the common spotted orchid, frog orchid and lady's slipper. On dry heaths the mountain aven can make a beautiful display and the Lapland rhododendron prospers on the fells.

**FAUNA** The reindeer is emblematic of Lapland and is undoubtedly the most eye-catching of the region's animals. But it is far from the only one. Regrettably perhaps, insects are to be found everywhere, including midges, mosquitoes, blowflies and wasps. More happily butterflies can brighten up the terrain in summer.

**Birds** As many as 175 breeds of birds have been identified as breeding in Lapland. Most take advantage of the summer sun to nest and raise their young before flying south again. A few stick it out for the harsh winters, notably grouse, crows, woodpeckers and owls. You will find the biggest variety of birdlife and the largest numbers in the more temperate coastal areas. The long hours of daylight in summer can make birdwatching in Lapland particularly rewarding. There are large populations of breeding **ducks**, **sandpipers**, **greenshanks** and **dotterels**.

Inland there can be a disappointing lack of birds. If you're lucky, you may see the **snowy owl**, especially when rodent numbers are high, as well as rough-legged buzzards and eagles. More common are the **meadow pipit**, **wheatear** and **willow warbler**. **Snow bunting**, **willow grouse** and the **Siberian jay** are often seen, and on fell heaths you might encounter golden plover. The brambling and the three-toed woodpecker are quite common, but don't expect to get close enough to start counting digits. On fast flowing rivers the water ouzel likes to dive for fish. In swamp areas the sandpiper, ruff, crane and **bean goose** are happy to get their feet wet.

# Mammals

**Land mammals** Having originated from the wild caribou, Lapland's **reindeer** are now domesticated and semi-tame. They are plentiful – literally running into hundreds of thousands – and hard to miss, although they move about depending on the season and the available grazing. Every square millimetre of their bodies is covered in fur and to provide extra insulation each hair is hollow.

The Sámi have traditionally depended on the reindeer for their meat, hides, bones and oil. They provide not only food, but materials for clothing, tents, fuel and tools. The herdsmen round up their reindeer in summer into specially made corrals, where the fawns are marked with the same mark as their mother's. These roundups can make for impressive photo opportunities if you're lucky enough to catch one. There's a second roundup every autumn when the reindeer that are to be slaughtered are separated from the herd. This is also the time for a stock-take and to treat the animals for parasites.

The rutting season, when the males fight for supremacy, is September to October and the bulls can weigh up to 150kg at this time of year. They then shed their antlers in November, unlike the females (cows), which keep theirs all year round. Reindeer herds attract predators, notably the **bear**, **lynx** and **wolverine**, but visitors are extremely unlikely to spot any of them. They generally hunt at night and are very timid. The brown bear can weigh over 300kg, but it is the much smaller wolverine that poses the biggest threat to the reindeer, killing the deer by biting into its neck and hanging on with its teeth until death.

**Elk** are also prone to attack. These huge, antlered, herbivorous creatures are usually found close to the pine forests. Unlike reindeer they prefer to be alone, although in winter small clusters can be seen. The **Arctic fox** is well adapted to the harsh climate as it has small extremities, apart from a huge tail, which it can wrap around itself for extra warmth. Even the soles of its feet have fur on them and when the outside temperature drops as low as –30°C it can keep its body temperature at a comfortable +40°C. Arctic foxes are fearless and inquisitive, and about the size of a small dog.

Smaller still is the **lemming**, whose reputation for mindless self-destruction is undeserved. In fact lemmings do not get together in large numbers and jump off high cliffs in acts of mass suicide. Rather they potter about on the tundra, dig burrows and eat a lot. The Norway lemming is particularly colourful but not famous for its friendliness. The myth probably came about because of the cyclical over-population of lemmings. At these times they seem to panic that the food is going to run out and head off in large numbers to find more fertile territory.

**Marine mammals** On the face of it, the **orca** has little in common with the Norwegian lemming, but it too suffers from an unearned reputation. They are better known as **killer whales**, creating an image of huge bloodthirsty monsters prowling the deep on the lookout for anything to kill. In fact they are very intelligent, social and surprisingly gentle. They are also one of the most common whales off the coast of Lapland and very impressive to watch. They generally live in large pods of around 20 animals, have distinctive black and white bodies, and the males have large dorsal fins.

**Minke whales** are much smaller, sleeker and not at all carnivorous. They are mostly grey in colour and generally less striking to watch. But fortunately for them the whale's only predator, man, has shown limited interest in them and their numbers are plentiful. The white-beaked **dolphin**, though small, is actually a close relative of the orca whale. They travel in large groups and go surprisingly far north for animals that can't cope well with ice. Although they are protected by a thick layer of blubber that keeps them warm, it is not unusual for dolphins to get trapped in pack ice and die.

# 2

# Practical Information

Undoubtedly the most magical time to be in Lapland is **winter**. Snow is thick on the ground at this time of year, activities are in full swing and it's the only time you can see the northern lights. However, this is the busiest time of year for the tourist industry and accommodation is at a premium during the winter months; it always pays to book well in advance to ensure a bed for the night.

In general, the winter season starts in late November/early December, peaks at Christmas and New Year, and runs through to around Easter, though destinations such as Icehotel in Swedish Lapland stay open for several weeks beyond the end of the peak season. It's worth remembering that daylight is in short supply during winter and that Christmas and New Year are the darkest time of the year – the sun barely skims the horizon at the Icehotel. Snow cover helps considerably in brightening things up by reflecting the little light there is. See *Travelling in winter* on page 25 for suggestions of what to bring if you travel at this time of year.

Snow usually melts in May (or mid-June in more mountainous areas). **Spring** in Lapland, though shortlived, is glorious: trees burst into leaf seemingly overnight, flowers emerge from their enforced period of winter hibernation, carpeting the plains in a mêlée of reds, yellows and blues and the birds start to return – and sing. Within a matter of weeks the short but hectic Lapland **summer** is in full swing with the Midnight Sun adding to the attractions of this time of year. In tourist terms, summer is usually counted as mid-June to mid-August, the period when everything is open and there's a marked spring in people's step. After the middle of August certain museums and other services start to close down. If you're thinking of hiking or canoeing, summer is the perfect time of year to visit Lapland, though be prepared for swarms of Scandinavia's infamous mosquitoes, which are present from the beginning of June until early August.

By August, the first frosts are generally felt somewhere in Lapland, marking the beginning of the slow return to winter. However, the frost is responsible for one of the most breathtaking spectacles of the Lapland year: the Finns call it *ruska*, nature's last stand before winter, when the leaves on birch, aspen and mountain ash trees turn bright yellow or scarlet red, bathing the hillsides in an orgy of colour. It's hard to predict the exact time this happens, though generally the sight is at its most spectacular between mid-August and mid-September. **Autumn** is the time to come to Lapland to enjoy the nature's fruits – this is when the region's forests are bursting with berries, mushrooms and various herbs ripe for picking. The exact time of the first snows varies from year to year but there's usually snow cover somewhere in Lapland by October.

Distances between attractions in Lapland are always greater than you think and it's important to bear this in mind when planning a trip. The distance from Karesuando, for example, at the very tip of Swedish Lapland, to the North Cape is still a whopping 500km. It makes sense, therefore, on a short trip to concentrate on a particular area of Lapland and explore that thoroughly rather than hurtling from town to town and spending all your time on the road.

In **winter**, Lapland's two blockbuster attractions are **Icehotel** at **Jukkasjärvi** near Kiruna in Sweden and **Santa Claus** at either **Rovaniemi** on the **Arctic Circle** or **Kakslauttanen** near Ivalo, 260km further north. The main draw in Norway is the **North Cape**, which is accessed via Alta. One day is enough for the attractions at Icehotel, though, of course, if you visit Kiruna as well you should add in one or two more; it's perfectly feasible to visit Icehotel over a **weekend** and be back at work on Monday morning.

For trips to Santa Claus, allow two to four days depending on how many activities you want to include. Although there are plenty of one-day charter flights to Lapland during the winter months specifically aimed at visiting Santa Claus, such a flying visit will give you the briefest glimpse of Lapland (it will already be dark when you get there); remember, too, that a direct flight from Britain to Lapland is around 4–5 hours one-way.

Although it is possible to visit all of these destinations on one trip, it will entail driving 1,800km in icy conditions and isn't recommended for first time visitors. If you're looking for a two-centre break of a week in Finnish Lapland, a good option is to combine a visit to Rovaniemi or Kakslauttanen with a husky safari out of **Muonio**; the distance between Rovaniemi and Muonio is 230km, Kakslauttanen to Muonio is 300km.

In **summer** the main place to head for is undisputedly the **North Cape**. Consider starting your adventure at Alta, the closest main airport to the Cape, and perhaps also visiting the Sámi settlements of **Karasjok** or **Kautokeino**, to make a

## DISTANCES IN LAPLAND (KM)

|  | Alta | Arctic Circle | Hammerfest | Honningsvåg | Ivalo | Kautokeino | Kirkenes | Kiruna | Murmansk | Narvik | North Cape | Rovaniemi | Sortland | Tromsø |
|---|---|---|---|---|---|---|---|---|---|---|---|---|---|---|
| Alta |  | 859 | 142 | 210 | 347 | 131 | 572 | 449 | 797 | 519 | 238 | 500 | 638 | 405 |
| Arctic Circle | 859 |  | 1000 | 1013 | 1205 | 985 | 1422 | 505 | 1655 | 331 | 1044 | 1359 | 388 | 597 |
| Hammerfest | 1000 | 142 |  | 180 | 370 | 273 | 541 | 590 | 768 | 861 | 208 | 656 | 782 | 548 |
| Honningsvåg | 1013 | 210 | 180 |  | 338 | 342 | 562 | 603 | 736 | 729 | 35 | 824 | 849 | 616 |
| Ivalo | 1205 | 347 | 370 | 338 |  | 282 | 239 | 491 | 286 | 926 | 369 | 286 | 1028 | 797 |
| Kautokeino | 985 | 131 | 273 | 342 | 282 |  | 452 | 322 | 680 | 647 | 370 | 373 | 766 | 533 |
| Kirkenes | 1422 | 572 | 541 | 562 | 239 | 452 |  | 769 | 243 | 1090 | 590 | 473 | 1210 | 977 |
| Kiruna | 505 | 449 | 590 | 603 | 491 | 322 | 769 |  | 756 | 175 | 635 | 337 | 329 | 382 |
| Murmansk | 1655 | 797 | 768 | 736 | 286 | 680 | 243 | 756 |  | 1325 | 767 | 551 | 1450 | 1196 |
| Narvik | 331 | 519 | 661 | 729 | 926 | 647 | 1090 | 175 | 1325 |  | 757 | 512 | 202 | 259 |
| North Cape | 1044 | 238 | 208 | 35 | 369 | 370 | 590 | 635 | 767 | 757 |  | 655 | 877 | 644 |
| Rovaniemi | 1359 | 500 | 656 | 624 | 286 | 373 | 473 | 337 | 551 | 512 | 655 |  | 569 | 577 |
| Sortland | 388 | 638 | 782 | 849 | 1028 | 766 | 1210 | 329 | 1450 | 202 | 877 | 569 |  | 378 |
| Tromsø | 597 | 405 | 548 | 616 | 797 | 533 | 977 | 382 | 1196 | 259 | 644 | 577 | 378 |  |

week's holiday. Alternatively, make the journey directly to the Cape starting from either Kiruna or Rovaniemi; once again, you should allow a week for this trip. Another option for a week's holiday would be to combine a visit to Kiruna with an excursion to the **Lofoten islands** in Norway. With a couple of weeks at your disposal you could extend this journey to include the North Cape by flying into either Tromsø in Norway or Kiruna in Sweden, then heading across to the Lofoten islands *en route* to the Cape and then return from there via Karasjok or Kautokeino to Rovaniemi in Finland. From here you could fly home or continue south to **Luleå** in Sweden, where there's a greater range of flight options to take you south.

## TOUR OPERATORS

Although Lapland is geared up for individual travel, with a full range of accommodation and transport options to ensure a trouble-free stay, there are a number of tour operators who also specialise in holidays to the region. The main ones are listed below.

### AUSTRALIA
**Bentours International** ↘ 02 9241 1353; e info@bentours.com.au; www.bentours.com.au. Selling trips onboard the Norwegian coastal ferry, Hurtigruten, as well as trips to the North Cape, hiking tours along the Kungsleden trail in Sweden & the Icehotel at Jukkasjärvi.

### CANADA
**Great Canadian Travel Company** ↘ 204 949 0199; www.greatcanadiantravel.com (email via website). Trips to the North Cape & Norwegian Lapland.

### UK
**Canterbury Travel** ↘ 01923 822388; e info@santa-holidays.com; www.santa-holidays.com & www.laplandmagic.com. The market leaders in 1–5 day trips to see Santa Claus have an impressive range of departures from most UK regional airports.
**Discover the World** ↘ 01737 218800; e enquiries@discover-the-world-co.uk; www.discover-the-world.co.uk/lapland. The only company selling the direct flight from London Heathrow to Kiruna & the UK's largest tour operator to the Icehotel in Jukkasjärvi. Experienced & well-respected specialist operator with years of experience in arranging independent holidays to Lapland.

Options include short winter breaks to Lapland & the Icehotel as well as skiing under the Midnight Sun & even breaks at Sweden's Space Centre.
**Scantours** ↘ 020 7554 3530; e info@scantours.co.uk; www.scantours.co.uk. Northern lights, Santa Claus, ice hotels, husky safaris – these people have got most things covered.
**Taber Holidays** ↘ 01274 875199; e info@taberhols.co.uk; www.taberhols.co.uk. A wide range of Lapland holidays from this Yorkshire-based tour operator – everything from the Alta igloo hotel in Norway to dog sledding at Harriniva in Finland.

### USA
**5 Stars of Scandinavia** ↘ 800 722 4146; e info@5stars-of-scandinavia.com; www.5stars-of-scandinavia.com. The American specialist in holidays

to the region including a 7 night Arctic adventure special covering Norwegian, Finnish & Swedish Lapland.

## RED TAPE

European Union, American, Canadian, Australian and New Zealand nationals need only a valid passport to enter Finland, Norway or Sweden – and, hence, Lapland – for a maximum period of three months. All other citizens should contact the appropriate embassy for visa information.

# ⓔ EMBASSIES

Since Lapland crosses national borders and is not an independent country, it has no embassies or consulates of its own. Instead, the national governments of Finland, Norway and Sweden are the point of contact for all affairs relating to Lapland.

## AUSTRALIA
**Finland** ☎ 02 6273 3800;
ⓔ sanomat.can@formin.fi; www.finland.org.au/fi
**Norway** ☎ 02 6273 3444;
ⓔ emb.canberra@mfa.no; www.norway.org.au

**Sweden** ☎ 02 6270 2700;
ⓔ sweden@iimetro.com.au; www.swedenabroad.com

## CANADA
**Finland** ☎ 613 288 2233; ⓔ embassy@finland.ca;
www.finland.ca
**Norway** ☎ 613 238 6571; ⓔ emb.ottawa@mfa.no;
www.emb-norway.ca

**Sweden** ☎ 613 244 8200;
ⓔ ambassaden.ottawa@foreign.ministry.se;
www.swedenabroad.com

## UK
**Finland** ☎ 020 7838 6200;
ⓔ sanomat.lon@formin.fi; www.finemb.org.uk
**Norway** ☎ 020 7591 5500;
ⓔ emb.london@mfa.no; www.norway.org.uk

**Sweden** ☎ 020 7917 6400;
ⓔ ambassaden.london@foreign.ministry.se;
www.swedenabroad.com

## USA
**Finland** ☎ 202 298 5800;
ⓔ sanomat.was@formin.fi; www.finland.org
**Norway** ☎ 202 333 6000;
ⓔ emb.washington@mfa.no; www.norway.org/embassy

**Sweden** ☎ 202 467 2600;
ⓔ ambassaden.washington@foreign.ministry.se;
www.swedenabroad.com

# ✈ GETTING THERE AND AWAY

Given the tremendous distances involved in reaching Lapland, even from elsewhere in Scandinavia, the only feasible way of getting there is **by air**. Naturally, it is possible to drive to Lapland as part of a greater European tour, but consider just how far it is: London to Kiruna, for example, is 3,000km.

**LAPLAND'S AIRPORTS** The main airports to use in Lapland are Kiruna (KRN), Luleå (LLA), Narvik/Harstad (EVE), Tromsø (TOS), Rovaniemi (RVN) and Ivalo (IVL), but flying to Lapland will generally entail first reaching one of the Nordic capitals (Stockholm, Oslo, Helsinki) and then changing planes for a domestic flight to one of the airports listed above; see 'Getting to Scandinavia' below for information on how to reach the Nordic capitals. The only exception to this rule is the new SAS direct flight from London Heathrow to Kiruna operating in partnership with the British tour operator Discover the World (see above). It runs three times per week between December and April and a new direct flight operated by Norwegian from London Stansted to Tromsø which runs twice weekly.

**CHANGING PLANES** Domestic flights to Lapland leave from Stockholm Arlanda (ARN), Oslo Gardermoen (OSL) and Helsinki Vantaa (HEL) airports. There are currently no flights to Lapland from the secondary Scandinavian airports used by Ryanair. Accordingly, if you choose to fly to Scandinavia with Ryanair and arrive at either Stockholm Skavsta (NYO) or Oslo Torp (TRF) you will have to change airports and get to either Arlanda or Gardermoen to continue your journey; you should allow at least three or four hours to do this.

**DOMESTIC AIR ROUTES TO LAPLAND** Below we've listed the most useful domestic routes and airline websites to consider when planning a trip to Lapland. The duration of the flight up to Lapland is roughly 1½ to 2 hours, depending on destination. If bought in advance, it is possible to pick up a single ticket from around £35/$65.

### Finnish Lapland
**Helsinki-Enontekiö** www.finnair.com
**Helsinki-Ivalo** www.finnair.com

**Helsinki-Rovaniemi** www.finnair.com & www.blue1.com

### Norwegian Lapland
**Oslo-Alta**
**Oslo-Kirkenes**

**Oslo-Narvik/Harstad**
**Oslo-Tromsø**

All routes operated by SAS: www.sas.no, & Norwegian: www.norwegian.no

### Swedish Lapland
**Stockholm-Arvidsjaur** www.skyways.se
**Stockholm-Kiruna** www.sas.se & www.flynordic.com

**Stockholm-Luleå** www.sas.se & www.flynordic.com

**GETTING TO SCANDINAVIA** The best transit airports to aim for when heading for Lapland are Stockholm Arlanda, Oslo Gardermoen or Helsinki Vantaa. Copenhagen's Kastrup airport, although the biggest hub in Scandinavia, has no direct flights to Lapland and is worth avoiding for that reason.

**From the UK** There are direct flights to Stockholm, Oslo and Helsinki from several UK airports, including Aberdeen (ABZ), Bristol (BRS), Edinburgh (EDI), Glasgow (GLA), London City (LCY), London Gatwick (LGW), London Heathrow (LHR), London Stansted (STN), Manchester (MAN) and Nottingham East Midlands (EMA). Some flights only operate during the summer months. A return ticket usually costs from £100/$190. Useful websites are:

**British Airways** www.ba.com (LHR to ARN, OSL & HEL)
**City Star Airlines** www.citystarairlines.com (ABZ to OSL)
**Finnair** www.finnair.co.uk (LHR, MAN & EDI to HEL)
**Norwegian** www.norwegian.no (LGW, STN & EDI to OSL)

**Scandinavian Airlines** www.flysas.co.uk (LHR, LCY & MAN to ARN & OSL; BRS & GLA to ARN)
**Sterling** www.sterling.dk (LGW & EMA to ARN; EMA & EDI to OSL; EDI to ARN)

**From the USA and Canada** The best fares from the USA and Canada to Scandinavia are to Stockholm and Helsinki. Oslo has only a handful of flights and fares are correspondingly higher. Direct flights are operated by the following airlines:

**Continental** www.continental.com (Newark to Stockholm & Oslo)
**Finnair** www.finnair.com (Boston to Stockholm; Boston, New York & Toronto to Helsinki)

**Malaysia Airlines** (Newark to Stockholm)
**Scandinavian Airlines** (Chicago & Newark to Stockholm)
**US Airways** (Philadelphia to Stockholm)

High season fares are in the region of US$1,000, falling to US$650 in the shoulder season and as low as US$500 in low season.

**From the rest of the world** Getting to Lapland from elsewhere in the world naturally involves reaching one of the Scandinavian gateways first, from where connections are available as described above. If you want to buy a through ticket to Lapland, the best options are Scandinavian Airlines and Finnair, which will be able to offer connections through their Stockholm and Helsinki hubs respectively from several destinations in Asia and Australia, sometimes using codeshare flights with their partners. A good place to start your research is an online travel website such as Expedia, Opodo or Travelocity.

## ✚ HEALTH AND SAFETY with Dr Felicity Nicholson

The health risks while travelling in Lapland are minimal and health care is of an excellent standard. Language (except occasionally in Finland) is rarely a problem and health workers are generally proficient in English. Reciprocal health arrangements between European Union countries entitle all EU citizens to free or discounted medical treatment within Swedish and Finnish Lapland. Norway, although not part of the EU, also provides EU nationals with similar cover to that they can expect in the EU under the terms of the EEA (European Economic Area) agreement.

Non-EU nationals are obliged to pay for medical treatment in full and should therefore make sure they have up to date travel insurance.

Two particular hazards to bear in mind when travelling in Lapland are the heightened risk of road accidents as a result of the large number of wild animals on the road, especially reindeer, and the effects of cold during the winter months.

**TRAVEL CLINICS AND HEALTH INFORMATION** A full list of current travel clinic websites is available from the International Society of Travel Medicine (*www.istm.org*). For other journey preparation information, consult www.tripprep.com. Information about various medications may be found on www.emedicine.com.

## WOMEN AND GAY TRAVELLERS

Women travelling alone are unlikely to encounter any problems. Nordic males are generally well mannered and far too shy to create trouble. On Friday and Saturday nights, though, when the beer starts to flow, it's obviously sensible to keep your wits about you, but, once again, you are unlikely to become the target of abusive behaviour. Gay travellers will have to forego the pleasures of gay bars and clubs while in Lapland – quite simply, there is no gay scene whatsoever. Attitudes towards homosexuality are generally tolerant, though the views of unmarried lumberjack types may not be the most enlightened. The sight of a same-sex couple walking hand in hand through a remote Lapland village, particularly with a large Sámi community, is likely to cause quite a stir so it's probably best to keep outward shows of affection to yourselves.

## WHAT TO TAKE

Obviously, what to take on a holiday to Lapland depends on when you're going. In winter, for example, you'll need to be properly kitted out with cold-weather gear and the like. For detailed advice, see Winter Lapland: what to bring, pages 24–5. In summer, the relatively mild climate doesn't require any particular items of clothing, though it can be useful to have a decent **waterproof jacket** since the heavens can open at any moment. If you're considering hiking, a good pair of **sturdy waterproof boots and trousers** are essential, and it is worth taking a **waterproof cover for your rucksack** if you have one. Consider taking an **alarm clock** (or your mobile phone) for early-morning buses and ferries. If you're planning to take non-digital photographs during your stay, you'll save lots of money by buying your **films** at home rather than in Lapland where they are more expensive and hard to find.

The Finnish, Norwegian and Swedish electricity supply is 220V and all plugs are the northern European two-pin standard, for which **adaptors** are readily available at major airports. If you're taking a **laptop** computer with you, consider taking along a **patch cable** so you can connect to the internet in hotels with no WiFi connection.

**TRAVELLING IN WINTER** The Lapland winter is not to be taken lightly and in order to enjoy a visit between October and May, when the cold is at its most intense, it's essential to come prepared. The key to surviving the chill is to wear several **layers of clothes**, preferably made of cotton, which acts as an effective insulator; forget jeans and synthetic materials – you'll freeze to death. It's worth considering wearing longjohns to help keep your legs warm, though they can be a little cumbersome at times. In addition to a warm and snug winter coat, you should bring a thick woolly hat, scarf, gloves and the thickest socks you have. If you fail to keep your head and feet warm, you risk losing up to 50% of your body heat.

Hiking boots or other stout shoes are an absolute must – preferably the type that have a deep tread to help you walk on the compacted, polished snow that covers city streets in winter. Don't expect roads and streets to be cleared every time it snows – it simply is impractical. Instead take extreme care when walking on snowy or icy pavements or roads, even those that have been treated with salt or sand, because they can still be extremely slippery.

**MAPS** The best **maps** of Lapland are Pohjoiskalotti by Finland's Genimap (1:800 000), or the more detailed Nordkalotten (1: 700 000) by either Norway's Cappelen or Sweden's Kartförlaget.

These maps are best bought in the countries concerned. If bought abroad, for example, in the UK, they are much more expensive.

## $ MONEY AND BANKING

Annoyingly, three currencies circulate in Lapland: Norway uses the **Norwegian krone** (plural *kroner*; official international abbreviation NOK); Sweden, the **Swedish krona** (plural *kronor*; offical international abbreviation SEK); and Finland, the **euro** (EUR). Since they are not interchangeable (you cannot spend Norwegian kroner in Sweden, for example), you'll be forced to convert one currency into another if you are visiting more than one country. Notes and coins are in circulation in all three countries.

We have given prices in the local currency of each country. For example, prices marked as *kr* in Norway are in Norwegian kroner, and prices marked as *kr* in Sweden are in Swedish kronor. Prices in Finland are given in euro.

The best way to get money in Lapland is by using a **debit card** that has a Cirrus facility on it. This makes it possible to withdraw money from cashpoints much as you would at home. Although there is a small charge levied by banks for this purpose, it is much less than you would pay in bank commissions when exchanging travellers' cheques. Cashpoints machines are commonplace and appear

*Ariadne Van Zandbergen*

**EQUIPMENT** Although with some thought and an eye for composition you can take reasonable photos with a 'point-and-shoot' camera, you need an SLR camera if you are at all serious about photography. Modern SLRs tend to be very clever, with automatic programmes for almost every possible situation, but remember that these programmes are limited in the sense that the camera cannot think, but only make calculations. Every starting amateur photographer should read a photographic manual for beginners and get to grips with such basics as the relationship between aperture and shutter speed.

Always buy the best lens you can afford. The lens determines the quality of your photo more than the camera body. Fixed fast lenses are ideal, but very costly. A zoom lens makes it easier to change composition without changing lenses the whole time. If you carry only one lens, a 28–70mm (digital 17–55mm) or similar zoom should be ideal. For a second lens, a lightweight 80–200mm or 70–300mm (digital 55–200mm) or similar will be excellent for candid shots and varying your composition. Wildlife photography will be very frustrating if you don't have at least a 300mm lens. For a small loss of quality, tele-converters are a cheap and compact way to increase magnification: a 300 lens with a 1.4x converter becomes 420mm, and with a 2x it becomes 600mm. Note, however, that 1.4x and 2x tele-converters reduce the speed of your lens by 1.4 and 2 stops respectively.

For photography from a vehicle, a solid beanbag, which you can make yourself very cheaply, will be necessary to avoid blurred images, and is more useful than a tripod. A clamp with a tripod head screwed on to it can be attached to the vehicle as well. Modern dedicated flash units are easy to use; aside from the obvious need to flash when you photograph at night, you can improve a lot of photos in difficult 'high contrast' or very dull light with some fill-in flash. It pays to have a proper flash unit as opposed to a built-in camera flash.

**DIGITAL/FILM** Digital photography is now the preference of most amateur and professional photographers, with the resolution of digital cameras improving the whole time. For ordinary prints a 6 megapixel camera is fine. For better results and the possibility to enlarge images and for professional reproduction, higher resolution is available up to 16 megapixels.

Memory space is important. The number of pictures you can fit on a memory card depends on the quality you choose. Calculate in advance how many pictures you can fit on a card and either take enough cards to last for your trip, or take a storage drive on to which you can download the content. A laptop gives the advantage that you can see your pictures properly at the end of each day and edit and delete rejects, but a storage device is lighter and less bulky. These drives come in different capacities up to 80GB.

in even the smallest village. The use of **credit cards** such as Visa and MasterCard is widespread and provides another way of paying for goods and also, of course, for withdrawing cash on credit.

**Banking hours** in Norway are usually Monday–Friday 08.30–15.30 (17.00 or 18.00 on Thursday); in Finland banks tend to be open Monday–Friday 09.15–16.15; in Sweden service hours are 09.30–15.00 (till 17.30 on Thursday).

**BUDGETING** Costs in Lapland vary widely from country to country. The most expensive part of the region is Norwegian Lapland where prices are punitive.

Bear in mind that digital camera batteries, computers and other storage devices need charging, so make sure you have all the chargers, cables and converters with you. Most hotels have charging points, but do enquire about this in advance. When camping you might have to rely on charging from the car battery; a spare battery is invaluable.

If you are shooting film, 100 to 200 ISO print film and 50 to 100 ISO slide film are ideal. Low ISO film is slow but fine grained and gives the best colour saturation, but will need more light, so support in the form of a tripod or monopod is important. You can also bring a few 'fast' 400 ISO films for low-light situations where a tripod or flash is no option.

**DUST AND HEAT** Dust and heat are often a problem. Keep your equipment in a sealed bag, stow films in an airtight container (eg: a small cooler bag) and avoid exposing equipment and film to the sun. Digital cameras are prone to collecting dust particles on the sensor which results in spots on the image. The dirt mostly enters the camera when changing lenses, so be careful when doing this. To some extent photos can be 'cleaned' up afterwards in Photoshop, but this is time-consuming. You can have your camera sensor professionally cleaned, or you can do this yourself with special brushes and swabs made for the purpose, but note that touching the sensor might cause damage and should only be done with the greatest care.

**LIGHT** The most striking outdoor photographs are often taken during the hour or two of 'golden light' after dawn and before sunset. Shooting in low light may enforce the use of very low shutter speeds, in which case a tripod will be required to avoid camera shake.

With careful handling, side lighting and back lighting can produce stunning effects, especially in soft light and at sunrise or sunset. Generally, however, it is best to shoot with the sun behind you. When photographing animals or people in the harsh midday sun, images taken in light but even shade are likely to be more effective than those taken in direct sunlight or patchy shade, since the latter conditions create too much contrast.

**PROTOCOL** In some countries, it is unacceptable to photograph local people without permission, and many people will refuse to pose or will ask for a donation. In such circumstances, don't try to sneak photographs as you might get yourself into trouble. Even the most willing subject will often pose stiffly when a camera is pointed at them; relax them by making a joke, and take a few shots in quick succession to improve the odds of capturing a natural pose.

*Ariadne Van Zandbergen is a professional travel and wildlife photographer specialising in Africa. She runs The Africa Image Library. For photo requests, visit www.africaimagelibrary.co.za or contact her on ariadne@hixnet.co.za.*

Norway has long had a reputation as one of the most expensive countries in the world to visit – sadly, this is still very much the case. If anyone can explain to me why something as basic as a pizza should cost upwards of 150kr, I am eager to learn. You should expect to pay two or three times more than home for just about anything you want to buy. A main course in a restaurant, for example, will cost around 250–350kr; a beer is in the region of 65kr.

Mercifully, Swedish and Finnish Lapland are different. Sweden is the cheapest of all the Nordic countries and in many circumstances you'll pay less for things than you would at home. The filling daily set lunch available in restaurants everywhere, for example (*dagens rätt*), costs around 65–75kr and includes a main dish, salad, bread, a soft drink and coffee – that's a fantastic deal for just £5/US$9.50. Alcohol is cheapest in Finland, where half a litre of beer, for example, costs around €4; in northern Sweden it's normally around 55kr. Tipping and bargaining are not expected in Lapland, though you may wish to round up a restaurant bill to the nearest large number, for example, 280kr becomes 300kr, as a small sign of your appreciation.

Accommodation in Finland and Sweden costs significantly less than in Norway. Transport costs are roughly the same throughout Lapland and, given the huge distances involved, represent good value for money.

When budgeting for a trip calculate that you should be able to get by on £25/US$45 per day in Sweden and Finland (£40/US$75 in Norway) staying in hostels, eating lunch and seeing the sights; having the odd drink and staying in hotels will push prices up to around £60–75/US$100–130 in Sweden and Finland (£100–130/US$190–240 in Norway).

# GETTING AROUND

Although distances are often long and journeys between towns can take several hours (if not all day in some circumstances), travel around Lapland is straightforward. The public transport system in all three countries is efficient, and more often than not runs on time. In Sweden **trains** run from Luleå northwest to Gällivare, Kiruna and Riksgränsen before crossing the border to Narvik in Norway. There are trains between Gällivare, Jokkmokk and Arvidsjaur running on the privately operated single-track **Inlandsbanan** (*www.grandnordic.se*) between mid-June and early September. In Finland rail services effectively expire at Rovaniemi although there is an occasional service as far north as Kolari (which until recently had been stopping at Tornio; latest details at www.vr.fi).

In Norway, all transport north of Narvik is by **bus**; services run all the way to Kirkenes in the far east of the region and are described in the text. Both Finland and Sweden have a comprehensive bus network, and in the summer months there are cross-border services between Finland and Norway which can help you get around the region as a whole; once again details are given in the text. In Norway, the Hurtigruten coastal **ferry** provides a relaxing way of travelling up and down this highly indented coastline, as do the Hurtigbåt express ferries which operate over shorter distances.

**Flights** too can be particularly useful, especially to cover some of the grinding distances between towns in Norwegian Lapland; the key airline to look out for here is Widerøe (*www.wideroe.no*). Another airline worth considering for hopping between Luleå, Kiruna and Tromsø is Barents Airlink (*www.barentsairlink.se*), which can help you save hundreds of kilometres. As we went to press, the Swedish low-cost airline, Fly Nordic, also announced plans to fly between Luleå and Kiruna.

However, getting around **by car** is always going to be the most convenient way of seeing Lapland. Not only are you free of the tyranny of timetabling but you can get well off the beaten track beyond the reach of most buses. **Car hire** though is pricey and you may well find it cheaper to arrange car hire before you go; airlines sometimes have special deals. Once again, Sweden and Finland are considerably cheaper than Norway, where even the Sultan of Brunei would think twice before hiring anything larger than a Nissan Micra. On the whole, expect to pay upwards of £250/$475 a week for a small car. Across Lapland the rules of the road are strict: there's a speed limit of 30km/h in residential areas, 50km/h in built-up areas and

80–90km/h on other roads. Speed cameras exist and penalties are high – particularly in Norway where on-the-spot fines can reach 5,000kr and more.

## CAR HIRE AGENCIES The main car hire agencies represented in Lapland are:

**Avis** Norway `\` 81 53 30 44; Finland `\` 0870 60 60 100; Sweden `\` 0770 82 00 62; www.avis.com **Europcar** Norway `\` 67 16 58 20; Finland `\` 0403 062 444; Sweden `\` 08 462 4848; www.europcar.com **Hertz** Norway `\` 67 16 80 00; Finland `\` 020 11 22 33; Sweden `\` 0771 211 212; www.hertz.com

## ACCOMMODATION

Inevitably, accommodation is going to be your biggest expense, particularly in Norway, where staying in **hotels** can be extremely pricey. However, they are of a universally high standard and more often than not have free WiFi internet access. In Sweden, in particular, much reduced weekend (Fri & Sat night) and summer prices (generally mid-Jun to mid-Aug, every day) can bring the cost of a night tumbling down. Unfortunately, many hotels suffer from an identity crisis – there are countless mundane concrete blocks across Lapland which have little character to charm the visitor. More pleasing are the ubiquitous **guesthouses** dotted across the region, which are often family-run and much more homely alternatives to the anonymous hotels. **Youth hostels** can be found in several towns offering double rooms and accommodation in dorm beds, as well as access to a communal kitchen and sauna. **Campsites** generally have **cabins** sleeping 2–6 people and can be an economical (and infinitely more cosy) alternative to a guesthouse giving you self-catering facilities.

### ACCOMMODATION PRICE CODES

The hotels and guesthouses in the guide have been graded according to price, based on the cost of the least expensive double room in high season. Where two prices appear after an entry the first refers to high season, the second to low season and/or weekend rates (ie: $$$/$$). Although we have given one price code for both Norwegian kroner/Swedish kronor (abbreviated to kr) to cover prices in Norway and Sweden, remember that prices in Sweden will be cheaper (when converted into your own currency) since one Norwegian krone is not equal to one Swedish krona. For example, 500 Norwegian kroner is approximately £44/$84, whereas 500 Swedish kronor is roughly £38/$72. For Finland we have given prices in euros.

| | | |
|---|---|---|
| **Top of the range** | $$$$$$$ | over 1,500kr/€160 |
| **Luxury** | $$$$$$ | 1,200–1,500kr/€130–160 |
| **Top range** | $$$$$ | 1,000–1,200kr/€110–130 |
| **Mid range** | $$$$ | 800–1,000kr/€85–110 |
| **Average** | $$$ | 600–800kr/€65–85 |
| **Budget** | $$ | 350–600kr/€40–65 |
| **Shoestring** | $ | under 350kr/€40 |

## EATING AND DRINKING

**FOOD** In the bigger towns and cities across Lapland you will find a wide range of eateries. In addition to the regular Nordic restaurants serving **traditional specialities** such as Arctic char and reindeer in its various guises (see below), over recent years there has been a profusion of Thai restaurants, which can make a tasty change to the ubiquitous pizzerias which line the streets of northern Scandinavia. Chinese restaurants and burger bars are common. In smaller towns, hotel restaurants are generally the best place to find quality food. Cafés can be a good place to pick up an open sandwich piled high with various topping such as prawns or meatballs, though they are generally closed on Sundays. It is generally not necessary to book a table in a restaurant in Lapland.

**Breakfast** is a perfect way to fuel up for the day. Hotels and guesthouses in all three countries provide a generous help-yourself buffet (included in the room rate) with yoghurt, cereals, ham, cheese, bacon, egg, herring, coffee and juice. You simply take what you want and return to the table as many times as you like.

**Lunch** varies from country to country. In Norway it consists mostly of a sandwich bought from a café, whereas in Sweden (and sometimes in Finland where it's called *lounas*) you should look out for the set lunch special, the *dagens rätt*, which offers an extremely economical way of enjoying a good meal. Between Monday and Friday from 11.00 to 14.00, most restaurants serve the *dagens rätt*, which generally consists of a choice of two or three main dishes, plus salad, bread, a soft drink or a low-alcohol beer and coffee – all for around 65–75kr. By switching your main meal of the day to lunchtime, you'll save a packet.

Eating **dinner** à la carte in the evening is a more expensive undertaking, although much more so in Norway than in Sweden and Finland. Many mid-range restaurants in Lapland serve local specialities, in particular **reindeer**. There are several main varieties to try: *renskav* is thin slices of stirfried reindeer meat (a bit like kebab meat to look at), usually served in a creamy mushroom sauce with mashed potatoes and lingonberries; *souvas* is salted reindeer meat, which is cold smoked and served in small rounds; the other main alternative is a regular steak of reindeer meat, mouthwateringly tender and very lean (reindeer meat has no natural fat).

**DRINK** Finland is the cheapest country in which to buy alcohol, closely followed by Sweden, with Norway off the scale. All three Nordic countries operate a restrictive system of **alcohol** sales aimed at limiting the amount of alcohol people consume. State-run stores known as Vinmonopolet (Norway), Alko (Finland) and Systembolaget (Sweden) are open office hours Monday–Friday and generally on Saturday morning and are found in the larger towns and villages across the region. They are never open in the evening, on Sunday or on public holidays. These shops are the only place to buy wine, strong beer and spirits – the only alcohol available in supermarkets is beer with a maximum alcohol content of 4.5°, in the case of Finland and Norway, or a watery 3.5° in Sweden. Naturally, alcohol is available in restaurants and bars at higher prices than in the stores. In Norway you should expect to pay 65–85kr for half a litre of beer in a bar; in Sweden around 45–55kr; and in Finland about €4–5.

## PUBLIC HOLIDAYS AND FESTIVALS

Despite the restricted sale of alcohol throughout Lapland, there's certainly no shortage of the stuff during **midsummer** celebrations, the most important public holiday of the year, which takes place between 21 and 23 June in Sweden and Finland. Festivities centre around the maypole, an old fertility symbol, which is erected at popular gatherings across the north of Scandinavia. There's much dancing and drinking into the light night – and severe hangovers the next morning. The biggest **Sámi festivals** in the region are the Kautokeino Easter Festival (see pages 115–16) and the late-August Storstämmningshelgen in Arvidsjaur (see page 44). Other public holidays are:

## FINLAND
1, 6 January
April Good Friday, Easter Sunday, Easter Monday
1 May, Ascension Day, Whit Sunday
23 June (Midsummer Day)
1 November All Saints Day
6 December (Independence Day)
25, 26 December

## NORWAY
1 January
April Maundy Thursday, Good Friday, Easter Sunday, Easter Monday
1, 17 May (National Day), Whit Sunday, Whit Monday
25, 26 December

## SWEDEN
1, 6 January
April Good Friday, Easter Sunday, Easter Monday
1 May, Ascension Day, Whit Sunday
6 June (National Day), 23 June (Midsummer Day)
1 November All Saints Day
25, 26 December

 # SHOPPING

Across Lapland you'll be presented with dozens of opportunities to pick up locally produced **handicrafts** of Sámi design and origin: attractively carved wooden knives and forks (with or without engraving), hollowed out birch knots in the shape of drinking cups, leather goods in various shapes and sizes made of reindeer skin and jewellery are just some of the items on sale. It's possible to pick up a **reindeer skin** (most reasonably priced in Finland), though you should make sure when you buy it that the animal was slaughtered in the autumn since it will moult less; you should take care not to get the skin wet since that can cause the hair to fall out. Try to buy any of the above directly from Sámi-run stalls or businesses and you'll be sure that the money is going back into the local community, a much more satisfying experience than giving your money to a national chain store in Luleå, for example, selling mass produced trinkets for the tourist market. Although Norway operates a system of tax-free shopping, as it is not part of the European Union, you will always find prices higher than in Sweden and Finland, even taking your return tax into account.

 # ARTS AND ENTERTAINMENT

In Sámi the words for 'art' and 'artist', as they are perceived in western cultures, are relatively new. However, traditional Sámi art, which includes music, storytelling and handicrafts, are all key pillars of the indigenous culture of Lapland, which has a history spanning several millennia. The prehistoric rock carvings, for example, discovered 30 years ago near Alta in Norway, are an artistic impression of man's inseparable link to nature – a characteristic of Sámi art when seen from a non-indigenous perspective. Art for art's sake has rarely existed in the Sámi community since utensils and other items were created for their practical rather than aesthetic value. However, in the modern age, Sámi artists have begun to express a Western conception of art, drawing on the ancient culture of their indigenous heritage for inspiration, which has helped the wider community create an identity for itself.

When it comes to non-indigenous art, it's Norway that has the most developed scene. Northern Norwegian artists such as Axel Revold are well represented in exhibitions across Norwegian Lapland, particularly in Tromsø and Henningsvær in the Lofoten islands. There are specialist museums dedicated to paintings produced in the north at the turn of the last century, a period widely regarded as the golden era of contemporary art from this part of the country. A key recurring element in these paintings is the powerful nature of Norwegian Lapland.

## MEDIA AND COMMUNICATIONS

**RADIO** Although there are now **radio stations** in all three countries transmitting in Sámi, it's unlikely you'll have anything to do with them, other than tuning in perhaps for curiosity's sake. The best source of **English-language radio news** is the BBC World Service, which can be received during the mornings and evenings across Scandinavia; see www.bbc.co.uk/worldservice for times and frequencies. Alternatively, during hours of darkness you may be able to receive BBC Radio 5 Live on 693kHz medium wave, although reception is patchy.

**TELEVISION** National **television** carries a short daily bulletin of Sámi news. State-run licence-fee funded television (NRK in Norway, SVT in Sweden and YLE in Finland) all operate a couple of channels in their respective countries, complementing the respective offerings of commercial stations TV2 (Norway), TV4 (Sweden) and MTV (Finland, though not the music channel you're no doubt familiar with). Many programmes are imported from Britain or the US and shown with subtitles.

**NEWSPAPERS** All countries support a number of national and regional newspapers, though unless you speak one of the Scandinavian languages it's unlikely you'll have much call for them. In larger libraries it is sometimes possible to find **English-language newspapers** and in some towns they are also available for sale, though this is the exception rather than the rule.

**TELEPHONES AND THE POST OFFICE** In the land of Nokia and Ericsson, there's little call for public telephones and most have now disappeared. **Mobile phone** coverage is virtually 100% and you will find it useful to have one. However, it's a good idea to buy a local SIM card to eliminate roaming costs. They are available from telephone stores, Telenor in Norway, Telia in Sweden and Sonera in Finland and occasionally also from newsagents.

In Sweden the **post office** has ceased to exist. Instead you buy stamps from supermarkets, filling stations or hotel receptions. In Norway and Finland the post office lives on offering the range of services you're accustomed to. Stamps can also be bought from newsagents.

**INTERNET** Most hotels offer free WiFi internet connection, which is great if you're travelling with your own laptop. Alternatives are to access the net at most tourist offices for a small fee, or for free at town libraries where you will most likely have to book a slot for later in the day and come back at your allotted time. Internet cafés have yet to make their mark in Lapland since everybody has internet access at home.

# TIME

Time in Norway and Sweden is the same. It is always one hour ahead of Britain and Ireland at Greenwich Mean Time (GMT) in winter, and GMT plus two hours in summer; six to nine hours ahead of the continental US. Finland is two hours ahead of the UK and seven to ten hours ahead of the continental US. Daylight saving is in operation, as in Britain and Ireland, from late October to late March.

*Brown bear*

*Elk*

# Part Two

## THE GUIDE

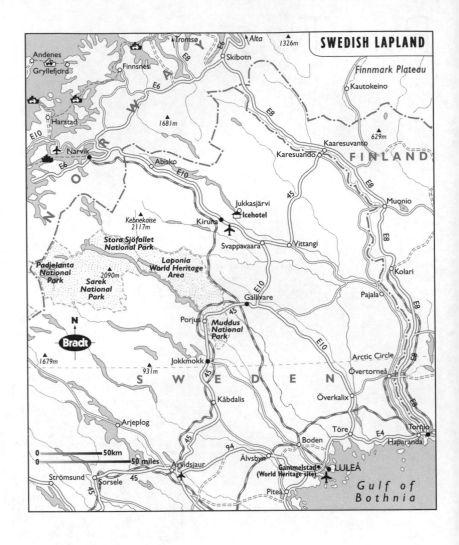

SWEDISH LAPLAND

# 3

# Swedish Lapland: Luleå to Riksgränsen

Stretching from the upper reaches of the Gulf of Bothnia to the high fells that delineate Sweden's northern borders with Norway and Finland, the immense expanse of forest and upland terrain that is Swedish Lapland is home to no fewer than eight national parks, Sweden's highest mountain and vast tracts of uninhabited, unsullied land that are as large as some European countries. If you travel here you will experience a land that is entirely dominated by nature: pine and spruce forests cloak the hills, mighty rivers roar down the valleys to the coast and crystal-clear mountain lakes punctuate every landscape. Its towns and villages, many with a sizeable Sámi community, are few and far between. Pleasant, easy-going places, nonetheless, they make a fine introduction to Lapland, and can be explored by train as well as car since Swedish Lapland has the area's greatest concentration of rail routes. The further north and west you travel within the region, the more reindeer you will come across. In the summer months, they graze on the high fells northwest of Jokkmokk and Gällivare, while during the winter months they can often be seen in the forests on the outskirts of towns where they dig for lichen in the snow. They can also be a particular hazard on the roads in winter since they are attracted by the salt and sand which is thrown down to assist driving.

You will find the region's best-known attraction, **Icehotel**, in Swedish Lapland. It is built of blocks of ice hewn every winter from the frozen Torne river, which stands tall until the spring thaw in May. Nearby **Kiruna**, with its new direct flights to London, is as good a gateway as any to this part of Lapland and provides easy access to **Abisko** which, thanks to its clear skies, is the best place in Lapland to view the **northern lights**. On the Arctic Circle, **Jokkmokk** is the location for the region's oldest and most enjoyable market, a mammoth event, which attracts ten of thousands of visitors every February. **Arvidsjaur**, further south, has an equally strong Sámi history and culture, witnessed by its impressive collection of Sámi church dwellings, Lappstaden. **Luleå**, on the other hand, is a modern, thoroughly Swedish city, with an impressive bar and restaurant scene, top-notch accommodation and excellent transport links to the rest of the region. Yet, it is also the site of **Gammelstad**, a UNESCO World Heritage listed collection of 400 knotted wooden cottages neatly gathered around the most stunning medieval church in Lapland.

## LULEÅ

With a population of 73,000, Luleå (Julev in Sámi; Luulaja in Finnish) is the biggest city in Lapland, and bills itself as the capital of Swedish Lapland, although, arguably, Kiruna has a stronger claim to the title thanks to its location north of the Arctic Circle. Either way, Luleå is one of the best gateways to Lapland thanks to its busy airport and good bus and train connections. It is also an excellent place to rest either side of a trip further north; its restaurant and bar scene is the best for miles around, prices are reasonable (unlike in Lapland's second city, Tromsø) and the impressive UNESCO World Heritage Site, Gammelstad, is just down the road.

**SOME HISTORY** Founded by Swedish king Gustav II Adolf in 1621 on the site of nearby Gammelstad (Old Town) with its medieval church and attendant church cottages, Luleå quickly grew thanks to its superb, though small harbour. However, a combination of falling sea levels and rapid land elevation soon rendered the harbour useless and it was decreed in 1649 that the entire town should up sticks and move to its current location at the mouth of the River Lule. Barely two hundred years later, virtually the entire place was burnt to the ground in a devastating fire; only a handful of buildings escaped the flames. Things improved with the arrival of the new railway line, Malmbanan, in the late 1880s, which enabled iron ore from the mines at Kiruna and Gällivare to be transported to Luleå by train for shipping via the Gulf of Bothnia. Today Luleå is a likeable, vibrant, go-ahead sort of a place, which is fast developing into a world-renowned hi-tech metallurgical centre, thanks to its research programmes and expansive steel industry. There is also a technical university here, which lends the city's wide open streets and airy public squares a pleasant, youthful air.

**GETTING THERE** Taking a flight to **Luleå airport** (*airport code LLA; www.lfv.se/lulea*) is an excellent way of arriving in Swedish Lapland. The airport, 10km southwest of the city, is served by several **airlines**, flying from/to a whole host of destinations: Stockholm (SAS and Flynordic); Gothenburg (City Airline); Kirun (Barents Airlink and Flynordic); Murmansk, Pajala and Tromsø (Barents Airlink); Umeå and Östersund (Nordic Regional); and Sundsvall (Direktflyg). The airport bus into town costs 45kr; a taxi is 180kr. The **train** and **bus** stations are barely five minutes' walk from each other, at the eastern end of the town centre. Luleå has direct trains from/to Stockholm, Gothenburg, Kiruna and Narvik.

**TOURIST INFORMATION** The tourist office (❧ *0920 45 70 00;* e *turistbyra@lulea.se; www.lulea.se;* ⊕ *09.00–19.00 Mon–Fri; mid-June to mid-Aug Sat & Sun 10.00–16.00*) is in Kulturens Hus, Skeppsbrogatan 17, a straightforward ten-minute walk from the bus station west all the way along Skeppsbrogatan. There's internet access here and in the adjoining library.

**WHERE TO STAY** Luleå has a large range of modern, central hotels, the pick of which we have detailed below. Prices at weekends and in summer drop significantly making non-peak hotel rooms an absolute bargain. For such a relatively large city, it is unusual for the youth hostel not to be affiliated to the national youth hostel association, STF, but it is a good standard and relatively central.

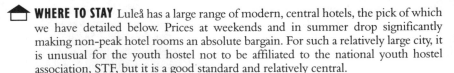

⌂ **Best Western Arctic** Sandviksgatan 80; ❧ 0920 109 80; e rec@arctichotel.se; www.arctichotel.se. An inviting hotel, close to the train station, with newly renovated contemporary Nordic-style rooms. The attractive corner suites are spacious & bright. Free wireless internet access & a good sauna & jacuzzi on the 5th floor. $$$$$$/$$$$
⌂ **Elite Stadshotell** Storgatan 15; ❧ 0920 27 40

00; e info.lulea@elite.se; www.lulea.elite.se. Built in the 1890s with a touch of French Renaissance style, this is undoubtedly the grandest place to stay in Luleå with a wide range of rooms featuring period furniture & sumptuous drapes. $$$$$$/$$$$
⌂ **Amber** Stationsgatan 67; ❧ 0920 102 00; e info@amber-hotell.se; www.amber-hotell.se. A pretty

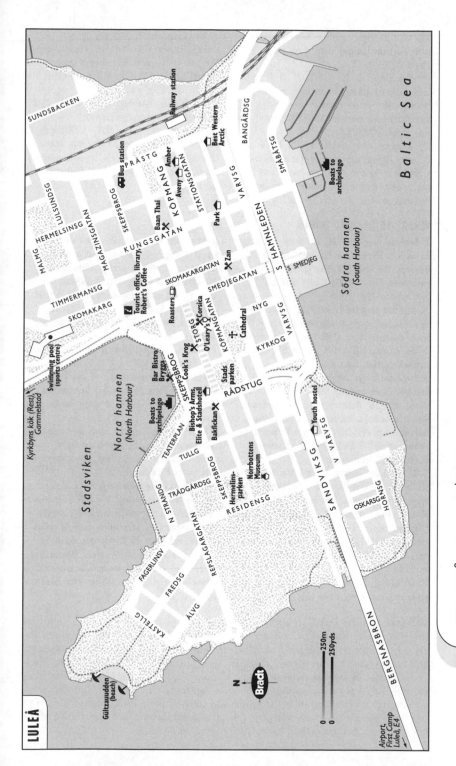

**LULEÅ**

Stadsviken

*Baltic Sea*

SUNDSBACKEN

Railway station

Bus station

PRÄSTG

Best Western
Arctic

Amber

KÖPMANG

Aveny

BANGÅRDSG

Boats to
archipelago

STATIONSGATAN

VARVSG

SMÅBÅTSG

Baan Thai

SKEPPSBROG

KUNGSGATAN

Park

MALMG

HERMELSINSG

LULSUNDSG

MAGAZINSGATAN

TIMMERMANSG

SKOMAKARG

SKOMAKARGATAN

Zan

SMEDJEGATAN

S SMEDJEG

S HAMNLEDEN

Södra hamnen
(South Harbour)

Tourist office, library,
Robert's Coffee

Roasters

Corsica

O'Leary's

STORG

Cathedral

KÖPMANGATAN

NYG

VARVSG

KYRKOG

Swimming pool
(sports centre)

Kyrkbyns kök (Rest),
Gammelstad

Norra hamnen
(North Harbour)

Bar Bistro
Brygga

Boats to
archipelago

SKEPPSBROG

Cook's Krog

Bishop's Arms,
Elite & Stadshotell

Bakfickan

Stads
parken

RÅDSTUG

Youth hostel

SANDVIKSG

V VARVSG

TEATERPLAN

TULLG

Hermelins-
parken

Norrbottens
Museum

SKEPPSBROG

TRÄDGÅRDSG

N STRANDG

RESIDENSG

OSKARSG

HORNSG

REPSLAGARGATAN

FAGERLINSV

FREDSG

ÄLVG

KASTELLG

Gültzauudden
(beach)

N

Brädt

0        250m
0        250yds

BERGNASBRON

Airport,
First Camp
Luleå, E4

39

little hotel offering a home-from-home experience in an old timber building close to the train station. $$$$/$$$

🛏 **Park** Kungsgatan 10; 📞 0920 21 11 49; e hotellet@parkhotell.se; www.parkhotell.se. A small family-run place in the centre of town with comfortable newly renovated, though still rather plain rooms. $$$$/$$$

🛏 **Aveny** Hermelinsgatan 10; 📞 0920 22 18 20; e birgitta@hotellaveny.com; www.hotellaveny.com. A hotel that's built its reputation on providing cosy, homely rooms at a respectable price. Always a warm welcome from the staff. $$$$/$$

🏕 **First Camp Luleå** 📞 0920 603 00; e lulea@firstcamp.se; www.firstcamp.se/lulea. About 5km west of the centre in Karlsvik. A great riverside location with views of the city. Cabins available $$. Open year round.

🛏 **Youth hostel** Sandviksgatan 26; 📞 0920 22 26 60; e luleavandrarhem@telia.com; http://web.telia.com/~u92017710. A 15min walk from the centre & located beside a busy main road. The cheapest place in the city with simple dbl rooms at $$ & dorm beds $. Cooking facilities available.

## ✖ WHERE TO EAT AND DRINK

✖ **Baan Thai** Kungsgatan 22. One of the best places for lunch in Luleå with a Thai buffet for 69kr. Otherwise, Thai mains are 99kr, Chinese predictables 99kr or 119kr. A large beer is good value at 39kr.

✖ **Bakfickan** Storgatan 11. An elegant Mediterranean-style restaurant serving a tasty range of meat & fish dishes: gratinated salmon (199kr); Arctic char with shiitake mushrooms (219kr); & reindeer fillet with cep mushrooms (245kr). Lunch is 75kr.

✖ **Bar Bistro Brygga** Skeppsbrogatan. Also known as BBB, this ship & adjoining floating pontoons moored alongside Skeppsbrogatan is an inordinately popular place for a bite to eat & a drink during the summer months. Everything from burgers to moules marinière & fried salmon all in the range of 100–200kr. Recommended.

♀ **Bishop's Arms** Storgatan 15. Busy British-style pub in the centre of town with a wide choice of beers. Extremely popular watering hole.

✖ **Cook's krog** Storgatan 17. ⏱ Closed Sun. Long-established, popular steakhouse, which is the best in town. Mains 190–252kr. Also has smoked reindeer steak with Västerbotten cheese & horseradish cream for 245kr.

✖ **Corsica** Nygatan 14. French-style (though not overly authentic) meaty mains such as steak in grand marnier sauce or steak cordon bleu. Mains around 119kr; lunch featuring Swedish home cooking, pasta buffet or pizza is 69kr.

✖ **Kyrkbyns kök** Lulevägen 1, Gammelstad. Absolutely the most sophisticated cuisine in Luleå, specialising in local delicacies such as grouse, reindeer & Arctic char; mains excellent value at around 195kr.

♀ **O'Leary's** Köpmangatan 31. ⏱ from 17.00 Mon–Thu & Sun, 16.00 Fri & 13.00 Sat. The American-style sportsbar is one of Luleå's liveliest bars. Big screens showing live matches, plus a wide choice of beers & spirits. Tex-Mex menu, too.

☕ **Roasters** Storgatan 43. Luleå's most popular coffee house with sunny outdoor seating in summer. The best coffee in town, plus a choice of light snacks & sandwiches.

☕ **Roberts Coffee** Skeppsbrogatan 17. In the entrance to the Kulturens Hus complex, this popular pan-Sweden chain is now in Luleå with gorgeous cakes, sandwiches & an excellent range of coffees.

✖ **Zan** Smedjegatan 10. An adorable, chi-chi little restaurant where Persian food meets Western. Mains in the range 150–230kr, for example, a tasty skewer of chorizo, peppers & onion with baked potato for 150kr.

**THE CITY** Central Luleå occupies a rectangular-shaped peninsula at the mouth of the River Lule. Running east–west across the promontory and right through the ciy centre, Storgatan is Luleå's main street, lined with shopping malls, restaurants and cafés. At its western end, Rådhustorget square is dominated by the Neo-Gothic redbrick **domkyrkan** (*cathedral;* ⏱ *Mon–Fri 10.00–15.00*), which was built in 1893 to replace the previous church destroyed in the city fire six years previously; at 67m high, it is the tallest and most striking building in Luleå. The interior's plain white brick walls serve to accentuate the size and appearance of the enormous chandelier, which hangs above the aisle.

**Norrbottens Museum** (*Storgatan 2;* ☼ *10.00–16.00 Tue–Fri, noon–16.00 Sat & Sun; free*) is a ten-minute walk west from the cathedral along Stationsgatan. It is informative and has a collection of exhibitions on regional history during the 1900s, and on local Sámi life and culture. Upstairs, in a small cinema, Filmrummet, a collection of films is available for viewing; you choose the one you want to watch. Since it is not always on show, ask if the museum can let you watch the eye-opening film that was shown on Swedish television about a young Sámi woman, born in the south, returning to Lapland to find her roots (it is in Swedish with English subtitles). Even with Sámi blood, the woman has to struggle to be accepted into Sámi society in nearby Jokkmokk.

**Konstens Hus Arts Centre** (*inside Kulturens Hus at Skeppsbrogatan 17;* ☼ *10.00–18.00 Mon–Fri, noon–16.00 Sat*) There's more culture at Konstens Hus, which shows a changing collection of work from Swedish artists and sculptors.

**Gültzauudden beach** Occupying a windy location at the western extremity of the Luleå peninsula, Gültzauudden beach is a small sandy strand that's ideal for catching the rays or taking a quick dip. Indeed, on sunny days, it seems virtually the entire population of the city is here enjoying the sunshine. From the town centre you can walk here in about 20 minutes by taking Skeppsbrogatan west, then doing a dog-leg right into Residensgatan and then left Repslagargatan, then, finally, turn right into Fredsgatan, which leads all the way to the beach.

**GAMMELSTAD** One of Lapland's top sights, Gammelstad (*www.lulea.se/gammelstad*), 11km northwest of Luleå, was added to the UNESCO World Heritage list in 1996. It is an outstanding example of what's known in Swedish as a *kyrkstad*, a '**church town**' consisting of over 400 **timber cottages**, which were used on Sundays and during religious festivals by people attending services in the spectacular late medieval **stone church**, Nederluleå kyrka, around which they are grouped. The cottages provided overnight accommodation for parishioners who lived too far away to make the journey to the church and back in one day.

**Nederluleå kyrka** The city of Luleå originally grew up around Nederluleå kyrka, which was built during the 15th century and inaugurated in 1492. The opulence of the building is a clear sign of the economic prosperity of the town at the time, which was based on fur trading in the Lapland interior and salmon fishing on the coast. Originally intended as a cathedral, this is the largest church in Sweden north of Uppsala. Indeed, the lookout slit in the eastern gable suggests it was a useful fortification during periods of unrest, allowing boiling oil to be poured over unexpected visitors. The interior is ornate in the extreme. The altar screen with its finely carved wooden figures was made in Antwerp around 1520 at great cost to the local farmers who were presented with the bill. The ornate pulpit replete with dashes of gilt dates from 1712 and is the work of local carpenter, Nils Jacobsson Fluur.

**The church town cottages** Of Sweden's 71 church towns, only 16 remain today, the largest and best preserved of which is Gammelstad, which consists of 408 gnarled wooden cottages. The combination of a strongly felt duty to attend church and the long distances involved in getting here, led to the construction of the church town in the mid-1500s. The ad-hoc placing of the cottages suggests that the church town grew successively over the years, with cottages being added as and when they were needed. Miraculously, the *kyrkstad* has never been subject to fire. Traditions live on in Gammelstad and the cottages are used by parishioners three to four times every year when special 'church weekends' are held or when confirmations take place shortly before Midsummer.

### Friluftsmuséet Hägnan: the Hägnan Open-Air Museum (⊕ *Jun to mid-Aug daily 11.00–17.00; free*) Just down the hill from the cottages, Friluftsmuséet Hägnan is a rustic collection of old farmstead buildings spanning three centuries. They come from farms across Lapland and have been rebuilt in their original form to accurately portray country life from the 1700s onwards. Rural skills such as sheep-shearing and flatbread making are also occasionally displayed.

**LULEÅ ARCHIPELAGO** With over 700 islands, the archipelago off Luleå is unique: it is the only one in the world surrounded by brackish water. The archipelago is renowned for its rich birdlife and a profusion of wild berries, such as the delicious Arctic raspberry and the orange-coloured cloudberry, which ripen in late summer. Ideal for walking or lazing on the rocks, the islands can be reached by *M/S Ronja* from Luleå's southern harbour between mid-June and mid-August; see www.lulea.se/english for timetables (choose the Luleå archipelago link) or ask at the tourist office which also has information about (limited) accommodation options in the archipelago; a return ticket to any of the islands costs 200kr. The main islands to aim for are: **Brandöskär**, remote and known for its hilly terrain; **Hindersön**, a pastoral farming island; **Kluntarna**, an island of small fishing hamlets and pine forest; or **Klubbviken** (actually a bay on the island of Sandön), which has the advantage of the best beaches and more frequent ferry connections.

**MOVING ON FROM LULEÅ** Train lines in Lapland are rare. However, Luleå is on the Swedish rail network and has daily **trains** north to Gällivare, Kiruna, Abisko and Narvik; departures are currently at 06.15, 11.40 and 16.43 (only as far as Kiruna). Journey time to Kiruna is about four hours; Narvik is seven and a half hours. Trains also run south from Luleå at 16.57 (for Stockholm and Gothenburg) and 21.10 (Stockholm); full details at www.connex.se. **Buses** connect Luleå with Haparanda every few hours, as well as Arvidsjaur, Jokkmokk and Pajala. Although there are also services to Gällivare and Kiruna, it is a much more enjoyable journey by train. For bus times see www.ltnbd.se or call ✆ 0771 100 100 or e lanstrafiken@ltnbd.se. The airport bus leaves from the bus stop across from the Bishop's Arms on Storgatan.

## ARVIDSJAUR

Arvidsjaur (Árviesjávvrie in Sámi, meaning 'generous water'), 155km due west of Luleå, lies in the heart of Sámi territory. Archeological finds suggest that the Sámi lived in this area of northern Sweden long before the first settlers from the south arrived in the late 1500s. However, it was they who built the first chapel here in 1560 on the site of the original Sámi marketplace. In 1605, Karl IX declared Arvidsjaur as a church town in order 'to Christianise the Lapp lands' and to make it easier for the Sámi to attend church. With the discovery of silver in the mountains to the northwest of the village in the 1620s, Arvidsjaur developed into a staging and supply town. The Sámi community existed in parallel to that of the silver pioneers, gathering on market days and for important religious festivals. In the 18th century they built their own **church town**, a handsome collection of solid wooden huts known as **Lappstaden**, still standing today, which constitutes Arvidsjaur's main attraction.

**GETTING THERE** Appropriately enough, the **train station** is located on Järnvägsgatan, from where it is an easy five-minute stroll up either Stationsgatan or

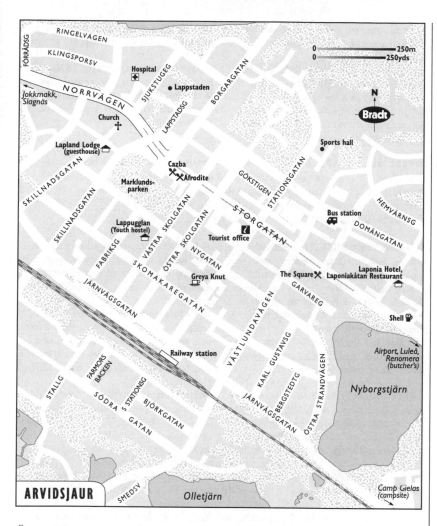

Östra Skolgatan, which run parallel to each other towards the town centre, to the **tourist office** at Östra Skolgatan 18C. **Buses** arrive at the bus station on Västlundavägen, two blocks east of the tourist office. **Flights** from Stockholm arrive at the airport, 15km east of the centre; a taxi into Arvidsjaur costs around 65kr.

**TOURIST INFORMATION** The tourist office at Östra Skolgatan 18C, behind the pharmacy, has **internet** access (⊕ *mid-Jun to mid-Aug Mon–Fri 09.30–18.00, Sat & Sun noon–16.30; rest of year Mon–Fri 08.30–noon & 13.00–16.30;* ✆ *0960 175 00;* e *arvidsjaurlappland@arvidsjaur.se; www.polcirkeln.nu*).

**WHERE TO STAY** There's not a whole lot of choice when it comes to finding somewhere to stay in Arvidsjaur.

🏠 **Laponia** Storgatan 45; ✆ 0960 555 00; e info@hotell-laponia.se; www.hotell-laponia.se. The most upmarket option largely catering for the test drivers who come here in the winter months. Some

rooms have their own kitchen & sauna. There's a good swimming pool & sauna complex, too. $$$$$$/$$$$$
🏠 **Lapland Lodge** Östra Kyrkogatan 18; ➘ 0960 137 20; e lapland.lodge@telia.com; www.laplandlodge.eu. A new venture with comfortable, unadorned rooms close to the church; WiFi connection available; $$$/$$$$ in winter.
🏠 **Lappugglan** Västra Skolgatan 9; ➘ 0960 124

13; e lappugglan@hem.utfors.se. Arvidsjaur's private youth hostel with dbl rooms but no dorm beds. $$
Å **Camp Gielas** Järnvägsgatan 111; ➘ 0960 556 00; e gielas@arvidsjaur.se; www.gielas.se. The town's campsite with cabins ($$$) beautifully situated beside Tvättjärn Lake, 1km or so east of the town centre. $

✖ **WHERE TO EAT AND DRINK** For **self-catering**, it is hard to beat Renomera (*Larstopsvägen 22*) which sells juicy chunks of reindeer meat, elk and all varieties of fish including locally caught Arctic char. The store is located at the eastern end of the village, just before the junction of Routes 94 and 95. It is marked as *renslakteri* (reindeer slaughterhouse) on some maps.

✖ **Afrodite** Storgatan 10. A large selection of pizzas & steaks, as well as a couple of Greek dishes, including the unusual variant, reindeer *souvlaki* for around 100kr.
✖ **Cazba** Storgatan 8. Pizzas are the speciality at this simple restaurant on the main road. Prices hover around the 100kr mark.
☕ **Greya Knut** Stationsgatan 20. The best café in town, also serves light lunches for around 75kr. There's outdoor seating in summer.

✖ **Laponiakåtan** Storgatan 45. A Sámi *kåta* (tent) is the location of this summertime restaurant at Hotell Laponia, which specialises in barbecued meats, particularly reindeer. Reckon on 250kr for a main course.
✖ **The Square** Storgatan 34. Gourmet food in exquisite surroundings at the best restaurant for miles around. Local specialities such as reindeer steak & Arctic char expertly rustled up by owner & chef, Margan Lundin. Mains go for around 300kr.

**LAPPSTADEN** From the tourist office, it is a walk of around ten minutes west along the main street, Storgatan, and then right into Lappstadsgatan, to reach the fascinating Lappstaden (☉ *mid-Jun to mid-Aug daily guided tours 10.30 & 18.00; 30kr; at other times, free*), a tightly grouped cluster of square wooden huts, which make up the Sámi **church town**. The site is all the more remarkable since a couple of blocks of modern flats have been plonked unceremoniously next to the old buildings, making an awkward juxtaposition. Built in the 18th century as accommodation for people who couldn't make the journey to church and back in one day, eighty or so have survived today, thanks to the dogged preservation work of local schoolteacher, Karin Stenberg. Lappstaden is composed of 52 storage huts, raised off the ground on poles for added protection from the elements, and 29 *kåtor*, living-huts, about 4m$^2$ and with pyramid-shaped rooves. These dwellings are set on low wooden walls and built in traditional Forest Sámi style. They have a sloping trap door to allow the smoke from the fire to escape. Inside there was traditionally an earthen floor covered with birch twigs although now a concrete floor is more common. Today, the huts are still used during the Storstämningshelgen festival, which takes place during the last weekend of August and is a great time to be in Arvidsjaur for the accompanying events such as reindeer lassoing competitions, musical concerts and all-round merriment.

**ACTIVITIES AROUND ARVIDSJAUR** One of the most enjoyable things to do while in Arvidsjaur is to visit the **Båtsuoj Sámi Center** (➘ *0960 130 14; e same-id@algonet.se; www.algonet.se/~same-id*) in the village of **Gasa**, 70km west of the town along Route 45 towards Slagsnäs. This is not only one of the best places to see **reindeer** at close quarters, but it is also a chance to meet herders and learn more about their animals. Amazingly, there's a chance to see the dying art of milking a reindeer, a custom which was once commonplace when the Sámi lived a nomadic lifestyle and used everything their animals produced. A short visit to the Center of around an hour or so, including coffee and a chance to taste dried reindeer meat sitting around the fire in a *kåta*, costs 200kr per person. A longer half-day trip, which also features a dinner of reindeer meat, potatoes and cloudberries, information about the local flora and about the old shamanistic religion of the Sámi, is 500kr.

**River rafting and steam train rides** With departures from the Burmabron bridge 45km north of Arvidsjaur (the point where Route 45 crosses the Pite river), Arvidsjaur offers one of the very few opportunities in Lapland to go **river rafting** (*tours daily Jul to mid-Aug, 10.00, noon & 15.00; 395kr*). All equipment such as safety helmets and life jackets are included in the price. You can either meet at the bridge or arrange for a pickup from Arvidsjaur for an extra 80–120kr per person. At 400km in length, the Pite river is one of Lapland's great watercourses, rising at Sulitelma in the mountains of the interior and flowing into the Gulf of Bothnia at Piteå, south of Luleå.

In summer a steam train pulling vintage coaches leaves Arvidsjaur station for the popular return journey west to Slagnäs along the **Inlandsbanan railway** line (*between Jul & mid-Aug Fri & Sat 17.45; 190kr*). There's a restaurant car on board and the train stops at Storavan lake for a swim and a barbecue.

**Akkanålke Mountain and Auktsjaur spring** For some truly spectacular views of the sweeping forest and mountainous terrain of this part of Lapland, head west along Route 45 towards Slagnäs and take a left turn for Hedberg/Storberg (just before the hamlet of Kläppen). From opposite Järtajaure lake, a car track leads off to the left for Akkanålke Mountain (750m). Translating from the Sámi as 'shoulder of the big mother', the peak is a sacred place to the local indigenous people and associated with a myth about the local Sámi woman, Rich Maja, born in 1661, who lived up here with her reindeer. Every morning she would don reindeer-calf skins and, on her knees, play her magic drum so hauntingly that her reindeer would be enticed down from the fells and back to her farm.

Just beyond the turn which leads up to Akkanålke, there's a **sandy beach** in Storberg at the southern edge of **Järtajaure Lake**.

Heading in the opposite direction from Arvidsjaur, Route 45 crosses the Inlandsbanan rail track after about 25km and passes through the hamlet of **Auktsjaur**. Just beyond the village there's a track leading off to the left, which leads to an enchanting **spring**, set deep in the forest, full of crystal clear water around 6–7°C. The spring is just 150m from the gravel road and reached along a section of duckboarding.

## JOKKMOKK

Winning the prize for Lapland's most unusual name, Jokkmokk (Jåhkåmåhkke in Sámi) is the Swedish version of the original Sámi name, meaning 'bend in the river'. Squeezed into one particular *mokk* in the Lule river, the town of Jokkmokk, 160km north of Arvidsjaur, is one of Swedish Lapland's oldest settlements. As part of a royal reorganisation and categorisation of villages in Lapland in the 17th century, Karl IX decided that Jokkmokk, until then just a winter gathering place for the local Sámi, should have a church and a market. The winter market, known as **Jokkmokks marknad**, is still going strong and recently celebrated its 400th

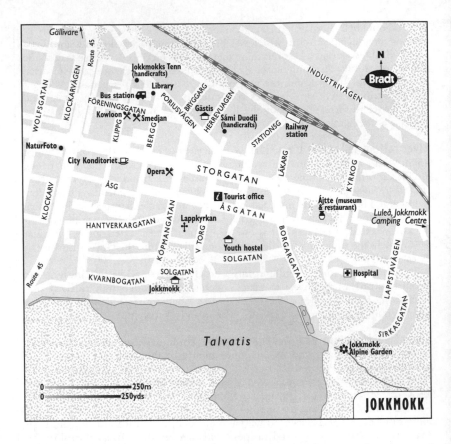

anniversary. Held over the first weekend in February, the event draws around 30,000 people and is the best time to be in town, when the streets are full of stalls and any number of events.

Today Jokkmokk is a thriving, go-ahead sort of a place, that's home to around 3,200 people including a sizeable Sámi community. Indeed, there's not only a further education college teaching subjects such as reindeer husbandry and ecology entirely in Sámi, but also an interesting Sámi museum, Ájtte.

**GETTING THERE** Jokkmokk's **train station** is located on the northeastern edge of the town along Järnvägsgatan. However, Jokkmokk is not a big place and from here it is barely a five-minute stroll up Stationsgatan to reach the town centre and the main street, Storgatan, which runs in an east–west direction. The **bus station** is centrally situated behind the Folkets hus building off Porjusvägen, which leads towards Storgatan.

**TOURIST INFORMATION** The tourist office (✆ 0971 222 50; e turist@jokkmokk.se; www.turism.jokkmokk.se; ⊕ mid-Jun to mid-Aug Mon–Fri 09.00–19.00, Sat & Sun 10.00–18.00; mid-Aug to mid-Jun Mon–Fri 08.30–noon & 13.00–16.00; during the winter market Thu–Sat 09.00–18.00, Sun noon–16.00) overlooks the main street from Stortorget 4. **Internet** access is available at the tourist office as well as the town library on Porjusvägen opposite the bus station.

## ⌂ WHERE TO STAY

⌂ **Jokkmokk** Solgatan 45; ☎ 0971 777 00; ℮ info@hoteljokkmokk.se; www.hoteljokkmokk.se. Much improved in recent years, this refurbished, lakeside hotel is the best place to stay in Jokkmokk. Go for a room overlooking the lake (not the car park), if possible. Huge restaurant in the shape of a *kåta* with Sámi paintings & a stuffed reindeer for authenticity. Fabulous sauna suite with attractive red & white tiles in the basement. $$$$$$$/$$$$

⌂ **Gästis** Herrevägen 1; ☎ 0971 100 12; ℮ info@hotell-gastis.com; www.hotell-gastis.com. More centrally located than its rival, the Jokkmokk, though the overall feel of the place is less appealing. Brightly decorated rooms & a new sauna section. $$$$$

Å **Jokkmokk Camping Center** Notudden; ☎ 0971 123 70; ℮ campingcentre@jokkmokk.com; www.jokkmokkcampingcenter.com. Beside the River Lule, 3km southeast of the town centre along Route 97. There are 2–6 berth cabins here, too, from $$$.

⌂ **Youth hostel** Åsgatan 20; ☎ 0971 559 77; ℮ info@jokkmokkhostel.com; www.jokkmokkhostel.com. ⏲ Reception 08.00–10.00 & 17.00–19.00 (to 20.00 in summer). An old timber house opposite the tourist office set back in a pretty little garden. Rooms are a little on the cramped side. $

## ✗ WHERE TO EAT AND DRINK

✗ **Ájtte** Kyrkogatan 3. A good & popular choice for lunch (70kr). Otherwise, there's also a selection of local specialities such as *renskav* 125kr, *souvas* (165kr) & Arctic char (145kr).

⊡ **City Konditoriet** Storgatan 28. Sandwiches, cakes & coffee from this perfectly OK café in the town centre.

✗ **Hotel Jokkmokk** Solgatan 45. Dinner-only restaurant in the main hotel with a selection of local dishes for around 170kr. The pleasant views over the lake make this restaurant the most pleasant dining experience in town.

✗ **Kowloon** Föreningsgatan 3. Jokkmokk's Chinese restaurant with lunch for 65kr plus a wide selection of Chinese mains for 99kr. This being Lapland, the restaurant serves pizzas.

✗ **Opera** Storgatan 36. The best place to try reindeer, which is always part of the set lunch (65kr). Alternatives include pizzas (80kr), Greek salad (60kr), *pytt i panna* (80kr) or schnitzel (100kr).

✗ **Smedjan** Föreningsgatan 11. A fry-up place with burgers & other Swedish home-cooking options for 80kr.

**THE TOWN** The best Sámi **museum** in Swedish Lapland (⏲ *mid-Jun to mid-Aug daily 09.00–18.00; early May to mid-Jun & mid-Aug to early Sep Mon–Fri 10–16.00, Sat & Sun noon–16.00; rest of year Tue–Fri 10.00–15.00; 50kr*), the appropriately named Ájtte (Sámi for 'storage hut'), at Kyrkogatan 3, is the main sight in Jokkmokk and just a brief walk east along Storgatan from the town centre. Assembled around a circular apex known as the 'round room', the museum is composed of several exhibition halls detailing the life, culture and ecology of Lapland. Although labelling is in Sámi and Swedish only, it is easy to follow the displays, which begin with the pioneers who came to this part of Sweden in the 1600s, following on with a thorough section on traditional costumes and silver spoons. These gave the owner prestige and were an important status symbol in society. Next there is a display of taxidermy. The museum has chosen to ignore the fact that stuffed animals are not to everyone's taste and gone for a full-on display of the work of its resident taxidermist, Göran Sjöberg, whose stuffings have won several competitions: think what you will, the collection of owls – including an eagle owl (*Bubo bubo*), Ural owl (*Strix uralensis*) and great grey owl (*Strix nebulosa*) – are truly impressive, and the massive golden eagle (*Aquila chrysaetos*) has to be seen to be believed. Ájtte rounds off with a small section on the Laponia world heritage area, in the mountains northwest of Jokkmokk (see *Swedish Lapland's national parks*, page 52).

**Jokkmokks fjällträdgård: the Jokkmokk Alpine Garden** (⏲ *mid-Jun to mid-Aug Mon–Fri 11.00–17.00; early Jul to mid-Aug also Sat & Sun noon–17.00; 25kr or 50kr* *including entrance to Ájtte*) One block east of the museum, past the swimming pool and local school, a right turn from Storgatan into Lappstavägen will bring you to Jokkmokks fjällträdgård, a delightful alpine garden overflowing with local plant species. Even before the garden was established, the area along the banks of the Kvarnbäcken stream was particularly rich in alpine plants. Experts have now created areas within the garden that reflect the flora found in different habitats such as: mountaintops, southfacing slopes, windy ridges and marshes. There's even a small section on edible plants which the Sámi have traditionally used.

**Naturfoto wilderness photographs** If the pictures of mountain vegetation on display at the alpine garden grabbed your attention, you may want to see more of the work of local wilderness photographer, Edvin Nilsson, who also worked as a warden in the Sarek National Park, northwest of Jokkmokk. Naturfoto in Klockartorget square at the corner of Klockarvägen and Storgatan is a gallery of his work open in summer (⊕ *Jul & Aug Mon–Fri 10.00–18.00, Sat & Sun 10.00–15.00*). It is a good place to buy coffee-table books, postcards and posters.

**Lappkyrkan: the Lapp Church** Jokkmokk's first church was built in 1607 on the orders of Karl IX whose dream was to create an Arctic empire covering the whole of northern Scandinavia; churches were his way of nailing land for Sweden. A new church was built in 1753, but it burnt to the ground in 1972, leaving nothing but a pile of charred remains. Today, the church that stands on the same spot, between Köpmangatan and Västra Torggatan, is an exact replica of the original and is curiously still known by its politically uncorrect name, Lappkyrkan. The church is surrounded by a double wooden wall which served as storage space for coffins (and bodies) during the winter months when the ground was frozen. Come the thaw, the coffins were then buried in the adjoining graveyard. The church's unusual octagonal design and oddly proportioned tower are of Sámi design, as are the colours of the interior – the blues, reds and yellows you will no doubt be familiar with from the Sámi flag.

**Shopping** Jokkmokk is a good place to pick up genuine Sámi handicrafts. At the small gallery and shop of **Sámi Duodji** (*Porjusvägen 4;* ⊕ *10.00–15.00 Mon–Fri*), you will find a limited but tasteful collection of knives, jewellery and leatherware. The tourist office has a list of local handicraft producers who sell directly from their workshops.

Alternatively, **Jokkmokks Tenn** (*Järnvägsgatan 19;* ⊕ *06.30–16.00 Mon–Thu, 06.30–13.00 Fri*), one block north of the bus station, is a family-run business producing quality pewterware such as bowls, flower vases and ornate drinking spoons of Sámi design.

**The winter market** With origins from 1602, when Karl IX decided there should be a market in Jokkmokk to generate tax revenue for his many wars, the great winter market is *the* event of the year in Swedish Lapland when Jokkmokk's population swells by ten times. Attracting over 30,000 visitors, this fun annual event is held on the first Thursday, Friday, Saturday and Sunday of February and it is a fantastic time to be in town, when the whole place takes on a Wild West atmosphere. The streets are lined with stalls sagging under the weight of everything from bear skins to wooden knives – needless to say, much alcohol is consumed during the event and many people end up buying all sorts of unwanted knick-knacks. There are **reindeer races** held on the frozen lake, Talvatis, behind Hotel Jokkmokk, a fantastic spectacle as man and beast delight the crowds as they hurtle around the specially prepared track on the ice.

A smaller and less-thrilling historical market is now held on the preceeding Monday–Wednesday, when people dress in traditional costume and put on theatrical performances, speaking Swedish, naturally. It takes place at the eastern edge of the lake where Jokkmokk was first established.

**Accommodation** during the market is generally booked up two years in advance; if you fail to find anywhere to stay at the last minute, consider Arvidsjaur or Gällivare instead and take the bus into Jokkmokk.

**ACTIVITIES AROUND JOKKMOKK** Between them, the local adventure companies, Jokkmokkguiderna (�‌ *0971 122 20;* e *info@jokkmokkguiderna.com; www.jokkmokk guiderna.com*) and Outdoor Lapland (�‌ *070 260 0537;* e *outdoorlapland@telia.com; www.outdoorlapland.com*) provide just about every kind of tour you can imagine. Both companies specialise in kayaking, canoeing and hiking. There's little to choose between them, although Jokkmokkguiderna is generally a little less expensive. A day's canoeing, for example, booked with them, costs 590kr; hiking for a day in the Muddus National Park is 640kr.

**NORTHWEST OF JOKKMOKK: KVIKKJOKK** A classic Swedish mountain village, 127km northwest of Jokkmokk, Kvikkjokk (Huhtáan in Sámi) is surrounded by towering, snow-capped peaks reaching over 2,000m in height. The drive here along twisting Route 805 is one of the most stunning in Lapland, hugging the northern shore of the hauntingly beautiful ribbon-shaped Saggat lake and offering jaw-dropping views of the unspoilt upland terrain that stretches north and west of here; take a look at the map of this part of Sweden and you will soon see that man has made very few inroads in this remote corner of the country.

In the 17th century tiny Kvikkjokk was at the centre of the silver mining industry and even had its own smelting works. The famous botanist, Carl von Linné, visited in 1732 and was totally overwhelmed by the beauty of the mountains and their rich flora. Indeed, it was here, as a schoolboy, that the revivalist preacher, Lars Levi Laestadius, first developed an interest in botany, and that he met the girl who was later to become his wife, Brita Cajsa Alstadius; the Laestadius family lived in Kvikkjokk from 1808 to 1816.

Today, the village is used as a gateway for the surrounding national parks, and, in particular, the **Kungsleden trail** (see pages 63–4), which passes through the settlement.

### 🔺 Where to stay and eat

🏠 **Kvikkjokk fjällstation mountain lodge** �‌ *0971 210 22;* e *kvikkjokk@stfturist.se;* ⊕ late Feb to late Apr & mid-Jun to mid-Sep. Gorgeously situated beside the rushing torrents that form the upper reaches of the River Lule. Rooms with shared facilities, & kitchen, & sauna. B/fast & some evening meals. $$

**Bus** #47 runs here from Jokkmokk once daily (*Mon–Fri 15.10, Sat & Sun noon*), terminating at the village church.

## GÄLLIVARE

It is hard to like Gällivare (Jiellevárre in Sámi), a grim, northern town 90km north of Jokkmokk, which owes its existence to the iron ore mines up the road in neighbouring Malmberget. Unlike many other inland settlements in Lapland, Gällivare doesn't lie on a river and, consequently, colonisation of the area by outsiders was slow; for centuries the only inhabitants hereabouts were the indigenous Sámi community. However, with the arrival of the railway line to Luleå

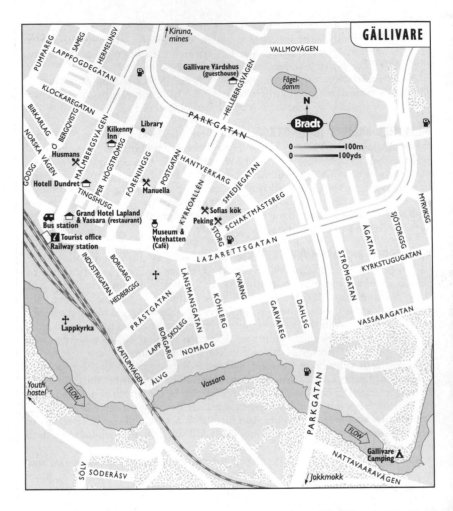

in 1888, the town began to grow as the newly opened iron ore mines, now one of the most important sources in Europe, began to expand. Gällivare is the terminus of the great Inlandsbanan railway which runs here in summer all the way from Mora in the province of Dalarna, a distance of 1,067km. Today, the town is home to around 8,400 people (including a sizeable Sámi community), many of whom are employed in iron ore production. Incidentally, an unusually large number of local people have been found to suffer from the rare genetic disorder, CIPA, which stops the body from feeling pain or reacting to extremes of temperature; there are almost as many reported cases in the Gällivare district as in the entire United States.

**GETTING THERE AND TOURIST INFORMATION** The **train station** is at Centralplan 3, next to the tourist office. **Buses** use the adjoining bus station. Gällivare's **tourist office** (✆ 0970 166 60; e turistinfo@gellivare.se; www.visit.gellivare.se; ⊕ mid-Jun to mid-Aug daily 08.00–22.00; rest of year Mon–Fri 08.00–17.00) provides **internet** access (10kr per 15min).

# WHERE TO STAY

**Grand Hotel Lapland** Lasarettsgatan 1; ☎ 0970 77 22 90; e info@grandhotellapland.com; www.grandhotellapland.com. The smartest place to stay in town right opposite the station with tastefully appointed rooms & a decent sauna suite overlooking the station. $$$$$$$$/$$$$

**Gällivare Värdshus** Hellebergsvägen 5; ☎ 0970 162 00; e info@gallivarevardshus.com; www.gellivarevardshus.com. Uninspiring rooms in a modern block that won't be the highlight of your stay. Free wireless internet connection & sauna. $$$$$/$$$$

**Kilkenny Inn** Per Högströmsgatan 9; ☎ 0970 77 22 80; e info@kilkenny.nu; www.kilkenny.nu. Sharing the same building as the Kilkenny Inn, this modern hotel has been recently renovated & in a homely rather than chain hotel style. $$$$$/$$$$

**Hotell Dundret** Per Högströmsgatan 1; ☎ 0970 550 40; e hotelldundret@bredband.net; www.hotelldundret.se. Homely, good-value guesthouse in the centre of town with dbls sharing facilities. $$$

**Gällivare Camping** Malmbergsvägen 2; ☎ 0970 100 10; e info@gellivarecamping.com; www.gellivarecamping.com. A pleasant riverside location for this campsite off Route 45 towards Jokkmokk. Cabins from $$

**Youth hostel** Barnhemsvägen 2A; ☎ 0970 143 80; e info@explorelapland.com; www.explorelapland.com. Across the tracks (via the metal bridge) from the train station, accommodation here is in compact log cabins. Excellent sauna. $

# WHERE TO EAT AND DRINK

**Husmans** Malmbergsvägen 1. A greasy-spoon fastfood café which serves lunch (65kr) all day from 09.00.

**Manuella** Storgatan 9. The place in Gällivare for decent steaks (from 69kr), pizzas (55kr) & pasta dishes (60kr).

**Peking** Storgatan 21B. A rather tired though long-standing Chinese restaurant (*closed Mon*) with main dishes for 110kr or pizzas at 85kr. The daily lunch is 75kr.

**Sofias kök** Storgatan 19. Swedish home cooking *par excellence* with *renskav, souvas* & meatballs for 70–75kr. The lunch buffet is 68kr.

**Vassara** Lasarettsgatan 1. The best place for lunch at just 73kr. Otherwise, Lapland specialities in the range 130–239kr, such as ovenbaked Arctic char. A selection of Swedish home-cooking classics every evening.

**Vetehatten** Storgatan 16. Gällivare's most popular café serving open sandwiches, pastries & cakes.

**THE TOWN** Other than the mines (see below), the only sight in Gällivare of any significance is the church, **Lappkyrkan** (⊕ *Jun–Aug daily 10.00–15.00*), down by the river, near the western end of Prästgatan. Known as the 'one öre church', as every household in Sweden had to contribute the princely sum of one öre (100th of a krona) towards its construction in 1747, it is a delicate timber building that seems a world apart from the rest of the town centre, composed of sturdy, modern concrete blocks with quadruple-glazing against the biting Arctic winter. Having ticked off the church, you might want to have the briefest of glances around the town **museum** at Storgatan 16 (⊕ *11.00–15.30 daily; late Jun to early Aug Sat & Sun noon–14.00; free*), though its collection of coffee cups, mosquito traps and equally dull wood carvings by local man, Martin Stenström, who spent all his life living alone in a cabin in the woods, is unlikely to excite.

**The mines** The centre of Gällivare may be humdrum, but its mines are anything but. Located up in Malmberget (effectively a suburb of Gällivare, a ten-minute drive away), there are two mines to consider visiting: mining giant LKAB's underground **iron ore mine** (⊕ *mid-Jun to mid-Aug daily 09.30–13.00 & Tue, Thu 14.00–17.30; 220kr*) and the opencast **copper mine**, Aitik (⊕ *mid-Jun to mid-Aug Mon, Wed & Fri 14.00–16.30; 200kr*). Inevitably, of the two, the most impressive tour is to the underground mine. A bus takes visitors deep inside Malmberget mountain, driving 40km or so to one of the points where iron ore is sliced out of the earth at a depth of 1,000m below ground. Here you will see LKAB's giant

Swedish Lapland has no fewer than eight officially designated national parks. Three of them (Padjelanta, Stora Sjöfallet and Sarek) lie within the Laponia World Heritage area established in 1996 by UNESCO, who stated that this vast expanse of 9,400km$^2$ 'is one of the last and unquestionably largest and best preserved examples of an area of transhumance, involving summer grazing by large reindeer herds'.

**HIKING TRAILS** cross most of the parks, with the notable exception of Sarek, which is classed as extremely difficult and only suitable for experienced hikers; there are no overnight cabins, no marked trails, no bridges to cross the many streams and rivers and no access roads. The terrain is nature at its most wild and untouched: deeply cut valleys, vast mountain plateaux, sharp peaks and huge glaciers. On the other hand, Stora Sjöfallet is regularly visited by people walking the Kungsleden trail, which cuts through on its way to and from Abisko. The park is divided in two by Akkajaure lake and is accessible by road from Gällivare. Padjelanta has its own hiking route, too, the enjoyable and readily negotiable Padjelanta trail which runs from Kvikkjokk to Ritsem (northwest of Gällivare). Padjelanta (Sámi for 'the higher land') consists of a reindeer-grazing mountain plateau surrounded by the sizeable lakes of Vastenjaure and Virihaure, which is widely regarded as the most beautiful stretch of water in Sweden.

Muddus National Park (see *Activities around Jokkmokk*, page 49), sandwiched between Jokkmokk and Gällivare, is the most accessible. It is a world of ancient forest and great bogs, which attract a wide variety of birdlife. In the south the park is riddled with deep gorges. There are trails and overnight cabins.

**PRACTICALITIES** Hiking in the any of the national parks is not something to undertake on a whim as the weather can often be challenging (they are subject to heavy rain in summer). However, they do represent some of the last areas of pure wilderness in Europe and a hiking trip to any one of them is likely to leave a lasting impression. There's more information about all Swedish Lapland's national parks at www.fjallen.nu as well as from the tourist offices in Jokkmokk, Gällivare and Kiruna.

90-tonne earth-moving trucks, which emit a truly deafening noise, and learn more about the hi-tech mining operations on which Gällivare is so dependent for survival.

Aitik is one of Europe's largest copper mines, beginning production in 1968 and providing employment for 400 local people. The copper is mined in an open pit, about 350m deep, which is Sweden's largest gold mine since the waste rock contains both gold and silver deposits. A bus will whisk you around the pit and bring you up close to the enormous machines which do the business. All tours can be booked at the tourist office.

**MOVING ON FROM GÄLLIVARE** Between mid-June and early September the **Inlandsbanan train** trundles daily down the single line track bound for Östersund, 750km to the south, calling at Jokkmokk, the Arctic Circle, Arvidsjaur and Slagnäs on the way; departure is usually just after 07.00 (*latest details are at www.grandnordic.se*). The Inlandsbanan arrives into Gällivare from the south at 21.40. It is possible to reach Jokkmokk, Arvidsjaur (and Pajala) by bus; services operate daily, timetables are available at www.ltnbd.se. All-year daily services run northwest to Kiruna and on to Narvik at 09.28, 14.18 and 19.09 (to Kiruna only). In the opposite direction there are trains to Luleå at 07.07 (not Sun), 11.19 (Sun only), 15.25 and 19.47; connections south to Stockholm (changing at Boden, outside Luleå) are available on the latter two departures.

## KIRUNA

Swedish Lapland's best known and most northerly town, Kiruna (Giron in Sámi), 127km north of Gällivare, has got a big problem – it is sinking. Paradoxically, Kiruna owes its fortunes to the ugly, brooding iron ore mines which drive the local economy, yet they are also the cause of its woes. Subsidence from the mines over a kilometre below the town is causing the ground to slip and it is estimated that by just 2015 the railway station and the western edges of the town centre will be affected. In January 2007, plans were formalised to move the entire town to a new location to the northwest of its current site, near the hill of Luossavaara. The move will happen in stages according to a precise map which looks rather like radiation waves emenating from a nuclear explosion. The train station and the main E10 road will be the first to go, followed in turn by slices of the centres. Surprisingly, local people seem remarkably unperturbed by the prospect of their homes sinking from beneath their feet, perhaps because the move is being funded by the state-owned mining company, LKAB, which is promising to build brand new homes for everybody affected and because without the mines Kiruna would cease to exist.

**SOME HISTORY** Although the Sámi had lived on the tundra around what is now Kiruna for countless generations, the first pioneers from the south came here in the early 1600s. They opened an iron ore mine in 1647, yet it took a further two centuries for test drilling for ore to commence in Kiirunavaara mountain, at whose foot the town was later to be founded. The decision by the Swedish parliament to build a railway line to transport the ore to Luleå (and later Narvik) for shipping abroad proved a significant turning point in the town's development and provided the basis of Sweden's economic prosperity in the 19th century. However, not all MPs were in favour of the new-fangled railway; one even declared 'it serves no purpose to build railways over mountains and rivers... to lead them in the opposite direction to cultivation, and all this to receive a few wagonloads of butter and ptarmigan'.

Despite misgivings in Stockholm, the line went ahead reaching Kiruna at the turn of the 20th century and just two years later the final section to Narvik was opened by King Oscar II in 1903. From 1900 onwards, people were beginning to spend the winter in Kiruna, the population snowballed and by 1910 Kiruna counted a respectable 7,500 inhabitants. Keen to avoid the mistakes of Malmberget (Gällivare) where a shantytown had sprung up unchecked, the mine's first director, Hjalmar Lundbohm, wanted to make Kiruna a model community. He enlisted the help of one of the country's leading experts in architecture and social planning and the new town began to take shape. Even the town plan was adapted to the climate; streets were built following the contour lines of the land in a highly irregular pattern to prevent the Arctic wind from howling through the centre. Sadly though, many of the original wooden buildings were ripped down in the 1960s as Sweden was swept by a wave of urban renewal – today's dismal concrete blocks are the result.

**GETTING THERE** Kiruna **airport**, 10km east of the centre, is only linked to city by **airport bus** between June and mid-September (40kr). At other times of the year, a **taxi** is the only way to get into town (250kr). **Trains** arrive at the train station on

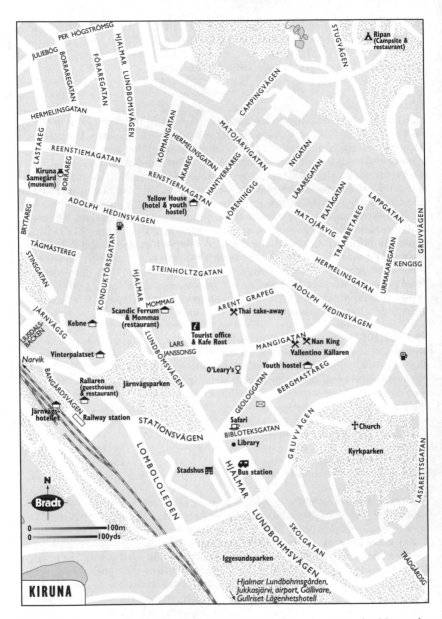

KIRUNA

Bangårdsvägen, a ten-minute walk below the town; from the station building, take the underpass below the E10 immediately outside, and head up through the small park, Järnvägsparken, to Lars Janssonsgatan, which leads into the town centre. **Buses** pull in at the bus station opposite the Stadshuset, off Biblioteksgatan, a couple of blocks east of the main square.

**TOURIST INFORMATION** The tourist office is in the Folkets Hus building in the square (↘ *0980 188 80;* e *info@lappland.se; www.lappland.se;* ⊕ *late Jun to mid-Aug Mon–Fri 08.30–20.00, Sat & Sun 08.30–17.00; rest of year Mon–Fri 08.30–17.00, Sat*

*08.30–14.00*) at Lars Janssonsgatan 17. **Internet** terminals are available here (*25kr for 20mins*), as well as at the library at Biblioteksgatan 4.

# 🏠 WHERE TO STAY

🛏 **Scandic Ferrum** Lars Janssonsgatan 15; ☎ 0980 39 86 00; e ferrum@scandic-hotels.com; www.scandic-hotels.se/ferrum. Smart, upmarket chain hotels with pleasantly decorated rooms. The superb top floor sauna suite and pool makes a stay here worth considering. $$$$$$$/$$$$$

🛏 **Kebne** Konduktörsgatan 7; ☎ 0980 681 80; e info@hotellkebne.com; www.hotellkebne.com. Smart, modern hotel with Nordic-style décor throughout. $$$$$/$$$$$

🛏 **Vinterpalatset** Järnvägsgatan 18; ☎ 0980 677 70; e vinterp@kiruna.se; www.vinterpalatset.se. Another of Kiruna's listed buildings from 1904 with wooden floors & a hint of French Renaissance elegance about the place. Each room is individually decorated with antique furniture. 4 cheaper, more basic rooms in the annexe at the rear. $$$$$/$$$$$

🛏 **Järnvägshotellet** Bangårdsvägen 7; ☎ 0980 844 44; e valfritt@jarnvagshotellet.com; www.jarnvagshotellet.com. The town's oldest hotel, originally built to serve folks arriving by train, & now a listed timber building with great character. However, it is right beside the train tracks & gets the full rumble of the iron ore trains as they pass by. $$$

🛏 **Rallaren** Bangårdsvägen 4; ☎ 0980 611 26; e info@hotelrallaren.se; www.hotelrallaren.se.

Individually decorated rooms with Sámi paintings, old-fashioned style furniture & wooden floors make all the rooms here an excellent choice. There's also 2 cosy wooden *lávvu* with bathroom immediately outside the main building for rent. Hot tub & sauna on site. $$$

🛏 **Gullriset Lägenhetshotell** Bromsgatan 12; ☎ 0980 109 37; e fabgullriset@kiruna.se; www.fabmf.se/gullriset. Perfect for self-catering: 3 different sizes of en-suite apartments, all with fully fitted kitchen. Access to sauna. Prices range from $$ to $$$ depending on size.

🏕 **Ripan** Campingvägen 5; ☎ 0980 630 00; e ripan@kiruna.se; www.kiruna.se. A 20min walk north of the centre, Kiruna's campsite has an open-air swimming pool & a number of cabins ($$) per night. Ice igloos available Dec–Apr ($$$$$$$ per night for 2 people).

🛏 **Yellow House** Hantverkaregatan 25; ☎ 0980 137 50; e yellowhouse@mbox301.swipnet.se; www.yellowhouse.nu. A budget hotel cum youth hostel offering plain, simple dbls ($$) sharing facilities or dorm beds ($). There's a fully fitted kitchen & a sauna.

🛏 **Youth hostel** Bergmästaregatan 7; ☎ 0980 171 95; www.kirunahostel.com. A popular choice right in the centre of town which fills fast. *Dbl* $$, *dorm beds* $.

# ✖ WHERE TO EAT AND DRINK

🍴 **Kafe Rost** Lars Janssonsgatan 17. Inside Folkets Hus (see page 54) with outdoor seating on the 1st floor balcony. Good cakes & open sandwiches, as well as *souvas* in pitta bread (70kr).

✖ **Mommas** Lars Janssonsgatan 15. ⏲ daily from 17.00, 16.00 on Fri. Closed Sun. Inside the Scandic Ferrum, this steakhouse is a Kiruna institution & a good place for your meaty fix: beef steak (265kr); lamb burger (139kr), *renskav* (139kr); grilled salmon (165kr). The bar here is a popular place for a drink.

✖ **Nan King** Mangigatan 26. ⏲ Closed Mon. Passable Chinese mains for 110kr; the lunch buffet is 70kr.

🍷 **O'Leary's** Föreningsgatan 11. The American sportsbar has finally opened in Kiruna with flatscreens everywhere you look showing the latest matches. Extremely popular place for a drink or a nibble from the TexMex menu.

✖ **Rallaren** Bangårdsvägen 4. Good, though limited, menu of local specialities, such as thinly sliced reindeer & elk meat with mashed potatoes (99kr); reindeer fillet in red wine sauce with stirfried veggies (225kr) or game meat gratin (149kr).

✖ **Ripan** Campingvägen 5. *The* place for top-notch Lapland cuisine: Arctic char in dill sauce (235kr); *souvas* in dark lingonberry gravy (265kr); cloudberry sorbet (115kr). A set 5-course gourmet menu featuring various Arctic delicacies is served for 455kr.

🍴 **Safari** Geologgatan 4. ⏲ Closed Sun. An attractive café with homemade sandwiches & pastries.

✖ **Thai Take Away** Föreningsgatan 17. Try to ignore the psychedelic paintings of Thai village scenes on the walls in these new premises, the food is good, though could do with spicing up a little. The lunch buffet is 75kr. Otherwise a wide selection of

3

vegetarian dishes at 99kr, or regular meat mains at 125kr. Singha beer available. ✗ **Valentino Källaren** Mangigatan 26. A cheap, cheerful & tiny place with 70-odd pizzas on the menu from 50kr. Also salads (from 60kr), various pasta dishes (59kr) & steaks (69–99kr).

**THE TOWN** Kiruna's sights are all linked to the town's mines in some way or other. The church, **Kiruna kyrka**, for example, on Kyrkogatan, was paid for by LKAB, the owner and operator of the mine and the town's main employer. Although the church has been voted Sweden's best looking religious building, the exterior is a bizarre neo-Gothic interpretation of a Sámi tent, full of sharp points and angles. The building was purposely designed not to resemble a church, since Hjalmar Lundbohm, who ordered its construction in 1907, didn't want references to any specific religion. However, the local bishop objected on hearing there wasn't even to be a single cross in the church. The plain cross on the altar was the compromise decision. Many of the details inside the church are of wrought iron – as you would expect. Even the tower of the **Stadshus** (Kiruna town hall), at the junction of Hjalmar Lundbohmsvägen and Stationsvägen, is of wrought iron. The open design is topped by a series of iron spikes, a clock and 23 bells, which chime a couple of times a day; it was designed by Swedish sculptor, Bror Marklund, whose striking work can often be seen adorning Sweden's public buildings. Inside the town hall, there's a small art collection on display and occasional exhibitions of local Sámi handicrafts.

**Lundbohmsgården** (*Ingenjörsgatan 1;* ☉ *08.00–16.00 Mon–Fri, Wed from 10.00; 35kr*) Mr Kiruna himself, Hjalmar Lundbohm (1855–1926), is remembered at Lundbohmsgården, an elegant manorhouse where the town's founding father once lived. Inside there's a potted history of Kiruna and its mines in black and white photographs as well as the great man's personal study just as he left it. Lundbohm travelled widely and actually spent more time living in Stockholm's chic Östermalm district than he did in Kiruna. His interest in art brought him into frequent contact with the great Swedish artists of the time, Anders Zorn and Carl Larsson, and he built up a considerable collection of paintings. He left his post as LKAB's managing director in 1920 and died six years later.

**Kiruna Samegård** (*Brytaregatan 14;* ☉ *07.00–noon &* *13.00–16.00 Mon–Fri; 20kr*) If all the talk of iron ore has dulled your senses, there's relief to be found at Kiruna Samegård, a considered exhibition of Sámi culture at a 20-minute walk from the town centre north along Hjalmar Lundbohmsvägen and then left into Adolf Hedinsvägen. There's a fair display of Sámi traditional costumes together with a *kåta* to have a look at. The souvenir shop is a good place to pick up a knicknack or two.

**The mine** (*tour: early Jun & late Aug daily 09.00 & 13.00; mid-Jun to mid-Aug daily 09.00, 11.00, 13.00 & 15.00; 240kr; duration 3hr*) Although the iron ore mine in Kiruna is the world's biggest, the tour is not a patch on what's available in Gällivare (see pages 51–2 for details). If, however, you are still keen to go underground, you can visit what LKAB calls its InfoMine, a sanitised tourist attraction, admittedly based on the real thing, but a little tame. After departing by bus from the tourist office in Kiruna, visitors are taken half a kilometre underground to the museum where exhibits, films and various multimedia presentations explain everything you ever wanted to know about iron ore mining – without getting your hands dirty.

**AROUND KIRUNA: ESRANGE AND KEBNEKAISE** Just 44km east of Kiruna, **Esrange** is Sweden's internationally renowned space research station. More than 500 rockets have been launched from this remote **space research base** in the Lapland

*top* **Fish drying rack, North Norway** (LM)
*above left* **Fishing boat, North Norway** (LM)
*above right* **Henningsvær, Lofoten islands, Norway** (JP) page 81

top     **Red-throated diver** (*Gavia stellata*)
**with fish for young, Finland**
(DT)

above left     **Wolverine** (*gulo gulo*),
**Bardu, Norway**
(PR) page 18

above right     **Puffin** (*Fracterula arctica*) **with**
**sand eels, Vesterålen**
**islands, Norway**
(DT) page 77

left     **Elk** (*Alces alces*), **Laponia World**
**Heritage Site, Swedish Lapland**
(PR) page 18

top left     **Husky, Rovaneimi, Finland** (DT)

top right     **Sea eagle** (*Haliaeetus albicilla*)**, Flatanger, Norway** (PR) page 77

above left     **Brown bear** (*Ursos arctos*)**, Finland** (DT) page 18

above right     **Red squirrel** (*Sciurus vulgaris*)**, Finland** (DT)

below     **Reindeer** (*Rangifer tarandus*)**, Finland** (DT) page 18

*top* Snowmobiling, Ylläs, Finland (LM)
*above left* Panning for gold, Tankavaara, Finland (LM)
*above right* Hiking, near Rovaniemi, Finland (LM)
*below* Camping beside a lake in Finnish Lapland (LM)

above left   **Sámi girl, Jokkmokk winter market, Sweden** (Arctic) page 48

top right   **Sámi man, Swedish Lapland** (PR) page 13

above right   **Sámi woman and reindeer, Muonio, Finland** (LM) page 93

below   **Reindeer statue, Sodankylä, Finland** (LM) page 116

*top* Painting of revivalist preacher, Lars Levi Laestadius, Jukkasjärvi church, Sweden
(JP) page 61

*above* Statue of polar bear, Hammerfest, Norway
(LM) page 152

*right* Prehistoric rock paintings, Alta, Norwegian Lapland
(LM) page 143

Aurora Borealis, Abisko, Swedish Lapland (PR) page 4

hills since the start in 1966. The base is used to launch helium-filled high altitude balloons which help with the study of the atmosphere and the monitoring of ozone depletion. Esrange is active in the reception and processing of satellite data. Due to the base's northerly location, the earth's polar satellites pass within coverage range on virtually every orbit. Four-hour-long **guided tours** (*all year round, leave tourist office Mon–Fri 09.15; 390kr; minimum 5 people*) to Esrange (including transfer from Kiruna and coffee and a sandwich) are available if enough people are interested.

From 2012, Virgin Galactic will own and operate private spaceships at Esrange and fly the first space tourists into the dark beyond. As otherworldly as it sounds, bookings are now being taken for the first liftoffs at www.virgingalactic.com. There'll be three days of pre-flight training before what the Virgin boss, Richard Branson, calls 'the most incredible experience of your life'.

**Kebnekaise** For those who can't afford, or indeed, don't want to go up in space, the next best thing has to be an ascent of Sweden's highest mountain, Kebnekaise (Giebmegáisi in Sámi; 2,111m). The mountain is accessed from the village of Nikkaluokta, 66km west of Kiruna, from where a hiking trail covers the last 19km to the foot of the mountain and the **Kebnekaise fjällstation mountain lodge** (✆ *0980 550 00;* e *kebnekaise@stfturist.se; www.stfkebnekaise.com;* ☉ *late Feb–Apr & mid-Jun to mid-Sep. Double room $$; dorm beds $*). The lodge has its own restaurant serving all meals, its own bakery as well as a sauna and a fully equipped kitchen for self-catering. There are two paths up the peak: the shortest one goes via the Björling glacier and is only recommended for expert climbers; the other, much longer, goes up the western face and is the one preferred by most visitors. Incidentally, Kebnekaise was first climbed, not by a Swede, but a Frenchman, Charles Robot, who made it to the summit in 1883.

There's a daily **bus** to Nikkaluokta from Kiruna, departing at 15.55. A boat leaves from Nikkaluokta after the bus's arrival, which can shorten the 19km hike to the mountain by 6km. From Kebnekaise, it is a 14km hike to the **Kungsleden trail** at Singi.

## ICEHOTEL AND JUKKASJÄRVI

If there's one thing that's put Lapland well and truly on the winter tourist trail, it is **Icehotel**. From Japan to Britain, the US to Italy, mention the name to any savvy traveller and everyone's heard about it, and, more often than not, wants to come here. In fact, such is Icehotel's popularity across the world that from December 2007 there will even be direct flights here from London (see below). Proof, if ever it was needed, that the man behind the project, Yngve Bergqvist, a southern Swede who moved to Swedish Lapland over thirty years ago, has struck gold.

Back in 1989 he hit on the idea of building a simple igloo here in the village of **Jukkasjärvi** (Sámi for 'meeting place by the lake'), 20km east of Kiruna, as a showcase for local Sámi handicrafts and art. Some of those first visitors wanted to sleep in the igloo – something that wasn't commerically possible in any part of Lapland at the time. A veritable niche in the market, Yngve developed the concept and Icehotel was born, gradually transforming sleepy Jukkasjärvi, a remote Lapland backwater, into a tourist blockbuster which now pulls in 40,000 visitors every year. True, the project has not been without its local critics over the years, who have complained that the soul of their village has been destroyed by hordes of tourists, and, indeed, planning permission for various projects has been refused by the local authorities. Be that as it may, Yngve has been bestowed with countless tourism awards and is heralded as the man who breathed new life and vigour into the local

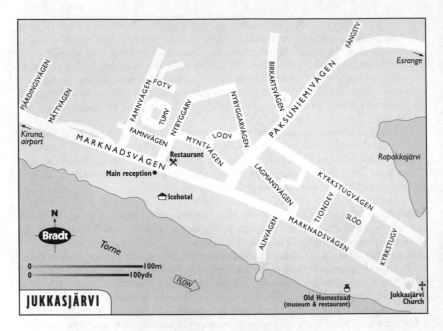

Map labels: FJARDINGSVÄGEN, MÄTTVÄGEN, FAMNVÄGEN, FOTV, TUMV, NYBYGGARV, FAMNVÄGEN, MYNTVÄGEN, LODV, NYBYGGARVÄGEN, BIRKARLSVÄGEN, PAKSUNIEMIVÄGEN, FANGSTV, Esrange, Kiruna, airport, MARKNADSVÄGEN, Restaurant, Main reception, Icehotel, LAGMANSVÄGEN, KYRKSTUGVÄGEN, Rapakkojärvi, N, Bradt, Torne, ALNVÄGEN, MARKNADSVÄGEN, TIONDEV, SLÖD, KYRKSTUGV, 0 ▬▬▬ 100m, 0 ▬▬▬ 100yds, FLOW, JUKKASJÄRVI, Old Homestead (museum & restaurant), Jukkasjärvi Church

economy, which had languished for years through lack of investment and interest from central government 1,300km away in Stockholm.

**ICEHOTEL** In late October each year work begins in earnest on the construction of Icehotel. Using blocks of ice hewn from the Torne river, which flows through Jukkasjärvi, artists and sculptors from across the world slowly give shape to the new structure which will consume around 4,000 tonnes of ice and 30,000 tonnes of snow. When complete, Icehotel covers around 5,000m² of ground space and stands proud beside the banks of the river until May, when winter finally releases its grip on Lapland and the entire structure melts away back into the river. Whether you stay here or not, if you are in Lapland during the winter season, you should make every effort to get here because Icehotel really is an amazing sight. Although the actual details of the design and interior decoration vary from year to year, the overall shape of the hotel remains the same: one long arched corridor, naturally lit at either end by giant ice windows, forms the main walkway, from which other corridors then branch off to the left and right leading to the bedrooms and suites. Intricately carved ice sculptures adorn the interior seemingly at every turn and only add to the overall sense of amazement most visitors feel. Beside the main entrance, there's the Icechapel, a smaller arched igloo, replete with ice pews and cross, which has become an inordinately popular place to tie the knot.

**Getting there** Kiruna airport (airport code KRN), barely a few kilometres from Jukkasjärvi, is the perfect gateway to Icehotel. The **airport** is currently served by SAS, which flies here from Stockholm Arlanda and Umeå; Flynordic operating from Stockholm Arlanda, Östersund and Luleå; and Baltic Airlink who connect Kiruna with both Tromsø and Luleå. New for the 2007/08 season, SAS will fly directly to Kiruna from London Heathrow three times per week, thus avoiding the need to change planes (and terminals) at Stockholm Arlanda; book with Discover the World (page 21), which is running the flights in partnership with SAS. An airport bus meets most arrivals and runs the 10km into Kiruna ( *Jun to mid-Sep* *only*). From Kiruna bus station, **bus #501** runs to Jukkasjärvi (*mid-Aug to mid-Jun Mon–Fri 7 daily; late Jan to mid-Apr also Sat & Sun 2 daily; rest of year Mon–Fri 4 daily, Sat & Sun 1 daily; 30mins*). If you are heading directly to Icehotel, which lies in the opposite direction, it makes sense to take a **taxi** here (250kr). There's only one road into Jukkasjärvi, Marknadsvägen, and Icehotel is located on its right-hand side as you enter the village. Undoubtedly the most fantastic way to arrive is by **dog sled**, which will meet you from your plane and pull you all the way to your bed. However, it is a pleasure that doesn't come cheap: 5,700kr for a maximum of four people (advance booking necessary).

**Practicalities** The Icehotel itself is only one part of the entire complex. The main **reception** is situated adjacent to the main car park beside the main road that runs through the village. In response to requests from previous guests a new **lounge** and **wine bar** is planned to provide a communal relaxation area for all overnight guests – something which has been lacking until now; it is due to open in late 2007 and will be open 24 hours. What's known as '**warm accommodation**' – a range of hotel rooms and chalets – is located immediately in front, and to the left, of the ice structure. The **restaurant**, open for breakfast, lunch and dinner, is across the road, diagonally opposite the reception building; in the basement there's a **bar**. A second bar, the Absolut Icebar is located inside the Icehotel itself, serving, you guessed it, Absolut vodka at 105kr a shot, in a glass made of ice. The **women's sauna** is located in this building, above the restaurant. At the time of writing the **men's sauna**, an inadequate affair with just five showers (Icehotel can accommodate 360 people at a time) was being closed, relocated and enlarged.

If you are staying in the Icehotel, you will be allocated your room on check-in and will be given a locker (in a heated cabin) in which to store your luggage since the hotel is open to **day visitors** (295kr entrance) until 18.00 daily. There's access from here to toilet facilities (also heated). When it is time to move into the room, the idea is you leave as many clothes as you dare in the locker and make a run for it – the temperature inside the Icehotel is pretty constant at around $-5°C$, whereas outside it can often be as low as $-30°C$. The sleeping bag you are provided with has been thermally tested and is designed to keep you warm in temperatures down to $-35°C$; it includes a special hood which you should draw over your head to avoid heat loss, leaving just your mouth and nose clear (this can be a little claustrophobic). In order to prevent sweating inside the sleeping bag, it is important to take all your clothes off and sleep naked; don't leave your clothes on the floor, though, because they'll freeze overnight, instead, stuff them right down inside the sleeping bag. Similarly, place your shoes on the bed beside you. You will be woken the next morning by cheery staff offering you a cup of warm lingonberry juice. Before breakfast it is a good idea to warm up with a morning sauna and a hot shower.

## Where to stay

**The Icehotel** (*Marknadsvägen 63;* ☏ *0980 668 00;* ✉ *info@icehotel.com; www.icehotel.com*) is open from early December until the end of April. Low season, which Icehotel calls its 'nice price period', runs from early to mid-December, early to late January and again from early to late April. All other times are classed as high season when you should be sure to book well ahead. Within each season, there is a price difference depending on whether your stay falls over a weekend (*Thu–Sun inclusive*) when prices are correspondingly higher. Below we've given the weekend price per room, first for the low season, then for the high season. '**Cold accommodation**' inside the Icehotel comes in various forms and prices: a regular **double room** costs 2,800kr/3,390kr; a **design suite** with more swanky adornments is 3,400kr/4,600kr; while, at the top of the range, a uniquely designed **art suite** (themes change from year to year) for that special occasion will set you back 3,800kr/5,300kr. **Beds** in all rooms are made of compacted snow and ice, raised off the ground and topped with a reindeer skin, on which you sleep in your sleeping bag.

For most people, the novelty of spending one night in the Icehotel is enough, and many people decide to stay on and book into the adjacent warm accommodation, which consists of regular double rooms and chalets. Known by the Sámi name *kaamos* meaning 'blue light', the double rooms (2,800kr/3,190kr), located in four separate buildings to the left of the Icehotel, are stylish in the extreme; Nordic-style minimalism complete with wood panelling and soft lighting. The chalets divide up into what Icehotel calls Nordic chalets, altogether more stylish and comfortable, and the more cluttered Northern Light chalets; although both have two separate bedrooms, the latter has a window in the roof allowing you to see the northern lights, weather permitting. Prices for both chalets are the same as those for double rooms.

Note that Icehotel is closed every year in May and between September and early December.

**✗ Where to eat** The **Icehotel restaurant** on Marknadsvägen, across from Icehotel, is the place to come for a warming breakfast; the extensive buffet is included in the price of all accommodation. An excellent buffet **lunch** (135kr) is served until 15.00 daily. Reservations are a good idea if you intend to have dinner here as demand for tables is high. Meals are a little pricey here but the quality of the food is excellent: à-la-carte starters weigh in at 125–230kr; mains, such as tasty fillet of reindeer with shiitake mushrooms, or ravioli stuffed with spinach and morel mushrooms, are in the range 195–290kr; and desserts cost are 125kr. The set Ice Menu costing 785kr merits a special occasion: it includes Arctic char from the River Torne, bleak roe with blini, smoked reindeer joint with stewed morels and basil cream, and elk cheese ice cream with berries from the forest; each cold course is served on an ice platter.

Aimed at complementing the main Icehotel restaurant, the **Old Homestead restaurant**, at the eastern edge of the village within the Homestead Museum area (a ten-minute walk east along Marknadsvägen from Icehotel; see below), is a more traditional place to dine. Housed in the former village school, the heavy wooden interior is typical of many buildings in Lapland and provides a more intimate dining experience. The excellent lunch buffet (95kr), although more limited in range than at the Icehotel restaurant, is just as tasty and is available until 16.00, whereas main dishes in the evening, such as steak, wild boar or salmon cost 165–240kr; there's always a vegetarian option on the menu.

For **self-catering** there's a small supermarket selling provisions just before the Old Homestead museum on Marknadsvägen.

**Activities** There is no end to the activities you can take from the Icehotel. The exact range of tours varies from year to year, but the old favourites are always available: a **snowmobile tour** lasting an hour and a half out into the forest around Jukkasjärvi (895kr per person with two people per machine; 800kr supplement for your own snowmobile); **Northern Lights tour** by snowmobile lasting four hours (1,750kr per person; once again a supplement is payable for your own machine) and a **dog sled tour** of one and a half hours costing 1,550kr per person including coffee and cakes by an open fire in the wilderness. Another interesting option is to spend a morning or afternoon with local Sámi people who'll give you an insight into their traditional way of life and let your try your hand at driving a reindeer sleigh; 1,475kr per person. Undoubtedly the most exhilarating of all the activities on offer is the chance to **drive** a SAAB car on a specially constructed **ice track**. With expert tuition on hand, both you and the car will be put through your paces out on the ice; 2,575kr per driver, an accompanying passenger pays half price. Be prepared to show your driving licence, and maybe to undergo a breath test.

**JUKKASJÄRVI VILLAGE** Other than Icehotel, the main attraction in Jukkasjärvi, a compact little village of barely 1,000 people, is the old Sámi **church** (⊕ *Jun–Aug 08.00–22.00 daily; rest of year 08.00–20.00*) hidden away, somewhat apologetically, at the eastern end of the main road, which ends here. A classic tall and narrow wooden structure built in 1608, and accordingly the oldest exisiting church in Swedish Lapland, the church is certainly attractive in its own right, but it is the startling **altarpiece** inside which really draws the eye and offers an insight into the Sámi's often uneasy relationship with alcohol. Ablaze with colour, the triptych was carved by Swedish artist, Bror Hjorth, whose work is favoured as adornment to many of Sweden's civic squares and buildings, it was carved and donated to the church by the big name in iron ore around here, LKAB, which operates the mines in Kiruna.

The man in the nasty brown suit, featured in both main sections of the altarpiece, is the revivalist preacher Lars Levi Laestadius, who worked as the Sámi minister in Karesuando from 1825. Laestadius took it on himself to free Lapland from alcohol abuse and to show the Sámi the way to enlightenment through his teachings: hence, the landlord stamping on a keg of beer; the return of a stolen reindeer; even confessions of sex by the couple with the long faces portrayed in the work. However, the Sámi really have the woman lit by a golden halo, Mary of Lapland (shown on the right of the altarpiece) to thank for their deliverance from evil. After meeting Mary, Laestadius found peace and conviction of his own beliefs and went on to found a religious movement which, to this day, still draws tens of thousands of followers across northern Scandinavia.

As you walked down Marknadsvägen to the church, you no doubt saw a collection of old wooden buildings on your right-hand side, just after the Icehotel complex: the **Homestead Museum** (Hembygdsgård). Guided tours of the museum are available (⊕ *10.00–17.00 daily; 90kr*), though, to be frank, the worthy collection of how-we-used-to-live-paraphernalia, such as spinning wheels and reindeer sledges, is unlikely to make the top line of your postcards home. It is a better idea simply to wander around yourself and pop into the nearby restaurant when you are done for a cup of coffee.

**Summer in Jukkasjärvi** Between June and August Icehotel lets its Kaamos double rooms and chalets at knockdown prices. Accommodation, which in the winter season costs up to 3,190kr per night, is available for just 900kr; there's no distinction between week and weekend prices. Although the main restaurant across the road from Icehotel is closed during the summer, it is still possible to get something to eat at the Old Homestead Restaurant (see above). There's certainly no shortage of activities on offer, though perhaps the two most rewarding are **whitewater rafting** on the River Torne (*duration 6hr; 750kr*) and a **cave tour** to the Kåppajåkka caves in search of stalactites and stalagmites (*duration 6hr; 680kr*). **Canoes** and **mountain bikes** are available for rent for 395kr per day.

## ABISKO

Thanks to its envious position as the driest place in the whole of Sweden, Abisko, 94km northwest of Kiruna, is not only the place to work on your tan during the summer when the sun never seems to stop shining, but it is the place of choice in winter to see the **Northern Lights** when, similarly, the sky here is often free of cloud, a prerequisite for observing the phenomenon. Lying in a rain shadow, Abisko has mountains that divide it from neighbouring Riksgränsen (the wettest place in Sweden) to thank for its sunny disposition. Though the village itself comprises little more than a couple of housing blocks, a supermarket and a filling station, the setting couldn't be better; sandwiched between Nuolja Mountain and the 70km long Torneträsk lake, a vast ribbon-like expanse of water, Abisko really has got it made. However, should you choose to come here, you are more likely to spend your time a couple of kilometres further along the main E10 highway, which links Abisko with Kiruna, at the excellent **Abisko Turiststation**, a cross between a regular youth hostel and a mountain lodge. Incidentally, it is also possible to reach Abisko by **train** from Kiruna; be sure, though, to alight at the station named Abisko Turiststation, not Abisko Ö (train speak for Abisko Östra, meaning east), which is the stop for the village and comes first when approaching from Kiruna.

**WHERE TO STAY AND EAT** Abisko Turiststation (✆ 0980 402 00; e info@abisko.nu; www.abisko.nu) is well signed from the main E10 highway and stands beside the road. It is open from mid-February to early May and then again from mid-June to the end of September. Prices for accommodation vary slightly between winter and summer. Double rooms ($$$) in the main building or in four-bed dorms ($) or self-catering rooms with a small kitchenette ($$) in the Keron buiding. There are cabins ($$$$) for rent with a fully fitted kitchen, living room and two bedrooms. There's a decent **sauna** both in the main building and in the Keron section, as well as a **wood sauna** down by the lake. The Turiststation's **restaurant** serves a buffet-style breakfast, lunch and dinner, and in the basement you will find a **bar** with superb views out over the Torneträsk lake. **Provisions** can be bought from the Fjällboden shop on site, or at the supermarket in the village. Opposite the store you will find Abisko's other eating option, the good-value **Lapporten Restauarang och Café** (🕐 11.00–18.00 daily), which serves a set dish of the day for 75kr and has an array of northern Swedish specialities at excellent prices: try the renskav (thinly sliced reindeer meat in a creamy sauce with mashed potato) for just 65kr.

## WHAT TO SEE AND DO

**Abisko Naturum** (Adjacent to the Turiststation; 🕐 early Jun to late Sep Mon, Wed, Fri & Sun 09.00–18.00, Tue, Thu & Sun 09.00–21.00; mid-Feb–May Wed 18.00–22.00, Thu–Sat 09.00–22.00, Sun 8.00–noon; www.abiskonaturum.nu; free). For a quick canter through the flora and fauna of this part of Swedish Lapland, the Abisko Naturum is worth a quick look. Inside you will find examples of some of the vegetation and wildlife in the surrounding national parks; though perhaps the most useful feature of the Naturum is the possibility to rent a backpack (50kr per day including a map and hiking information) if you are going trekking.

**Nuolja Mountain and Aurora Sky Station** Bearing down on tiny Abisko from a height of 1,169m, **Nuolja Mountain** is easily accessible by **chairlift** (linbana in Swedish; 120kr return). To get to the base station for the chairlift from the Turiststation, first cross the E10 and follow the Nuolja sign underneath the railway line, where you then turn right. At the summit you will find an agreeable **café** (which operates without electricity or running water) and one of the most breathtaking views in the whole of Lapland. As the chairlift whisks you to the top of the peak, you somehow forget that the view of Abisko and Torneträsk lake is behind you. The spectacular panorama is all the more amazing, then, when you get off the chairlift and enter the café – the village, lake and entire valley are laid out before you through floor-to-ceiling windows. Nuolja offers the best views of **Lapporten**, the U-shaped valley edged by identical twin peaks that has, over the years, become Lapland's most enigmatic sight; Lapporten was traditionally used by reindeering herding Sámi as an unmissable landmark during migration.

Tucked away in one corner of the café is a modest little room known rather grandly as the **Aurora Sky Station**, home to a scientific exhibition about the **Northern Lights** and containing all sorts of paraphernalia to measure and even hear the lights, such as audio amplifiers to listen to electromagnetic oscillations in the atmosphere, which often sound like a series of whistles, hisses and clicks. The sky station is open in connection with special tours to observe the aurora: at the time of writing, these were available on Tuesday, Thursday and Saturday between late August and late September and again, on the same days, from late February to mid-March; latest details are available at www.abisko.nu. Staff at the Turiststation are keen to attract visitors eager to learn more about the phenomenon (in understandable layman's terms) but unsure where to go to see the display. For just 235kr, you get a return trip on the chairlift and access to the sky station and all its instruments, plus there's an expert on hand to explain practically and theoretically what it is you are seeing (or indeed hearing).

**Hiking from Nuolja Mountain** From the top of the chairlift, there are a couple of enjoyable and easy marked hiking trails back down towards Abisko. You head south through dwarf birch woodland down to an impressive canyon within Abisko National Park from where you can follow the Kungsleden trail (see below) back to the Turiststation. Or, alternatively, you can head north on another trail which cuts down the hillside towards the village of Björkliden from where you can take the train the 7km back to Abisko.

**The Kungsleden Trail** Abisko marks the beginning of Sweden's best known **hiking route**, the Kungsleden trail, which stretches around 500km south to Hemavan and passes through one of Europe's last remaining wilderness areas. The trail's popularity means that it can get pretty busy, particularly during the peak Swedish holiday season between mid-June and mid-August. If you are looking for total isolation, this is probably not the trail for you, but if you can avoid the crowds, for example, by walking in September when the weather is still good and the glorious reds, yellows and oranges of the Lapland autumn are starting to appear, hiking this trail is an experience to cherish.

Alternatively, take a tent and choose the section of the trail where there is no overnight cabin accommodation – and consequently fewer hikers. STF (Svenska Turistföreningen; the Swedish Youth Hostel Association) maintain **overnight huts** and **hostels** between Abisko and Kvikkjokk (northwest of Jokkmokk) as well as between Ammarnäs and Hemavan at the southern end of the trail; they spaced at regular intervals, roughly every 15–20km or so, making it possible to hike between them comfortably in one day. There are no huts between Kvikkjokk and Ammarnäs, a distance of about 130km.

Passing through several national parks along its route, the Kungsleden is an easy trail to tackle as it is well marked, streams are bridged and duckboarding has been placed over areas of marshy ground. At one or two points along the route, it is necessary to cross lakes; a rowing boat is provided on each shore for this purpose, and, naturally, there must always be one boat on either shore for you to get across. This is what to do: first, row across in one boat, when you reach the second boat, tie it to yours and row back to your starting point; now leave one boat here and set out again across the lake and leave your boat on the other shore; this shuttling back and forth enables walkers coming in either direction to cross the lake.

**Getting to the Kungsleden: bus and train connections** The Kungsleden is readily accessible by public transport. **Trains** operated by Connex (*www.connex.se*) will whisk you to the starting point in Abisko, whereas, **buses** are available to collect you at the end of your hike at the following points: Nikkaluokta, Kvikkjokk, Jäkkvik, Adolfström, Ammarnäs and Hemavan. Other useful train stations (reached by buses coming down from the mountains) are: Jokkmokk and Arvidsjaur on the Inlandsbanan (*www.inlandsbanan.se*; see page 28); and Murjek and Luleå on the main line (*www.connex.se*).

**RIKSGRÄNSEN** A small mountain village 34km from Abisko, tucked up tight against the Norwegian border, Riksgränsen boasts that there's never any need for artificial snow. That's because the settlement is one of the wettest in the whole of Sweden, lying in the path of every low pressure system that sweeps in from the Norwegian Sea, hence, when it is not snowing here, it is raining. That said, Riksgränsen is a popular winter sports destination drawing holidaying Swedes from across the country to its sixty-odd peaks over 1,350m; skiing is generally possible until mid-June. Riksgränsen is really about the surrounding countryside, since there's not much to the place itself: a hotel, the train station and the E10 just about sums things up.

There are daily **trains** to Riksgränsen from Luleå, Gällivare, Kiruna and Narvik.

**Where to stay and eat** The top of the range Riksgränsen (✆ *0980 400 80;* e *info@riksgransen.nu; www.riksgransen.nu;* $$$$$$/$$$$$), opposite the train station, has a whole array of types of **hotel** accommodation including double rooms and self-catering apartments sleeping up to eight people. In summer individual bunks in the apartments are rented out as youth hostel style accommodation ($). **Food** is available in the hotel's main restaurant as well as in the bar. There's a well-appointed spa centre on site too, boasting several massage rooms as well as outdoor hot tubs.

Arctic fox

# 4

# Narvik and the Islands

West of Narvik, the Norwegian coast carves gracefully into the most breathtakingly beautiful archipelago of islands and skerries anywhere in Europe. The **Vesterålen Islands**, and particularly their southern neighbours, **Lofoten**, offer jaw-dropping scenery quite unlike any other part of Lapland. The combination of sheer, granite peaks, which run spine-like through the entire chain, set against the narrowest of foreshores, gouged into countless rocky inlets and sandy bays, is of such elemental beauty that you will find it hard to leave. Dotted with pretty little fishing villages and traditional *rorbuer* cottages perched on wooden stilts by the shore, the islands are the best place in Lapland to go **whale-watching**. Not only that, but every autumn there's a rare opportunity to snorkel with great pods of **killer whales**, drawn to the area by plentiful food supplies. Travel by boat is very much part of a visit to Lofoten and Vesterålen; the coastal scenery, always stunning, is at its most spectacular around the impossibly narrow **Trollfjord**, hemmed in between the two islands groups.

Although **Narvik** itself, destroyed during World War II, is not a handsome place, it is by far the best gateway to the islands; from here it is possible to reach Lofoten by both ferry and road. The highlight of any trip is end-of-the-road **Å**, a gorgeous little village squeezed between craggy mountains on all sides – the mountain and coastal scenery at the very tip of the Vesterålen/Lofoten triangle is monumental. You also shouldn't miss the island capital, **Svolvær**, and charming **Henningsvær** on the way, which both deserve a visit. At the opposite end of the archipelago, **Andenes** is the region's premier whale-watching centre and a good point from which to leave the islands in summer when there's a handy ferry route back to the mainland giving a head start on the journey north to Tromsø.

## NARVIK

Narvik's never going to win any beauty contests. Its purpose in life is pure and simple: it provides an ice-free port for the export of iron ore from the mines at Kiruna and Gällivare. The scene of fierce fighting in 1940 between German and British forces to gain control of the town's harbour and neutral Sweden's iron ore exports (which ultimately provided the raw material to keep the German war machine in production throughout World War II), the town centre was totally destroyed during four air attacks by German warplanes. Following the Nazi occupation, rebuilding began apace but won few accolades for aesthetics – today's soulless concrete blocks, which dominate the town centre wherever you look, were born out of necessity rather than a desire to please the eye. However, there's a certain gritty charm to Narvik, its ugly, brooding dockyards slap bang in the centre of town and plain for all to see, that give the place a pioneering edge. If you've tired of small, remote inland villages on your travels, you'd do well to spend a day or two here, recharging your batteries and enjoying the bustle and goings-on of the town

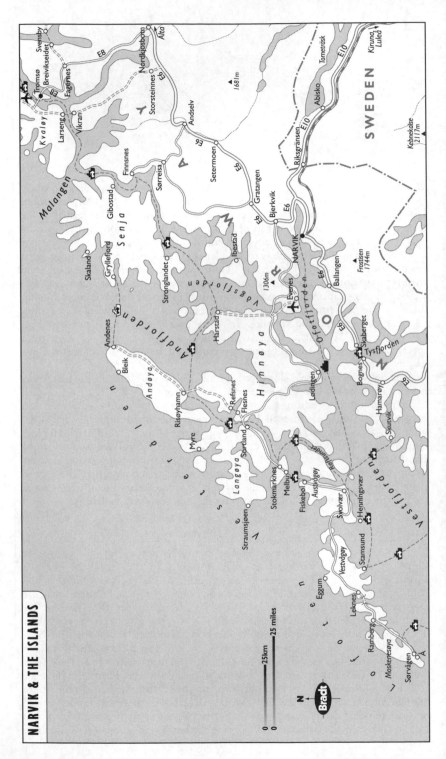

SWEDEN

Kiruna,
Luleå

Kebnekaise
2117m

E10

Torneträsk

Abisko

Riksgränsen

E10

168 Im

E6

Gratangen

Bjerkvik

E6

Frostisen
1744m

NARVIK

Ballangen

E6

Everes

1306m

Skaberget

Tysfjorden

Bognes

Hamarøy

Skutvik

Nordkjosbotn

Alta

E8

Svensby
Breivikseidet

Tromsø

Fagernes

E8

Larseng

Vikran

Kvaløy

Storsteinnes

E6

Andselv

Setermoen

E6

Finnsnes

Sørreisa

Gibostad

Skaland

Gryllefjord

Senja

Malangen

Stronglandet

Ibestad

Harstad

Vesteralen

Andfjorden

Andenes

Bleik

Risøyhamn

Myre

Andøya

Refsnes

Flesnes

Sortland

Straumsjøen

Stokmarknes

Langøya

Lødingen

Melbu

Fiskebøl

Austvågøy

Svolvær

Raftsundet

Henningsvær

Hinnøya

Ofotfjorden

Vestfjorden

Stamsund

Vestvågøy

Eggum

Leknes

Ramberg

Moskenesøya

Sørvågen

Å

N

Bradt

0  25km

0  25 miles

and its harbour. In recent years a rash of companies offering outdoor adventure sports has sprung up providing visitors with plenty to keep them busy. Incidentally, thanks to the Gulf Stream, spring comes much sooner here (and summer, mercifully, lasts that little bit longer) than on the other side of the mountains in Swedish Lapland; when it is −15C° in Kiruna, for example, with snow still thick on the ground, it can be above freezing in Narvik and the first spring flowers can be just starting to appear.

**GETTING THERE** Narvik is linked to Kiruna by both the E10 highway (later meeting the E6, which leads into town) and by rail. However, the **train** is by the far the best way to arrive; the ride is truly spectacular as the line seemingly splices right through the craggy, frost-shattered mountains which form the border with Norway. The train station is located on the northeastern edge of town, from where it is an easy five- to ten-minute walk southwest along Kongens gate (actually the E6) to the tourist office at no 57. The Hurtigbåt express passenger **boat** from and to Svolvær in the Lofoten Islands docks about 1km south of the tourist office at the quay beside Havnegata, which runs parallel to the E6 south of the town centre. Note that Narvik is not served by the Hurtigruten coastal steamer.

**TOURIST INFORMATION** The tourist office (↘ 76 96 56 00; e *post@ destinationnarvik.com; www.destinationnarvik.com;* ⊕ *Oct–Apr Mon–Fri 09.00–15.30; May to mid-Jun & mid-Aug to Sep Mon–Fri 09.00–16.00, also mid-Aug to Sep Sat 10.00–14.00; mid-Jun to mid-Aug Mon–Fri 09.00–19.00, Sat & Sun 10.00–17.00*) is at 57 Kongens gate, the single-standing concrete building painted blue on your right-hand side. There's **internet** access here for 10kr per 15 minutes.

**WHERE TO STAY** With just 18,500 inhabitants, Narvik isn't a big place and consequently there's not a great deal of choice when it comes to somewhere to stay but there is something for all pockets.

⌂ **Quality Grand Royal** Kongens gate 64; ↘ 76 97 70 00; www.choice.no. Although the hotel has changed hands several times in recent years it is still the smartest place in town with swanky Nordic-style rooms (all with free wireless internet) & some fine wood-panelling here & there which helps to retain a homely touch. $$$$$$/$$$$

⌂ **Victoria** Dronningens gate 58; ↘ 76 96 28 00; e post@victoria-hotel.net; www.victoria-hotel.net. Altogether more affordable & enjoying an equally central location. Comfortable, though less stylish rooms than the Grand Royal. $$$$

🅰 **Narvik Camping** Rombaksveien 75; ↘ 76 94 58 10; www.narvikcamping.com. The first thing of any significance as you come into Narvik on the E6 from the north; it is on your right-hand side & well signed. Camping & cabins (4 berth: $$$) available from late Feb to late Sep.

⌂ **Breidablikk** Tore Hundsgate 41; ↘ 76 94 14 18; e post@breidablikk.no; www.breidablikk.no. Does what it says on the can: *breidablikk* literally means 'wide view', and that's what you get from this hilltop guesthouse 2 blocks inland from the tourist office. Excellent, recently refurbished, tasteful rooms sharing facilities ($$) or dorm beds ($); b/fast buffet an extra 50kr. Recommended.

⌂ **Narvik Vandrarhjem** Dronningens gate 58; ↘ 76 96 22 00; www.vandrarhjem.no. A good central location for this comfortable youth hostel offering self-catering & washing facilities as well as internet. $

⌂ **Spor I Gjestegård** Brugata 2A; ↘ 76 94 60 20; e post@spor1.no; www.spor1.no. Housed in what was once the train station for Narvik's iron ore trains (Spor I means 'track I'), this guesthouse with unadorned, modern dbls ($$) & dorm beds ($) is perfect for self-catering with a good kitchen, TV room, bar & sauna. Also handy for the bus station.

4

## ✕ WHERE TO EAT AND DRINK

✕ **Astrupkjelleren** Kinobakken 1. This Narvik institution, housed in a battered old mustard-coloured timber building close to the tourist office, serves a choice of steaks, freshly caught fish & even reindeer for around 170–200kr per main dish.

🍽 **Kafferiet** Dronningens gate 47. The best of the town's cafés, set back from Kongens gate up a flight of stone steps. Of an evening this place mutates into a bar & a nightclub at w/ends.

✕ **Peppes Pizza** Kongens gate 66. Located towards the rear of the Storsenter shopping centre adjacent to the Quality Grand Royal (see above), there's a

good choice of pizzas & pasta dishes but prices at this national chain are not cheap. Reckon on 172kr for a medium-sized nothing-special pizza.

✕ **Rallar'n Pub & Kro** Kongens gate 64. Inside the Quality Grand Royal hotel, this eaterie offers the best balance between quality & price. A selection of burgers, pizzas, nachos & other meaty mains for around 150kr.

🍸 **Spor 1** Brugata 2A. The appealing pub attached to the Spor 1 guesthouse is one of the most sociable (& cheapest) places for a drink & a good place to meet other travellers.

**THE TOWN** Look at any map of Narvik and you will quickly see how the iron ore **harbour**, owned and operated by LKAB of Kiruna, totally dominates the town, engulfing about a third of it with loading quays, cranes, overhead walkways and railway sidings. At the time of writing the harbour was being rebuilt (a **tour** is normally available; ask at the tourist office for the latest details). Iron ore trains – often over a kilometre long and composed of a hundred or so wagons – make an oddly impressive sight as they trundle through town bound for the quayside and the end of their journey from Sweden.

**Ofoten Museum** (*Administrasjonsveien 3; www.museumnord.no;* ⊕ *Mon–Fri 10.00–15.00; also Sat & Sun late Jun to mid-Aug noon–15.00; 40kr*) Sandwiched between the Swedish Church and the Hurtigbåt quay, the harbourside Ofoten Museum contains a potted history of the harbour's development and its strategic importance for the town and the construction by navvies (some of whom paid with their lives) of the Ofotbanen railway across some of Lapland's harshest terrain. Completed in 1902, the new railway was crowned by the elegant former administration of NSB (Norwegian State Railways) which now houses the museum.

**Nordland Røde Kors Krigsminnesmuseum: War Museum** (*At the junction of Brugata & Kongens gate;* ⊕ *Jan–Apr Mon–Fri 11.00–15.00; May to early Jun & late Aug to mid-Sep daily 10.00–16.00; early Jun to late Aug daily 10.00–21.00; mid-Sep to Dec Mon–Fri 10.00–15.00; 50kr*) Predictably, Narvik's other museum is devoted to the five years the town spent under Nazi occupation; the Nordland Røde Kors Krigsminnemuseum is run by the Red Cross. The museum recounts the Battle of Narvik step by step which began on 9 April 1940, when ten German destroyers with 3,000 soldiers on board attacked the town, sinking two iron ore ships. The British responded attacking the German fleet and launching an air assault of the town a couple of days later. The battle raged for two months before the British withdrew due to the worsening situation in France; German occupation of Narvik began on 8 Jun 1940 and lasted until 8 May 1945. Sadly, all labelling in the museum is in Norwegian so ask for the leaflet in English, which summarises the main events of the campaign. It is not widely known that the Germans established two concentration camps east of Narvik. The Beisfjord camp was the scene of a massacre which cost 300 prisoners, all Serbs, their lives. Having dug their own mass grave, the prisoners were gunned down by camp guards, while others died in the flames when the Germans set fire to their barracks following a rebellion. The story is relayed in a moving video in English on the museum's ground floor.

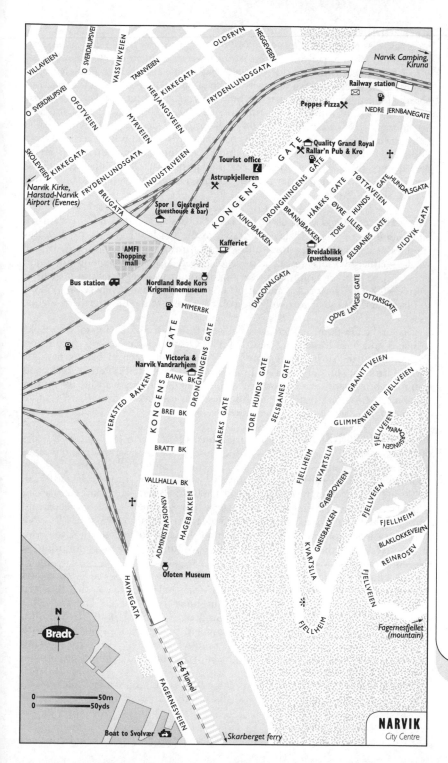

Narvik Camping,
Kiruna

Railway station

Peppes Pizza ✕

NEDRE JERNBANEGATE

Quality Grand Royal
Rallar'n Pub & Kro

Tourist office ℹ

Astrupkjelleren ✕

Spor 1 Gjestegård
(guesthouse & bar)

Kafferiet

Breidablikk
(guesthouse)

AMFI
Shopping
mall

Bus station

Nordland Røde Kors
Krigsminnemuseum

MIMERBK

Victoria &
Narvik Vandrarhjem

BANK BK

BREI BK

BRATT BK

VALLHALLA BK

ADMINISTRASIONSV

HAGEBAKKEN

Ofoten Museum

Fagernesfjellet
(mountain)

N

Bradt

0 ——— 50m
0 ——— 50yds

Boat to Svolvær

Skarberget ferry

NARVIK
City Centre

Narvik and the Islands NARVIK

4

VILLAVEIEN
O SVERDRUPSVEI
VASSVIKVEIEN
TARNVEIEN
KIRKEGATA
OLDERVN
HEGGEVEIEN
O SVERDRUPSVEI
OFOTVEIEN
MYRVEIEN
HERJANGSVEIEN
FRYDENLUNDSGATA
SKOLEVEIEN KIRKEGATA
FRYDENLUNDSGATA
INDUSTRIVEIEN
BRUGATA
KONGENS GATE
KINOBAKKEN
DRONGNINGENS GATE
BRANNBAKKEN
HÅREKS GATE
TØTTAVEIEN
ØVRE LILLEB
TORE HUNDS
SELSBANES GATE
HUNDSGATA
SILDVIK GATA
DIAGONALGATA
LODVE LANGES GATE
OTTARSGATE
GATE
DRONGNINGENS GATE
HÅREKS GATE
TORE HUNDS GATE
SELSBANES GATE
KONGENS GATE
VERKSTED BAKKEN
GRANITTVEIEN
FJELLVEIEN
GLIMMERVEIEN
FJELLVEIEN
MARMOR
SVINGEN
FJELLHEIM
KVARTSLIA
GABBROVEIEN
GNEISBAKKEN
FJELLVEIEN
FJELLHEIM
BLAKLOKKEVEIEN
REINROSEV
KVARTSLIA
FJELLVEIEN
FJELLHEIM
HAVNEGATA
E-6 Tunnel
FAGERNESVEIEN

Narvik Kirke,
Harstad-Narvik
Airport (Evenes)

## Other activities
**Fagernesfjellet and the cable car** (↘ 76 96 04 94; *www.narvikfjellet.no*; ⏰ *Jun–Sep*; *100kr return*) Weather permitting, one of the most enjoyable things to do in Narvik is to take the seven-minute ride on the town's cable car up Fagernesfjellet peak (656m) from where you can normally see the Lofoten Islands. It is a fine place to observe the Midnight Sun if you are here between mid-June and late July when the cable car runs until 01.00 (it runs until 21.00 at other times). A plethora of hiking trails criss-cross the mountain – the tourist office can help with details. During winter (roughly Nov to May) the cable car is a good way to access the ski slopes and cross-country trails available on the mountain. Skiing up here is pretty special since there are few other places in Lapland that offer such breathtaking views of the surrounding fjords and islands. There's more information from Narvik Skiing Center.

**Killer whale safaris and wreck diving** Between November and the middle of January large numbers of killer whales are drawn to the fjords off Narvik by plentiful supplies of herring. At this time tours operate from Narvik harbour to see the whales – either by zodiac inflatable or regular boat. There's the once-in-a-lifetime possibility to snorkel alongside these amazing animals. Full details are available from Orca Safari (*www.fcn.no*) and on ↘ 91 39 06 18 if you fancy snorkelling. A visit to Narvik at this time of year will give you the chance to see the Northern Lights, too.

One of the most unusual activities available from Narvik is diving to the wrecks of planes and ships lost during World War II. Over 50 planes and 46 ships lie on the bottom of the surrounding fjords – 39 ships went down in Narvik harbour alone. Naturally, you must be a qualified diver to attempt to reach the wrecks and you must bring your own equipment with you since it is not available for rent in Narvik. Application forms for diving need to be filled in – there's more information available from the tourist office.

**MOVING ON FROM NARVIK** From Narvik **buses** head north to Tromsø and Alta (from where there are connections to the North Cape; see page 149); and west to the Vesterålen and Lofoten islands. For Tromsø, #100, the Nord-Norgeekspressen, departs from the town's bus station Monday–Friday at 05.20, 13.00 and 15.00; Saturday 15.00; Sunday 13.00, 15.00 and 18.35, and takes about 4 hours 15 minutes. A single ticket is 360kr. For Alta there's just one departure on #815: at 13.00 Monday–Friday and Sunday arriving into Alta at 22.30. Note there's no bus at all on Saturday. If you are heading to the North Cape, you must first spend the night in Alta before continuing the next morning to Honningsvåg.

The Narvik-Lofoten Ekpressen (*1 daily; 6hrs 40mins*) runs via Sortland and Stokmarknes (in the Vesterålen Islands) to Svolvær and ultimately Leknes (Lofoten Islands). It is possible to reach Svolvær by **boat** from Narvik. The Hurtigbåt express passenger boat runs directly to Svolvær at 15.15 (*Mon–Fri & Sun; 3hrs 30mins*); alternatively on Tuesday, Thursday and Friday there's a bus at 16.10 to Skutvik, southwest of Narvik off the E6, from where there's a car ferry across to Svolvær, arriving 20.50, in time to make a northbound connection on the Hurtigruten, if needed.

Finally, **trains** run southeast to Sweden calling at Abisko, Kiruna, Luleå and all points south to Stockholm at 10.50 and 15.25; a final service at 19.30 operates as far as Kiruna.

The scenic highlight of any trip to Norwegian Lapland, the Vesterålen (pronounced *vester-oh-len*) and Lofoten (*loo-fut-en*) islands are a rugged triangular-shaped archipelago off Narvik. Though totally void of Sámi culture, these green, mountainous islands make a perfect antidote to the remote villages of the forested heart of Lapland, and are readily accessible from Narvik, itself linked to Swedish Lapland by train and road.

The **Vesterålen Islands** (literally *western isles*), predominantly Hinnøya, Langøya and Andøya, are the less dramatic of the two groups. Naturally, this being Norway, there are mountains wherever you look, but they are set back from the islands' towns and villages, often forming a backdrop to a view, rather than being the view themselves. From south to north the peaks become gradually less pronounced and craggy in nature – indeed, the north of Andøya is not mountainous at all but given over instead to enormous lowland peat bogs, cloudberry marshes and even coal deposits. Generally, there's a little more land available for farming in Vesterålen than Lofoten and as you travel around you will see tractors working narrow strips of precious flat land beside the coastline, although eking a living from agriculture so far north can never be more than borderline.

Settlements here tend to be nondescript, workaday affairs with few sights to set the pulse racing. The main centres to seek out are **Andenes**, a renowned base for **killer whale** safaris (see below), functional **Sortland** and **Stokmarknes**, from where the Hurtigruten begins its dramatic passage through one of the most spectacular stretches of the Norwegian coast, the narrow **Raftsundet** sound which separates Vesterålen from Lofoten. Branching off here, the impossibly tight 3km-long **Trollfjorden**, just 100m wide at its mouth, has to be seen to be believed; vertical rock walls towering to a height of 1,000m bear down on the huge ferries and inflatables which edge their way in here. Raftsundet notwithstanding, it is more the attraction of travelling through the spectacular mountain and fjordland scenery, and the prospect of what lies ahead in Lofoten, rather than visiting villages for their own sake, that draws people here.

The **Lofoten Islands** (literally named *lynx foot* by the Vikings after their supposed resemblance) really are something special. Overwhelmed by the 100km long **Lofotveggen** (Lofoten Wall), a spine of sheer, snow-clad granite peaks and ravines that runs the length of the archipelago and quite simply takes your breath away, it is clear to see how the extreme forces of nature have left their unforgiving mark on the geography of these islands. Smaller, narrower and infinitely more beautiful than their northern neighbours, the rearing mountains finally splinter into the Norwegian Sea beyond the beguiling village of Å in the south. Travel here is relaxed and enjoyable – the climate is generally mild and it is not uncommon for Lofoten to be bathed in warm sunshine while the mainland is depressed by heavy blankets of grey cloud. Spending the afternoon catching the rays on the rocks or the odd sandy beach or wandering through the winding backstreets of idyllic fishing villages is part of Lofoten's charm and it is hard to find anyone who doesn't succumb to this endearing side of island life.

The capital, **Svolvær**, is a good first place to head for; there's a fine selection of accommodation here, including plenty of traditional wooden fishermen's huts, *rorbuer* (see below), to choose from and some tasty fish suppers served up overlooking the harbour. However, it would be foolish to stop here and miss out on two of the islands' most endearing villages: picturesque **Henningsvær**, reached from the main road via a set of inter-connected islets, which huddles around its harbour proudly showing off its pretty painted houses, and laid-back **Å** (pronounced *oh*), a gaggle of wooden homes sitting snugly beneath the most impressive of peaks, seemingly at the end of the world.

**GETTING THERE AND AROUND** Travelling to and around both the Vesterålen and Lofoten islands takes time. If you have just a few days available, it is probably best to concentrate on just one group of islands, rather than to try to hurtle across the archipelago, wasting time waiting for bus and ferry connections. Distances are deceivingly long and roads are often exasperatingly wiggly, winding their way around deeply indented fjords and around obstinate mountains. Narvik is as good a place as any to begin a tour of the islands either with or without your own car.

**By car from south to north** With three or four days in hand, and to avoid doubling back on yourself, it is best to start in the Lofoten Islands, the most beautiful and scenically spectacular of the two island chains. From Narvik, first head southwest on the E6 towards Bodø then take Route 81 to **Skutvik** and the **car ferry** to Svolvær (✆ *76 11 82 45;* e *fergebooking@hurtigruten.com; www.hurtigruten. com; 4–6 daily; 2hr; 242kr for car & one passenger; reserve if travelling Jun–Aug*).

The best road connection between the Lofoten and Vesterålen islands currently involves taking the **car ferry** (*roughly every hour; 25mins*) operating between **Fiskebøl** (Lofoten) and **Melbu** (Vesterålen); both places are on the main trunk road, the E10, which runs south–north across the islands. However, as we went to press, a new tunnel was set to open replacing the ferry route; latest details available from the local tourist offices.

Having reached Sortland in the Vesterålen Islands, you have a choice of routes: either east to busy Harstad via the **car ferry** between **Flesnes** and **Refsnes** (*hourly; 25mins*); or north to Andenes, by far the better choice and a good place for whale and birdwatching, from where there's a **car ferry** (*summer only: Jun–Aug 2–3 daily; 1hr 40mins*) to Gryllefjord and ultimately north to Tromsø or south back towards Narvik.

**By public transport from south to north** Although more limiting, it is perfectly possible to see the best of the islands without your own car, travelling instead by **bus** and/or **ferry**. The route outlined above for car drivers is equally feasible by public transport. First take either the direct Hurtigbåt express **boat** from Narvik to Svolvær (see *Moving on from Narvik*, page 70). Then explore Lofoten by bus –

services operate once or twice daily from Svolvær as far south as Å (though often not at weekends; pick up a bus timetable from the tourist office before setting out). Return to Svolvær and continue by bus towards Sortland, the main transport interchange, from where you can pick up a connection for Andenes or Harstad, should you want to explore more of the Vesterålen Islands, or, alternatively, return to Narvik. There is a direct bus back Svolvær to from Narvik, or, of course, you could take the Hurtigbåt express boat back to the mainland.

**HARSTAD** The largest town in Vesterålen with a population of 23,000, Harstad's central position in the archipelago has always been its selling point. During the late 1800s, when plentiful catches of herring fuelled a boom in the local economy, the town became the perfect base for landing fish and transporting it to markets throughout the north thanks to its good road connections. As herring stocks dwindled, Harstad turned to shipbuilding and maintenance, the production of shipping and fishing equipment and even the import of coal from Spitsbergen to make a living. In more recent years, oil exploration has played a significant role in the local economy and today the northern headquarters of Statoil are here. If the number of heavy trucks which trundle into town today is anything to go by, Harstad is still a key player in the distribution of goods, which arrive here by cargo ship.

**Tourist information** Harstad is unlikely to be the highlight of any trip to Vesterålen, but if you reach here between ferries or buses, pop in to the tourist office (✆ 77 01 89 89; *www.visitharstad.com;* ☉ *mid-Jun to Aug daily 10.00–18.00; rest of year Mon–Fri 10.00–15.00*), at the bus station, Torvet 8, where there's plentiful information to tempt you to stay longer. **Internet** access is available for 20kr per 15 minutes, and at most of the main hotels for their guests.

## Where to stay

🏠 **Grand Nordic** Strandgata 9; ✆ 77 00 30 00; e resepsjon.gnh@nordic.no; www.nordic.no. Lives up to its name offering extremely elegant rooms in the centre of town. $$$$$$/$$$$

🏠 **Quality Arcticus** Havnegata 3; ✆ 77 04 08 00; e arcticus@quality.choicehotels.no; www.arcticus-hotel.no. The best hotel in town overlooking the harbour a short distance from the main square, Torvet, with Scandinavian-style décor throughout. $$$$$/$$$$

🏠 **Thon Hotel** Sjøgata 11; ✆ 77 00 08 00; harstad@thonhotels.no; www.thonhotels.no. A smart, though less chi-chi affair down on the quayside. $$$$

🏠 **Youth hostel** Trondenesveien 110; ✆ 77 04 00 77; e harstad.hostel@vandrarhjem.no; www.vandrarhjem.no. ☉Jun to mid-Aug. A couple of kilometres out of town along the road to Trondenes (see page 74). The best option for budget accommodation though rooms are a little spartan since the building is actually a school outside the summer season; you can walk into town in about 30min or take catch the local bus which runs hourly. Dbl room $$ & dorm beds $.

🏕 **Harstad Camping** Nesseveien 55; ✆ 77 07 36 62; e postmaster@harstad.camping.no; www.harstad-camping.no. Open all year round west of the town centre. $

## Where to eat

Harstad is large enough to support a fair number of eateries, most clustered around the main square, one of which, Restaurant De 4 Roser (see below), has justifiably earned a reputation for serving some of the finest fare in the north of Norway.

🍴 **Café De 4 Roser** Torvet 7B. A gloriously stylish continental style café serving French, English & American b/fasts (all day) for 89kr, homemade fish

burgers 130kr, plus a range of Mediterranean dishes such as goats' cheese salad 137kr & spinach & ricotta ravioli. Also, the best selection of coffees in town. Beer & smoothies available too.

**✘ Gründer** Fjordgata 2. A good choice if money is tight. This chain restaurant offers decent salads from 102kr; pasta & wok dishes from 129kr, tapas from 131kr as well as a series of quiche-like pies with chicken/bacon/beef or reindeer at 106kr.

**✘ Hoelstuen** Rikard Kaarbøs plass 4. Another upmarket restaurant for a special occasion with soft lighting & period furniture from the late 1800s. The food is French or Italian in inspiration & fish & meat mains cost around 270kr.

**✘ Milano** Strandgatan 18b. Tucked away beyond the Grand Nordic behind the main square, this dependable Italian chain has every pizza you could ever desire for around 150kr.

**✘ Restaurant De 4 Roser** Torvet 7B. Upstairs from the café, this top-notch restaurant is renowned for its expertly prepared fish (& meat) dishes which are truly mouthwatering; a main course here is around 279kr. Try the tasty fillet of fish topped with Serrano ham & cashew nuts (289kr) or the exquisite noisette of lamb with almond potatoes. Dinner only.

**The town and Trondenes** Having taken in the goings-on in the harbour and around the main square, there's little else to detain you in the town centre and it is a much better idea to either walk (30mins) or take the bus (the tourist office has details) to **Trondenes**, the original settlement of Harstad, located on the eponymous tapering peninsula to the east of town. On foot, from the tourist office, first follow Sjøgata, later becoming Strandgata and finally Skolegata as it snakes its way along the harbourside and then cuts up through town. Turn right into Hagebyveien (signed for Trondenes) and follow this road, passing an area of residential housing, until you reach Trondenes.

**Trondenes kirke: the church** (*guided tours late Jun to mid-Aug Sun–Fri at 16.00 & 17.00; 35kr*) The main item of interest, Trondenes kirke occupies a grassy knoll close to the water's edge. The church's setting is totally enchanting: surrounded by a well-kept graveyard and tall, swaying trees with snow-capped mountains in the background, there are good views from here back towards Harstad itself. Although the church's exact age is uncertain, it is thought it was completed on the orders of King Øystein Magnusson shortly after 1430, which makes it the northmost medieval stone church in Europe; remarkably, the exterior is close to its original state. During the late medieval period, the church served as the main place of worship for thousands of people across the entire north of Norway. It is likely that the current church was the third to stand here, replacing two other stave churches built in the 11th and 12th centuries. Inside, three ornate Gothic triptyches, fine examples of the medieval church art of northern Germany, adorn the altar and date from the 1400s. Unusually, the Baroque pulpit is equipped with an hourglass to dissuade the priest from engaging in lengthy ecclesiastical ramblings.

**Trondenes Historikse Senter: the Historical Centre** (*Trondenesveien 122; www.tdm.no; ☺ 08.00–16.00 daily; 70kr*) Next door to the church the Trondenes Historiske Senter is the place to get to grips with historical developments in this part of Norway through the imaginative use of multi-media exhibitions. Housed in a state-of-the-art building with a traditional turf roof, the heritage centre not only contains examples of original Viking artefacts discovered in the area but also recreates the sounds and smells of the period.

**Adolfkanonen: Adolf's gun** The other thing to see out at Trondenes is a massive World War II land-based gun, known as Adolfkanonen (Adolf's Gun), the only fortification from the war that has been restored, though its location inside a restricted military zone makes visits rather tricky (*guided tours early Jun to mid-Aug at 11.00, 13.00, 15.00 & 17.00; 30kr*). However, regulations stipulate that you must have your own transport to cover the couple of kilometres between the entrance gate, about 1km up the hill from the church, and the gun itself. This is not provided by the guided tour.

**Moving on from Harstad** Harstad is a good place from which to reach other destinations in Vesterålen and Lofoten by **ferry** and **bus**. The Hurtigruten sails south to Sortland, Stokmarknes and Svolvær (passing through the Raftsundet Sound and Trollfjorden) at 08.30. It sails north at 08.00 arriving in Tromsø at 14.30. A faster way of getting to Tromsø is to travel on the Hurtigbåt express boat, which sails there in just 2 hours 40 minutes (*Mon–Fri at 07.00, 10.00 & 16.00; Sat 07.30 & 15.00; Sun 16.00 & 20.00*). By bus there are direct services from Harstad to Sortland, from where connections can be made to other destinations such as Andenes and Svolvær. Car drivers might want to consider the car ferry which operates between Refsnes and Flesnes (*every hour; 68kr car and driver; 25mins*) as a way of shortening the journey between Harstad and Sortland. On leaving Sortland simply follow Route 83 signed for Sortland which will take you the ferry quay at Refsnes.

Incidentally, it can be useful to know just how far some of the other destinations in region are from here: Andenes (101km); Harstad (80km); Narvik (200km); Stokmarknes (27km); Svolvær (79km); and Tromsø (411km).

**SORTLAND** Try not to get stuck in Sortland, a dreary place utterly void of attractions (unless you consider the headquarters of the Norwegian Coastguard reason enough for your heart to flutter) just across the arching bridge, which links the two islands of Langøya and Hinnøya. Given its strategic location on the E10, you have no choice but to pass through here *en route* to Lofoten, and, indeed, Sortland is a major traffic junction and bus interchange point for the entire islands. Backed by jagged peaks and fronting the narrow Sortlandsundet sound, you'd have hoped that Sortland could have made more of its geographically stunning location. Sadly, the mundane parallel streets of modern concrete blocks do little to raise the spirits and you are best using Sortland as a place to stock up on provisions, fuel or bus timetables.

**Tourist information** Admittedly, Sortland's tourist office (✆ 76 11 14 80; *www.visitvesteralen.com;* ☺ *mid-Jun to mid-Aug Mon–Fri 09.00–18.00; Sat 10.00–16.00; Sun noon–16.00; rest of year Mon–Fri 09.00–16.00*) does its best to sell the town and is a good source of information on local bus routes (timetables are always posted in the window if the office is closed when you arrive). It is a five- to ten-minute walk west of the bus station at Kjøpmannsgata 2.

**Where to stay and eat** Should you find yourself in the unenviable position of having to spend the night here, perhaps waiting for the Hurtigruten, which sails southbound (for Svolvær and Raftsundet) at 13.00, or northbound at 03.00, the best place to stay is the **Strand Hotell** (✆ 76 11 00 80; *www.strandhotell.no;* $$$$$), Strandgata 34, one block back from the sound, with modern rooms just a stone's throw from the town centre and the main street. If you are here between June and August, you could try the simple B&B accommodation available at **Postmestergården** (✆ 76 12 10 41; e *asoelsne@online.no;* $$$) at Nordlysvegen 35. To get here from the town centre, first take the main E10, Vesterålsgata, back east towards the bridge across the sound, then, just before the bridge take Markvegen off to the left and then the first left again, Nordlysvegen. For eating, choices are severely limited: the cheap and cheerful **Milano** at Torggata 17 in the main square is the most economical place to fill and empty stomach with medium pizzas for two people costing just 85kr.

4

**NORTH TO ANDENES** It is the chance to go **whale-watching** from Andenes, a small and rather unattractive village at the northermost edge of Vesterålen, clinging to the very tip of Andøya island, that brings most visitors to the islands. There's reputed to be a 95–99% chance of seeing whales on the safaris which leave daily from the harbour – sperm and minke whales are found in relatively large numbers in the waters off Vesterålen's northern tip, but amazingly **killer whales** are also present, which are the big attraction, and good enough reason to sign up for a whale safari here rather than elsewhere. Sperm whales are seen on most trips though it is hard to predict whether other species will put in an appearance. However, Andenes's secret is its proximity to the continental shelf and the nutrient-rich feeding grounds in the vicinity, which draw whales to this area of the Norwegian coast. It is a good place to book **birdwatching trips**, in particular to see **puffins** or **sea eagles** (see below).

**Getting to Andenes by ferry from the mainland** Although it is possible to drive to Andenes along the E10 via Sortland, from whence Route 82 covers the last 100km or so north, a very useful ferry service operates between late May and mid-August from tiny Gryllefjord (reached along Route 86 northwest of Finnsnes, off the main E6 from Narvik) across to Andenes, cutting out the tiring and extremely wiggly drive across the Vesterålen Islands. Operated by **Senja Fergene** (❄ *76 14 12 03; www.senjafergene.no; passengers 140kr, cars 360kr*), the ferry crossing takes roughly 1 hour 40 minutes (*late May to mid-Jun & early Aug to mid-Aug 2 daily; mid-Jun to early Aug 3 daily*). Departure times from Gryllefjord are 11.00, 15.00 (when operating) and 19.00; from Andenes at 09.00, 13.00 (when operating) and 17.00.

**Tourist information** Andenes's tourist office (❄ *76 14 12 03; www.andoy.net;* ⊕ *mid-Jun to Aug daily 10.00–18.00; rest of year Mon–Fri 09.00–16.00;*), Hamnegata, is located down in the harbour by the lighthouse. The friendly staff can help with accommodation bookings as well as the whale safaris and transport enquiries.

## ⌂ Where to stay

⌂ **Norlandia Andrikken** Storgata 53; ❄ 76 14 12 22; e service@andrikken.norlandia.no; www.norlandia.no/andrikken. A hulk of a building with comfortable though run-of-the-mill modern rooms. $$$$$

⌂ **Grønnbua** (5 2-room apts, 15 1-room apts & 3 suites) Storgata 51; ❄ 76 14 14 99; e dag@rorbucamping.no; www.rorbucamping.no. 2 *rorbuer* known as Grønnbua I, built in 1938 for the town's fishermen & now converted into traditional-style 2-room apartments with kitchen, bathroom & private entrance, & the newly built Grønnbua II, which contains 1-room apartments & suites. *2-room*

apts $$, *1-room apts* $$$$, *suites* $$$$.

⌂ **Andøy Natursenter** Hamnegata 1; ❄ 76 14 12 03; e post@hisnakul.no; www.hisnakul.no. Located next to the Whale Centre & Hisnakul, the simple dbl rooms here are exceptionally good value, though, other than free wireless internet access, they include no frills. $

⌂ **Tusenhjemmet** Andenes harbour, ❄ 76 14 28 50; e service@andrikken.norlandia.no; www.norlandia.no/andrikken. Run by the Norlandia hotel, this shack down by the harbour functions as the town's youth hostel. Rooms & facilities are spartan. $

## ✗ Where to eat and drink

▣ **Jul Nilsen Bakeri & Konditori** Kong Hans gate 1. The town's best café & cake shop with a small selection of light lunches available.

✗ **Lysthuset Sørvesten** Storgata 51. Run by the owners of Grønnbua, the fresh fish here is quite

exceptional. Their grilled salmon with cucumber & sour cream salad is heavenly.

✗ **Restaurant Andrikken** Storgata 53. Another top-notch restaurant inside the main hotel with an emphasis on locally caught fish. Dishes are reasonably priced & expertly prepared.

Hvalsafari (✆ 76 11 56 00; www.whalesafari.no) operates daily from late May to mid-September and has two vessels with a capacity of 80 and 99 passengers respectively. They sail at 11.30 from Andenes harbour to the whale feeding grounds, though at times of increased demand there are departures at 09.30, 15.30 and 17.30. Booking at least a couple of days in advance is wise since the trips are often sold out weeks beforehand. The boats take around one hour to reach the whales and the entire trip lasts around 4–5 hours, costing 795kr, which includes entrance to the Whale Centre, a light meal on board and a certificate, which, frankly, you can live without. It is a good idea to have extremely warm clothes with you, including a hat and gloves, as it can get very cold out on deck waiting to see a glimpse of the whales. Expert guides are on hand to make sure you don't miss anything.

## What to see and do

**The Whale Centre** (⌚ *late May to mid-Jun & mid-Aug to mid-Sep daily 08.30–16.00; mid-Jun to mid-Aug daily 08.30–19.00; 60kr*) The town of Andenes itself holds few attractions. However, the Whale Centre right on the harbourside inside a former fish processing factory, forms part of the whale safaris and admission is included in the tours. The centre's remit is tourism, education and research – not easy bedfellows and the result is a rather dry interpretation of what awaits out on the safari itself. In addition to a film presentation about a whale feasting on a group of squid, the centre's prime exhibit is the complete skeleton of a 16m male sperm whale, which stranded on a nearby beach in September 1996. The bones were labelled and placed in nets in the sea to be thoroughly cleaned before being reassembled and put on display.

**The Northern Lights Centre** (⌚ *late Jun to mid-Aug daily 10.00–18.00; 30kr*) Slightly more engaging the Northern Lights Centre or Hisnakul, shares the same timber building as the tourist office and is, in effect, a simple natural history musuem with tired exhibits about local birdlife, fish species and the Northern Lights. Although the aurora borealis can be seen, weather permitting, across the northern skies during winter, Andøy boasts greater activity thanks to its location under the auroral oval. The Centre's displays on what exactly the aurora is and why it appears are its most interesting section.

**Puffin tours** Andenes makes a good base from which to go **birdwatching** (*trips daily lasting 90 mins Jun to mid-Aug 15.00, late Jun to mid-Aug additional tour at 13.00, from harbour in nearby village Bleik, about 10km southwest of Andenes; 300kr*). One of Norway's most spectacular seabird colonies on the island of Bleiksøya is just a 20-minute boat ride away. Home to 80,000 pairs of puffins and 6,000 pairs of kittiwakes, there's a chance to catch a glimpse of cormorants, razorbills and guillemots. Remarkably, the spectacular white-tailed sea eagle is seen on every trip according to the organisers.

**SOUTH TO STOKMARKNES** From Sortland, the E10 hugs the shore of Sortlandsundet as it heads the 27km southwest to Stokmarknes, famous, in Norway at least, as the birthplace of the Hurtigruten, the cruise specialists. As you cross the second of two bridges that lead into town you will catch sight of one of the line's former vessels, *Finnmarken*, standing high and dry beside the quayside currently used for Hurtigruten departures. Linked to the adjacent building,

Hurtigrutens Hus, by a walkway over the road, the ship forms part of the main attraction in Stokmarknes: the **Hurtigrutemuseet** (⊕ *mid-May to mid-Jun & mid-Aug to mid-Sep daily noon–16.00; mid-Jun to mid-Aug daily 10.00–18.00; mid-Sep to mid-May daily 14.00–16.00; 80kr*), an engaging collection of nautical paraphernalia that recounts the life and times of Norway's most famous shipping line.

The brainchild of local man, Richard With, Hurtigruten (literally 'the fast line') first saw the light of day in 1893, when, with financial support from the Norwegian post office, who were keen to find a reliable way to get mail to outlying districts of the country, the first vessel, *D/S Vesteraalen*, entered service sailing between Trondheim and Hammerfest. Seemingly everything from an old upright piano which once entertained passengers to a video film of the engine room of the *Harald Jarl* is on display in the museum, from which a lift leads to the walkway across the *Finnmarken*. Built in 1956 in Hamburg, the vessel was in service until 1993, joining the museum six years later. Walking around this empty ship, exploring its deserted restaurant, lounges and corridors, is a curiously unsettling experience – strangely ghostlike.

**Tourist information, and where to stay and eat** Like Sortland, Stokmarknes is another place you don't want to get stuck. The **tourist office** (⊕ ❭ *76 15 00 00; www.visitvesteralen.com; late Jun to mid-Aug Mon–Fri 10.00–19.00; Jul to mid-Aug Sat & Sun 11.00–16.00*) is at the entrance to the town, on the harbourfront on the first quay you come to as you drive in. If you want to spend the night here, the **hotel** in the **Hurtigrutens Hus** complex is your best bet (❭ *76 15 06 00; www.hurtigrutenshus.com; $$$$$$*); its sumptuous modern rooms look out over the harbour. For something to **eat and drink** look no further than the inordinately popular **Rødbrygga**, a creaking old timber building (painted red) next to *Finnmarken*, which serves up snacks and full meals throughout the day.

**RAFTSUNDET AND TROLLFJORDEN** One of the most remarkable sights in the whole of Norwegian Lapland is now on the doorstep. The **Raftsundet** sound is a 20km long strait, which separates the Vesterålen and Lofoten island groups – and it is through here that the Hurtigruten charts a careful course bound for Svolvær. From Stokmarknes the route first takes you under the arching bridge carrying the E10, past the airport, and seemingly straight towards a wall of sheer mountains. Roughly 45 minutes after departure, the ferries then make a sharp right turn to enter the strait: the scenery through the sound is spectacular, precipitous rock faces rising up from the sea, culminating in rows of craggy pinnacles and peaks which are dressed in snow even during the height of summer.

The highlight of the voyage through the sound comes when the superferries nudge their way into the narrowest of fjords, **Trollfjorden**, at roughly the halfway point. Barely 100m wide at its mouth, the fjord is edged by smooth, vertical walls of granite reaching up to 1,000m above sea level; it seems an impossible task to sail such a large vessel into such an impossibly tight inlet, but the ferries sail all the way to the head of the fjord, a distance of around 3km, before performing the most impressive of nautical pirouettes to turn round and inch their way out again. Needless to say when the announcement is made that the ferry is about to enter Trollfjorden, there's one almighty scrum on board to get the best views. If you can't get up front to watch the boat enter the fjord, standing aft is equally as good as you can still appreciate the fjord in all its geological splendour. One note of caution, however: during the winter months, the Hurtigruten doesn't sail into Trollfjorden because of the extreme risk of avalanches and rock falls; check with the ship before departure for precise conditions and information. Once back into Raftsundet, it is another hour or so to Svolvær.

Incidentally, if taking the Hurtigruten between Stokmarkes and Svolvær doesn't fit with your travel plans, you can still experience the Trollfjord – arguably even more breathtakingly – on a trip by **Zodiac inflatable** from Svolvær itself (see below).

**SVOLVÆR** The charming, waterside town of Svolvær makes a great introduction to the Lofoten Islands. True, it may not be as picture-postcard-perfect as the other small fishing villages to the south, but it is, nonetheless, an easy place to spend a couple of days simply chilling out in the harbourfront cafés and restaurants or heading out to the Trollfjord, if you missed it on your way here. In addition, Svolvær is one of the easiest places to reach in the entire island chain. Not only is the town served by the Hurtigruten, there are direct Hurtigbåt passenger boats and buses here from Narvik, plus a handy car ferry across the waters of Vestfjorden from Skutvik, a straightforward and much shorter drive from Narvik than heading here along the E10.

Backed by a ring of stubborn mountains, Svolvær's development has been limited by difficult terrain, so, instead, the town has spilled out seawards onto the islands which lie immediately offshore, all interlinked and connected to the town itself by a series of bridges and roads. Having said that, Svolvær is not a big place; the focus of life here is the main square towards the southern end of the town centre beside the harbour. Behind it you will find the two main streets, Vestfjordgata and Storgata, which run parallel to each other and are the location for most of the town's shops and other services.

**Tourist information** Usefully located in the main square, the tourist office (❧ 76 06 98 00; *www.lofoten.info;* ☉ *Sep to late May Mon–Fri 09.00–15.30; late May to early Jun Mon–Fri 09.00–16.00, Sat 10.00–14.00; early Jun to late Jun Mon–Fri 09.00–20.00, Sat 10.00–14.00, Sun 16.00–20.00; late Jun to early Aug Mon–Fri 09.00–20.00, Sat 09.00–20.00, Sun 10.00–20.00; early Aug to late Aug Mon–Fri 09.00–20.00, Sat 10.00–14.00*) has plentiful supplies of information about local accommodation, transport services and ideas on what to do with your day.

**Where to stay** Svolvær is the capital of Lofoten and consequently the largest place on the islands, and there's no shortage of places to stay here, though you should consider booking ahead during the summer months since it is a popular destination for holidaying Norwegians.

🏠 **Svinøya Rorbuer** Svinøya; ❧ 76 06 99 30; e post@svinoya.no; www.svinoya.no. The accommodation of choice in Svolvær on the island of Svinøya, accessed via the Svinøybrua bridge at the eastern end of Austnesfjordgata. 30 waterside *rorbuer* of different shapes, sizes & ages – some of which (no.18 for example) are original & over 100 years old. Others are newly built & contain more modern fittings. High season is Jun–Aug when prices are several hundred kroner higher than at other times of the year. There's a selection of comfortable, modern dbl rooms & suites in the new Minihotel behind the reception building. *Sgl high season* $$$$$, *2-bedroom rorbuer are from* $$$$$. *B/fast is included. Minihotel rates from* $$$$$$.

🏠 **Svolvær Sjøhuscamp** Parkgata 12; ❧ 76 07 03 36; e post@svolver-sjohuscamp.no; www.svolver-sjohuscamp.no. Another great central quayside location for these dbl rooms & apartments decked out with stripped pine walls, attractive blue tables & chequered curtains. *Dbls with kitchenette & TV cost* $$; *apts with kitchen, jacuzzi & balcony go for* $$$$$$$.

🏠 **Best Western Svolvær** Austnesfjordgata 12; ❧ 76 07 19 99; e post@svolvar-hotell.no; www.svolvar-hotell.no. A characterless, modern block on the edge of the town centre, though with perfectly respectable chain-hotel-feel rooms, which is worth a look if things are looking full elsewhere. $$$$$

🏠 **Rica Svolvær** Lamholmen; ❧ 76 07 22 22;

e rica.hotel.svolvar@rica.no; www.rica.no. Occupying the tiny island of Lamholmen in the middle of the harbour, accessed by the long causeway, Sjømannsgata, the Rica has accommodation in several attractive, maritime-style buildings located right on the water's edge. An excellent choice if Svinøya Rorbuer is full. $$$$$

🏠 **Anne Gerd's B&B** Marinehaugen 10; ☎ 99 52 99 45; e annegerd@online.no; www.annegerd.home.online.no. A homely B&B, roughly 20min on foot north of the centre, in a quiet residential area. *Dbls* $$–$$$ *per night.*

## ✗ Where to eat and drink

Undoubtedly, the most enjoyable place to eat and drink in town is down by the harbour, where, in summer, there are tables and chairs out on the quay, offering a perfect view of the harbour and all its goings-on – and a chance to work on your tan, weather permitting.

✗ **Bacalao** off Kirkegata on the quayside. A stylish, airy brasserie with lots of glass & chrome that can more than hold its own against the best of any big city. If the weather's not good enough to sit outside on the quayside, the interior here is more agreeable than the competition next door. Cheaper than its neighbour, the lunch menu here consists of ciabatta with cheese/ham/salad for 55kr, omelette at 85kr & open sandwiches for 55kr, whereas for dinner there's a range of large salads (from 99kr), baked potatoes (85kr), quiches with salad (85kr) & a selection of pizzas (from 135kr).

✗ **Børsen** Svinøya. Just to the right of the bridge as you cross on to Svinøya & the reception building for Svinøya Rorbuer, this atmospheric restaurant housed in a former fish warehouse dating from 1828 (much more enchanting than it sounds) is the place to come for a special occasion. With low ceilings, wooden beams & creaking floorboards, the candlelit ambience is the perfect place to enjoy top-of-the-range cuisine specialising in locally caught fish: try the traditional *boknafisk*, a cod dish with chopped boiled eggs, bacon chunks in a creamy sauce for 265kr. Mains all around the 250kr mark.

✗ **Du Verden** J E Paulsens gata 12. A more sophisticated menu than Bacalao, this place considers itself a more serious restaurant than the brasserie next door – & has prices to match: fish mains cost around 265kr, though at lunchtime you can find a selection of fishy delights, such as the excellent cream of fish soup with vegetables for 125kr.

## The town and activities

The reason to come to Svolvær is not to tick off a long list of tourist sights – there are none. Instead, the simple pleasure of wandering the streets in summer and sipping a coffee on the quayside is more than enough to keep most visitors happy for a few hours. However, once the attraction of begins to fade, there are two enjoyable activities worth considering from the town.

Operated by Lofoten Explorer (☎ 97 15 22 48, *www.lofoten-explorer.com*) from the harbour, **boat trips** leave daily at 11.00 and 14.00 from mid-Jun to mid-Aug for an unforgettable excursion by **high-speed Zodiac inflatable** to Trollfjord (400kr) and the surrounding bays and islands. Bookings can made at the company's office by the quayside and warm clothing is provided. If you missed the opportunity to travel by the Hurtigruten ferry through Raftsundet sound, calling in at Trollfjorden, this is an absolute must and one of the most memorable (and sensibly priced) excursions you can undertake while in Norwegian Lapland.

### Svolværgeita Mountain

Svolvær is the place from which to begin a **hike** to the twin peaks you can clearly see in the distance to the northeast of the town, known as Svolværgeita, the Svolvær goat. Climbed for the first time in 1910, the mountain's summit is composed of two noticeable horns, a distance of 1.5m apart. Daring, some would say, foolhardy climbers leap precariously from one horn to the other to crown their achievement of climbing the peak. A path begins beside the E10, a short distance outside of the town itself (ask the tourist office for precise directions), though you should only consider hiking to the very top if you are an experienced mountaineer. The pinnacles are vertical rock faces which can only be ascended with specialist equipment – and a good deal of bravery.

**Killer-whale safaris** Between mid-October and late January, one of the most breathtaking safaris imaginable operates from Svolvær: snorkelling with killer whales. Three local companies have joined forces to operate tours, under the name Orca Lofoten (✆ *45 83 27 10;* e *post@orca-lofoten.no; www.orca-lofoten.no*), both by regular boat and Zodiac – and the possibility, should you choose, to get into the water beside the killer whales and snorkel alongside them. Departure days vary from month to month (full details are available on the website) but are generally between Thursday and Sunday, most often on Friday and Saturday. The price of a safari by regular boat is 735kr; by Zodiac 950kr; and snorkelling is 1,800kr. Tours generally last four to five hours and all snorkelling equipment is provided and included in the cost. It is wise to book in advance to make sure that there is a departure on the day you would like and to ensure a place.

**Moving on from Svolvær** From Svolvær, the Hurtigruten sails south at 19.30 to Stamsund and north at 22.00 through Raftsundet to Stokmarknes, Sortland and Harstad (arrival 06.45). The quay is located in the centre of town, a short distance south of the main square. The Hurtigbåt express passenger boat to Narvik leaves from the quay beside the main square. Ferries to Skutvik sail from a separate quay about a kilometre away on the other side of the town centre; take the road towards Å and it is signed off to the left once you've gone through the short tunnel which leads out of town. When it comes to moving on from Svolvær, it can be useful to know the distances involved for onward travel since it is hard to know, just from looking at a map, how far places are given the highly indented nature of the coastline hereabouts. From Svolvær it is 26km to Henningsvær, 34km to the ferry at Fiskebøl, 70km to Stamsund, 134km to Å and 279km to Narvik.

**SOUTH TO HENNINGSVÆR AND Å** The beguiling villages of Henningsvær and the tersely named Å, together conjuring up the most exquisite combination of precipitous mountains and rugged coastal scenery Lofoten has to offer, make perfect day trips from Svolvær, or, in the case of Å, a wonderful off-the-beaten-track place to stay.

**Henningsvær** The drive out to tiny Henningsvær is simply gorgeous. The village is draped over the last island in a chain of skerries and islets which lie off the southwest corner of Austvågøy. Skipping from island to island, the minor road leading to the fishing village weaves its way around secluded sandy coves and rocky bluffs before it arches over a final narrow bridge and pulls into town. At the centre of the village is the harbour, a tight U-shaped inlet lined with handsome brightly painted houses and boatsheds and backed by jagged peaks rising precipitously from the sea. It is a scene from a postcard and really is as beautiful as you might imagine. However, in season, it attracts coachloads of camera-snapping visitors who swamp the little place and steal its charm. Try to time your visit to early morning or late afternoon and you should have the web of narrow lanes and passageways pretty much to yourself.

The quality of the light in the Lofoten Islands has attracted many artists to the area over the years, transforming the little village into a northern Norwegian version of Cornwall's St Ives. As you wander around, sooner or later you will come across **Galleri Lofotens hus** in Dreyersgate (⊕ *Jun–Aug 09.00–19.00 daily; 70kr*), which exhibits the work of northern Norwegian artists from the turn of the last century, widely regarded to be the golden age of Norwegian art. Over the gallery's three floors you will find paintings by the likes of Otto Sinding, Einar Berger and Gunnar Berg, as well as a collection of photographs mostly of the Lofoten Islands. There's a display of work by the contemporary artist Karl Erik Harr. There's more artwork plus a collection of glassware and ceramics available for perusal (and sale) at **Engelskmannsbrygga** (⊕ *late Feb to early Jun Tue–Fri 10.00–16.00, Sat & Sun noon–16.00; mid-Jun to mid-Aug daily 10.00–20.00*) in Dreyersgate by the main square.

## ⌂ Where to stay and eat

⌂ **Henningsvær Bryggehotell** ↘ 76 07 47 50; e booking@henningsvaer.dvgl.no; www.henningsvaer.no. The most atmospheric place to stay in Henningsvær is this harbourfront attractive, modern hotel surrounded by fishing boats & built on wooden stilts over the water. $$$$$

⌂ **Den siste Viking** at Misværveien 10 (↘ 90 57 42 08; e post@nordnorskklatreskole.no; www.nordnorskklatreskole.no. A more frugal choice located in the local mountaineering school & offering youth hostel style accommodation. $$

The **Klatrecafé** here serves up a decent selection of affordable Norwegian staples as well as beer and is a good meeting place. Finer fare is available from **Fiskekrogen** at Dreyersgate 19, which specialises in locally caught fish, in particular stockfish (dried cod).

**Å** Don't be fooled by the name, there's more to Å than first meets the eye. A pure scenic delight at the very end of the E10, this ravishing village of old timber buildings enjoys one of Lofoten's most special locations. A narrow foreshore, squeezed up tight against the churning waters of Vestfjorden, fights for space against the unforgiving rock wall of the Lofotenveggen mountains immediately behind. The resulting huddle of homes and fishing shacks, dating from the 19th century, makes Å one of the most delightful villages to stay in the islands and, thanks to its end-of-the-road location, a good place to escape the summer crowds.

A dozen or so of Å's buildings have been turned into the likeable **Norsk Fiskeværsmuseum** (⊕ *mid-Jun to mid-Aug daily 10.00–18.00; rest of year Mon–Fri 11.00–15.00; 50kr*), a detailed representation of life here in the late 1800s when the local fishermen were forced to pay rent for their homes in hard manual labour on the local merchant's farm. A couple of *rorbuer*, a boathouse and even a cod-liver oil plant have been preserved and offer a great insight into the hard – and dangerous – lives people lived in this part of Norway at the turn of the last century.

An enjoyable **hiking trail** from Å leads across Moskenesøya's ever-narrowing width to the island's west coast. Begin by following the southern shore of Å-vannet lake, before climbing over the ridge of mountains that forms the island's spine. Beyond here, it is a straightforward hike to the spectacular sea cliffs of the west coast. Don't attempt the hike in bad weather as low cloud can obscure the mountains.

⌂ **Where to stay and eat** There's a wide selection of *rorbuer* available in Å (*from 850kr per night*) as well as a **youth hostel** (*dorm beds 150kr*) and regular hotel double rooms in a building known as Salteriet (*500kr*). There's a restaurant and bar on site with light meals through the day and more substantial dishes in the evenings – fish is the speciality. It all comes under the management of **Å Rorbuer** (↘ *76 09 11 21; www.lofoten-rorbu.com*) who rents out boats from 500kr per day.

# 5

# From the Gulf of Bothnia to the Arctic Ocean

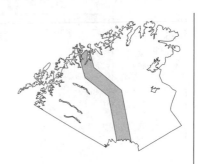

The trio of rivers that form the northern border between Sweden and Finland have created one of Lapland's most pastoral landscapes. Emptying into the Gulf of Bothnia, the River Torne flows lazily through flower meadows and undulating farmland dotted with haystacks drying during the long days of summer, passing sleepy villages where life takes on an enviably sedate pace. Gone are the dense pine forests and reindeer herds of the Lapland interior, here the whispers of the breeze through the birch trees and fields of grazing farm animals typify the southern stretches of the Torne valley. However, north of Pajala, where the Torne river swings inland, the landscape becomes progressively less tamed. Now, the swiftly flowing Muonio river forms the border between the two countries, land given over to farming is rare and the rounded fells which predominate north of here begin to show their face. Beyond Kaaresuvanto/Karesuando, the river changes course yet again, allowing the Könkämä river to take over the baton and run the final leg to the geographical point where Norway, Sweden and Finland all meet. The pastoral scenes of the valley's southern half are long gone, here the terrain is that of high, treeless tundra, the winters are long and hard and snow lies deep on the ground until well into May. Yet, as the land quickly falls away towards one of northern Norway's greatest expanses of open water, the Lyngen fjord on the Arctic Ocean, the warming influence of the Gulf Stream is clearly noticeable. Spring comes quickly here and temperatures are higher than those on the Gulf of Bothnia, where the chilling effect of the winter ice delays the onset of warmer weather.

The E8 highway runs the length of the valley from the Gulf of Bothnia to the Arctic Ocean and has two main uses. It provides a good access route to the North Cape (as far as Palojoensuu, from where Route 93 runs north to Alta via Enontekiö and Kautokeino) and it is the best way by far to reach Tromsø from central areas of Lapland. But it would be a shame simply to rush north without sampling some of the attractions en route: **Tornio** and **Haparanda** have the best choice of bars, restaurants and shopping for miles around, whereas **Muonio** provides ready access to Finland's biggest and best centre for **husky safaris**, or, alternatively in summer, **whitewater rafting**. The mark of the man who shaped northern Scandinavia more than any other, the revivalist preacher, Lars Levi Laestadius, is felt throughout the area: a museum and his grave are in **Pajala** and his former home is open for viewing in **Karesuando**. For hiking fans, **Kilpisjärvi** in the far north, has access to the three-country border post, **Treriksröset**, and some of Lapland's best high fell scenery.

**THE GULF OF BOTHNIA TO THE ARCTIC OCEAN**

## TORNIO AND HAPARANDA

Occupying a strategically important site either side of the Torne river at the head of the Gulf of Bothnia, Finnish Tornio (Torneå in Swedish; Duortnus in Sámi) and Swedish Haparanda (Haaparanta in Finnish) are to all intents and purposes the same place. If you are travelling by public transport between Finnish and Swedish Lapland, you are likely to pass through, as the hub of roads which radiate from here have made the towns a key transport interchange for inter-Scandinavian connections. Indeed, so commercially attractive is the towns' central location for the whole of northern Scandinavia, that the Swedish furniture giant, IKEA, opened its most northerly store in the world here in late 2006, drawing customers over a radius of hundreds of miles: according to the latest figures, people are now travelling to the Haparanda IKEA from as far afield as Tromsø and Murmansk. IKEA's strategic decision to open so far north has been a real boon for the local economy, since many other companies have followed the retailer's lead and set up here, too.

Crossing from Tornio to Haparanda, or vice versa, couldn't be easier: passport controls are non-existent and locals simply walk or drive from one country to the other without even batting an eyelid. A road bridge carries the main E4 highway across a small island which links one town with the other. A second smaller road, Krannigatan, to the east of the IKEA store forms the second link; on this road there isn't even a border post, just a camera monitoring road traffic. Although there are no must-see sights in either Tornio or Haparanda, both places are agreeable enough to while away a day or so, and, by evening, there's a positive buzz in the bars of Tornio.

**SOME HISTORY** Until 1821, when Haparanda was founded, there was only one settlement here: Tornio, which still today is the most lively and interesting of the two siblings. From 1105 until 1809, Finland was part of Sweden and Tornio, founded in 1621 and the oldest town in the whole of Lapland, served the Swedish crown's interests in the north by functioning as a key market town. However, following Sweden's defeat against Russia in the Great Northern War of the 1700s, Finland was ceded to Russia and Sweden consequently lost its most important trading centre in the north. It was soon decreed that Tornio should be replaced, and in the early 1820s Haparanda began to take shape – but over the ensuing decades never really matched its bigger Finnish brother in terms of size or vibrance. Today, the population of Haparanda is a mere 10,000, compared with Tornio's 25,000 and, accordingly, in most matters, it is Tornio that wears the trousers.

In the late 1990s, Haparanda and Tornio were declared a Eurocity – a European Union initiative which unites two adjoining towns or cities in two different countries. Although the label is now longer used, the spirit of co-operation and togetherness is very much alive. As you walk around, you will notice houses with television aerials pointing in different directions to pick up both Swedish and Finnish television and cash dispensers which issue notes in both Swedish kronor and euros, seemingly everything from central heating to the local fire brigade is centrally co-ordinated. The only thing that isn't is the time: there is still one hour's time difference between Tornio and Haparanda.

**TOURIST INFORMATION** The tourist office (*Finnish* \ *016 432 733; Swedish* \ *0922 120 10;* e *tourist@haparandatornio.com; www.haparandatornio.com;* ⊕ *Finnish time: Jun–Aug Mon–Fri 08.00–19.00, Sat & Sun 10.00–18.00; rest of year Mon–Fri 10.00–19.00, Sat & Sun 11.00–17.00*) is located in the Green Line centre by the bridge in Tornio. Inside there are two telephone lines, one handling calls from Finland, the other from Sweden; bilingual staff switch effortlessly from Swedish to Finnish depending on which phone is ringing.

## 🛏 WHERE TO STAY

🏠 **Stadshotellet** Torget 7, Haparanda; Swedish \ 0922 614 90; e info@haparandastadshotell.se; www.haparandastadshotell.se. A grand old place dating from 1900 full of wooden panelling & opulent chandeliers. The suites even have their own sauna. $$$$$$/$$$$

🏠 **Kaupunginhotelli** Itäranta 4, Tornio; Finnish \ 016 433 11; e info@torniokaupunginhotelli.fi; www.torniokaupunginhotelli.fi. A dowdy, rambling place that is desperately in need of renovation. Tired rooms with an unpleasant stale smell about them. The saving grace is its sauna & pool complex in the basement. $$$$/$$$

🏠 **E-city Bed & Breakfast** Saarenpäänkatu 39, Tornio; Finnish \ 044 5090 358; e matkakoti.e-city@pp.inet.fi; www.ecitybedandbreakfast.com. A family-run homely place in the centre of Tornio. B/fast included. $$

🏠 **Youth hostel** Strandgatan 26, Haparanda; Swedish \ 0922 611 71; e vandrarhemhaparanda@telia.com; www.haparandavandrarhem.se. The best choice for budget accommodation. *Comfortable dbls for* $$, *dorm beds just* $.

**TORNIO** Tornio is more a place to wander around the shops and nip in and out of cafés rather than somewhere to see the sights. However, there are one or two places worth investigating.

## 🍴 Where to eat and drink

♀ **Jetset** Satamakatu 3. A tiny little rock bar, tucked away on a street corner, that's popular with a younger crowd. A good place to start the evening off.

♀ **Josephine** Itäranta 4. The bar & nightclub complex inside Kaupunginhotelli is a popular place for a drink at w/ends.

🍽 **Karkiainen** Länsiranta 9. The best of the cafés in Tornio, & the only one that's open all w/end. Lights snacks & bar meals, too.

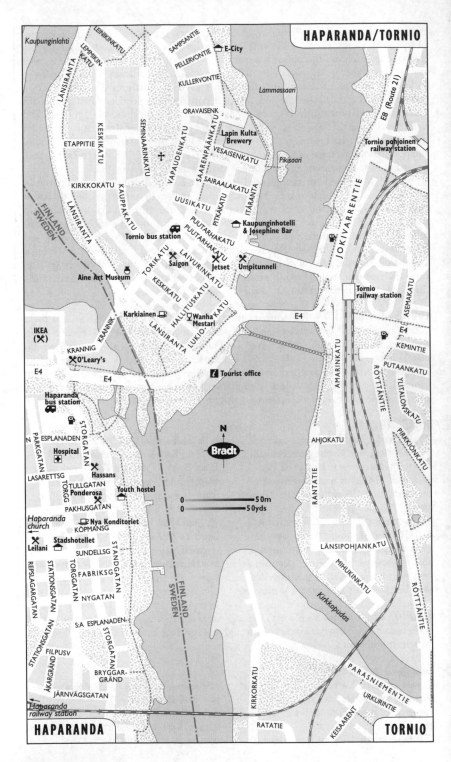

Kaupunginlahti

LEINIKINKATU
SAMPSANTIE
LEMMIKIN.KATU
PELLERVONTIE ⌂ E-City
KULLERVONTIE
Lammassaari
LÄNSIRANTA
ORAVAISENK
KESKIKATU
SEMINAARINKATU
VAPAUDENKATU
Lapin Kulta Brewery
ETAPPITIE
SAARENPÄÄNKATU
VESAISENKATU
Pikisaari
† KIRKKOKATU
KAUPPAKATU
LANSIRANTA
SAIRAALAKATU
ITÄRANTA
UUSIKATU
PITKÄKATU
Aine Art Museum
TORIKATU
PUUTARHAKATU
Tornio bus station
PUUTARHAKATU
LAIVURINKATU
Saigon ✗
KESKIKATU
Jetset ✗
Kaupunginhotelli & Josephine Bar
Umpitunneli
E8 (Route 21)
Tornio pohjoinen railway station
JOKIVARRENTIE
Tornio railway station
IKEA (✗)
KRANNIK
Karkiainen
HALLITUSKATU
WanhaKATU
Wanha Mestari
LÄNSIRANTA LUKIO
E4
E4
ASEMAKATU
KEMINTIE
KRANNIG
✗ O'Leary's
E4
E4
PUTAANKATU
YLITALONSKATU
ℹ Tourist office
RÖYTTÄNTIE
PIRKKIÖNKATU
Haparanda bus station
AMARINKATU
AHJOKATU
ESPLANADEN
STORGATAN
PARKGATAN
Hospital
RANTATIE
LASARETTSG
✗ Hassans
TULLGATAN
TORGG
Ponderosa
Youth hostel
PAKHUSGATAN
N
**Bradt**
Haparanda church
Nya Konditoriet
KÖPMANSG
✗ Leilani
Stadshotellet
SUNDELLSG
0 ————— 50m
0 ————— 50yds
STANDGATAN
FABRIKSG
TORGGATAN
LÄNSIPOHJANKATU
NYGATAN
REPSLAGARGATAN
STATIONSGATAN
S:A ESPLANADEN
STORGATAN
MIHUKINKATU
Kirkkopudas
FILPUSV
AKARGRÄND
BRYGGAR-GRÄND
PARASNIEMENTIE
RÖYTTÄNTIE
JÄRNVÄGSGATAN
URKURINTIE
Haparanda railway station
FINLAND SWEDEN
RATATIE
KIRKKORKATU
KEISARENT

✕ **Saigon** Kauppakatu 13. Not overly authentic (though good value) Vietnamese food such as fried chicken with pineapple for €8.50 or fried noodles with prawns & vegetables for €7.50.
✕ **Umpitunneli** Hallituskatu 15. A cavernous restaurant, bar & club all rolled into one that draws the crowds like nowhere else. A half-litre of beer is €4. An extensive menu featuring excellent Arctic char (€15.90) & fried chicken (€13.50) among others.
♀ **Wanha Mestari** Hallituskatu 5. One of Tornio's most popular bars, which is always full of locals. Can get a little drunken.

## What to see and do

**Aineen Taidemuseo: the Aine Art Museum** (*Torikatu 2;* ☉ *Tue–Thu 11.00–18.00, Fri–Sun 11.00–15.00;* €2) Tornio's Aine Art Museum was founded by local couple, Eila and Veli Aine, and traces its history, in one form or another, back to 1974. The aim of the museum is to show contemporary northern Finnish art, though there are often temporary exhibitions of modern European art, too. The museum's own collection contains a few classics: Elin Danielson-Gambogi's self-portrait, Werner Holmberg's *Midsummer Night in Tornio* and *Big Ida* by Unto Pusa.

**Lapin Kulta brewery** (*tours mid-Jun to mid-Aug Tue & Thu 14.00*) One of the best beers in Lapland, Lapin Kulta (literally 'Lapland Gold') was born in Tornio in 1873. At Lapinkullankatu, just to the north of the three bridges which span the River Tornio, the Lapin Kulta brewery runs free hour-long tours which kick off at the site's main gate.

**Tornio train station** Although the squat redbrick building beside Amarinkatu is nothing special to look at, it holds a significant place in Finland's history as Lenin returned to Finland and ultimately Russia after a period in exile through Tornio train station on 15 April 1917. His journey to Russia took him from Switzerland, through Germany by sealed train, then Sweden and finally Lapland. He had lived previously in the southern Finnish city of Tampere for two years after the failed revolution in Russia in 1905 and it was here that he first met Stalin. A plaque in Finnish and Russian on the side wall of the building commemorates his return to Finland *pakolaismatkaltaan*, 'as a refugee', bound for Helsinki and ultimately Saint Petersburg.

**HAPARANDA** Haparanda's residential streets make a more satisfying place to stroll around than Tornio's rather brash town centre, though there are really only two real sights to take in, here.

✕ **Where to eat and drink** Although it is hard to generalise, eating is generally cheaper in Sweden, but drinking is less expensive in Finland: witness the one-way traffic over the bridge every evening when thirsty Swedes head off in search of a drink or three in Finland.

✕ **Hassans** Storgatan 88. The cheapest pizzas in town (44kr), much better value than Leilani, though the restaurant itself is rather basic.
✕ **IKEA** Norrskensvägen 2. Swedish classics such as meatballs & smoked salmon are always on the menu here. Excellent prices & not nearly as cheesy as you might think.
✕ **Leilani** Köpmansgatan 15. A range of pizzas (56–78kr), Thai food (128–148kr) & Chinese mains (from 92kr). Lunch here is 70kr.
☕ **Nya Konditoriet** Storgatan 73. ☉ Closed Sun.
An excellent café with good pastries – & a good range of chocolates, too.
♀ **O'Leary's** Krannigatan 6. The American-style sportsbar has finally made it to Haparanda. Good for watching sports matches, though the beer is more expensive than in Tornio.
✕ **Ponderosa** Storgatan 82. A good range of Swedish regulars such as steak in pepper sauce (155kr), fried salmon in white sauce (125kr) & schnitzel (80kr).

## What to see and do

**Haparanda train station** Haparanda's imposing train station, erected in 1918, is the most impressive building in town. Constructed of red brick, replete with stone tower and lantern, it sits proudly atop a small hillock at the southern end of Västra Esplanaden and Stationsgatan. Although there are no longer any passenger services from the station, it is still possible to discern the two different track guages, Swedish and Finnish, which provided Sweden's only rail connection to the east. A metal plaque on the front wall of the station building commemorates the forced evacuation of people from northern Finland in the autumn of 1944, many of whom fled to Sweden through this station, as retreating German troops destroyed their homes. Plans are now being formalised to re-lay the track that connects Haparanda with Luleå so that services can resume, but it is likely to be some considerable time yet before it is possible to travel here by train.

**Haparanda kyrka: the church** (⊕ *mid-Jun to mid-Aug 07.00–15.00 daily*) Resembling a grain silo rather than a place of worship, Haparanda church on Östra Kyrkogatan has even won a prize for the ugliest building in Sweden. Completed in 1963 to replace the town's former wooden church which burnt down, the new structure of copper plate is something the townspeople of Haparanda have come to endure rather than love.

### MOVING ON FROM TORNIO AND HAPARANDA

Haparanda and Tornio are connected by the hourly (*06.00–18.00*) *RingLinjen* (in Swedish)/*KaupunkiLinja* (in Finnish) bus route. If you are heading for (or coming from) Rovaniemi via Kemi and need to cross the border to continue your journey in Swedish or Finnish Lapland, the bus is a handy link. From Haparanda **bus** station the Norrlandskusten bus runs every two to three hours to Luleå from where you can pick up trains north to Kiruna and Narvik or south to Stockholm and Gothenburg. Timetables are available from the tourist office or at www.ltnbd.se. At the time of writing Finnish **trains** were no longer calling at Tornio pohjoinen (Tornio north) station, but it was hoped that services would resume in the near future. If they do, Tornio pohjoinen station is not the same station as Tornio station (see above). Instead, it is 800m to the north and best reached on foot by the public footpath along the riverside, crossing Jokivarrentie, and continuing to the train tracks (see map on page 86). The station is little more than a gravelly platform with a forlorn-looking, broken-down shelter. Buy tickets from Tornio station (⊕ *09.00–16.00 Mon–Fri*).

## PAJALA AND AROUND

Heading north from Tornio or Haparanda, there's a choice of routes, which run parallel to each other either side of Torne river: the **E8** in Finland and **Route 99** in Sweden. To reach **Pajala**, 180km north of Haparanda, it is easiest to take Route 99, but it is equally possible to drive the E8 as far as Pello where you can cross the river into Sweden for the final leg of the journey.

> Almost at the top of the map lay Pajala, surrounded by brownish tundra, and that was where we lived. If you turned back a few pages you saw that Skåne was as big in area as the whole of northern Sweden, only green-coloured with farmland that was fertile as hell. It took many years for me to cotton on to the map scale and realise that Skåne would have fitted in between Haparanda and Boden.
>
> *From Mikael Niemi's* Popular Music, *on growing up in Pajala in the 1960s and 1970s.*

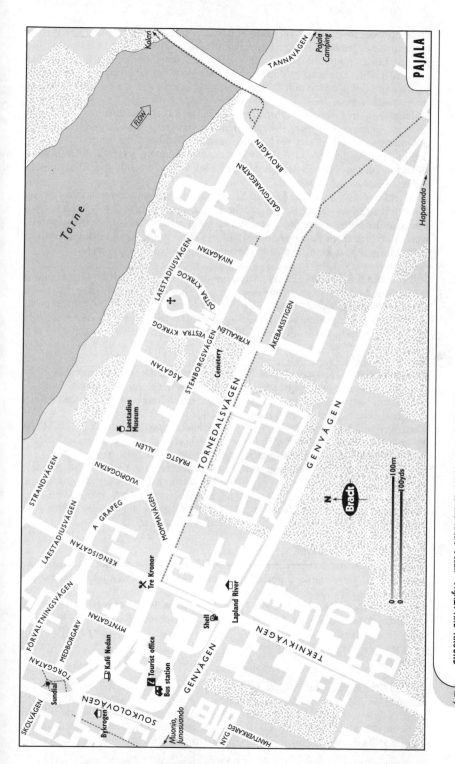

FLOW

Torne

Kolari

Tannavägen

Pajala Camping

Haparanda

GÄSTGIVAREGATAN

BROVÄGEN

LAESTADIUSVÄGEN

NIVAGATAN

ÖSTRA KYRKOG

VESTRA KYRKOG

ÅKEBARSSTIGEN

KYRKALLEN

Cemetery

STENBORGSVÄGEN

ÅSGATAN

TORNEDALSVÄGEN

PRÄSTG ALLÉN

Laestadius Museum

VUOPIOGATAN

STRANDVÄGEN

LAESTADIUSVÄGEN

KENGISGATAN

A GRAPEG

MOMMAVÄGEN

GENVÄGEN

Tre Kronor

Lapland River

Shell

TEKNIKVÄGEN

FÖRVALTNINGSVÄGEN

MYNTGATAN

MEDBORGARV

Kafé Nedan

Tourist office

Bus station

GENVÄGEN

SOUKOLOVÄGEN

Muonio, Junosuando

SKOLVÄGEN

TORGGATAN

Sundial

Bykrogen

HANTVERKAREG

DAN

N

Bradt

0 100m

0 100yds

Obligatory reading for any visit to this part of Lapland, *Popular Music*, by Pajala's most famous son, Mikael Niemi, provides an illuminating insight into what life was like in this forgotten corner of Sweden just a few decades ago, following the growing pains of teenager Matti, who's obsessed with becoming a rock star. Remote and unknown to much of the rest of the country (at least if the prejudicial maps in the school atlas in the above quote are anything to go by), Pajala has undergone a tremendous transformation in recent years, turning around its fortunes. In contrast to many other settlements in northern Scandinavia, the town is booming: new businesses are locating here, population is stable, and tourists are flooding in now that Pajala has finally been put on the map by *Popular Music*, a book owned by one in eight Swedes, and now a film, which recently played to sell-out audiences across the country.

In addition to the *Popular Music* trail you can follow around town (see below), Pajala has a few other sights, namely the largest sundial in the world and a small museum dedicated to the life and times of none other than Lars Levi Laestadius, who came here from Karesuando in 1849 and lived in the town until his death in 1861. His grave can be visited in Pajala cemetery (see below).

**TOURIST INFORMATION** Pajala's tourist office (☏ *0978 100 15;* e *info@ pajalaturism.bd.se; www.pajalaturism.bd.se;* ⊕ *mid-Jun to mid-Aug Mon–Fri 09.00–19.00, Sat & Sun 11.00–17.00; rest of year Mon–Fri 08.00–16.00*) can be found in the town's bus station beside Genvägen (Route 99), which runs through the centre of the town. **Internet** is available at Kafé Nedan, Tornedalsvägen 2.

## ⌂ WHERE TO STAY

⌂ **Bykrogen Hotell** Soukolovägen 2; ☏ 0978 108 15; e hotels@pajala.nu; www.bykrogen.se. Elegant rooms decorated with a touch of yesteryear make a nice change from the usual pan-Scandinavian minimalist design. $$$$$$/$$$$

⌂ **Lapland River** Fridhemsvägen 1; ☏ 0978 108 15; e hotels@pajala.nu; www.laplandriverhotel.se. Comfortable though rather bland dbl rooms in this modern hotel, which has a sauna. $$$$$$/$$$$

⌂ **Aurora Retreat** Prästgården, Junosuando; ☏ 0978 300 61; e info@auroraretreat.se; www.auroraretreat.se. A fabulous eco-friendly guesthouse in the village of Junosuando, 57km northwest of Pajala; see page 92 for more details. $$$

Å **Pajala Camping** Tannaniemi 65; ☏ 0978 741 80; e 0978.10322@telia.com; www.camping.se/bd08. Beautifully situated beside the graceful River Torneälven, the cabins here are the best place to stay in town. Snug 2-berth ones with cold water & a hotplate; or larger 4-berth cottages with a kitchen & bathroom. Also dorm beds. *2-berth* $, *4-berth* $$, *dorm beds* $.

## ✕ WHERE TO EAT AND DRINK

✕ **Bykrogen** Soukolovägen 2. The only Thai restaurant for miles around serving a good value lunch buffet (⊕ *11.00–14.00*) for 79kr. Alternatively, standards such as *pad thai*, green chicken curry & other rice & noodle dishes all costing 79–89kr. By evening, this place mutates into a sports bar with soccer matches shown on the big screens.

⌑ **Kafé Nedan** Tornedalsvägen 2. A pleasant café serving sandwiches, salads & light lunches. Internet access.

✕ **Tre Kronor** Tornedalsvägen 11. This basic but good value pizzeria has pizzas for 65–70kr, burgers at 65kr, as well as steaks costing 79–99kr.

**THE TOWN** Bombed by mistake by Soviet planes during the Winter War in the summer of 1940, several parts of the town, today home to around 2,000 people, were laid to waste. With Soviet funds, the damage was repaired and modern Pajala took shape. A pleasant, leafy place to stroll around, attractively located on the southern bank of the Torne river, Pajala stretches for a couple of kilometres between three main roads, Laestadiusvägen, closest to the river and location of the town museum, Tornedalsvägen, the main shopping street, and Genvägen (Route 99), the main east–west thoroughfare.

Arriving at the bus station, you will be confronted by a massive wooden model of the **great grey owl** (*Strix nebulosa*), plonked on a plinth beside the bus stops, which sweeps through the neighbouring forests. With eyes of black and yellow and a white crescent of feathers on its head, it is one of Lapland's most impressive birds of prey. The only other sight to speak of in the town centre is the world's largest **sundial**, which is located at the junction of Medborgarvägen and Torggatan, a 2 minute walk up from the bus station. With a diameter of 38m, this oversized clock tells the real solar time, which is generally around 20 minutes different from the regular time.

**Laestadiuspörtet: the Laestadius Museum** (*Laestadiusvägen 36; ☉ early Jun to mid-Jun & mid-Aug to late Aug Mon–Fri 10.00–17.00; mid-Jun to mid-Aug daily 10.00–18.00; 60kr*) From the sundial, head north on Torggatan towards the river and then right into Laestadiusvägen, where you will find the Laestadius museum also known as Laestadiuspörtet, which is actually the name of the red timber house where the revivalist preacher Lars Levi Laestadius (1800–61) lived while rector here from 1849 until his death. During his time in Pajala he was charged with inciting rebellion among the Sámi across the border in Norway (see page 112). Following the Kautokeino revolt, the criminalisation of revivalism caused many local people to shun the movement and, in Pajala in particular, resistance to Laestadius's radical ethics and morale led to confrontation. In 1853, the bishop decided that two separate church services should be held, one for Laestadians and one for regular churchgoers. This marked the first real split from the Church of Sweden and is regarded as the moment Laestadianism became a movement in its own right. Laestadius died in February 1861 and his grave can be seen in the middle section of the old churchyard on Kyrkallén, further east off Laestadiusvägen. The museum tells the story of Laestadius's life and his role as both a preacher, botanist and father of twelve children. There's a small café here serving light refreshments – though, naturally, no alcohol!

**The *Popular Music* trail** In order to get the most from Pajala, you really need to have read *Popular Music*. Anyone who has may want to visit some of the scenes Niemi describes in the novel. Bright yellow signposts dotted around the town proudly point the way to locations such as Vittulajänkkä, Paskajänkkä and the sewage works, where Matti and his friends hung out. The tourist office has a map of the sights for anyone who's keen to see more of Pajala the movie.

**Römppäviikko festival and Pajala market** Over 20 years ago, little Pajala made a big name for itself when it went public and declared that it needed women. There was quite simply a three-to-one gender imbalance in these parts and the gruff lumberjacks who lived and worked here had nobody to whisper sweet nothings to after a long day in the forest. The local authorities advertised in newspapers in the south of Sweden for single women to come to Pajala for a knees-up and possibly meet the man of their dreams. Sure enough, the story was picked up by journalists outside Sweden, the story appeared in newspapers across Europe, and before you could say 'timber!', busloads of women from across the continent were heading for Pajala for a drunken bash that the village has never forgotten. It was a great triumph: many of the amorous visitors decided to stay, and although several winters of temperatures of –30°C caused some to head south again, about 30 women have stayed the course and married local men. To mark the original event in 1987, the **Römppäviikko festival** (literally 'romp week'; *www.romppa.se*) is held during the last week in September every year. A riot of drinking, dancing, music – and bizarre sauna endurance competitions – makes the cultural festival the best time to visit Pajala.

A close second, though, is the **Pajala market**, which is held the second weekend after midsummer and with around 40,000 visitors is one of the biggest in the north of Sweden. People pour into town from far and wide to pick up bargains from the street stalls or simply to enjoy the smell of popcorn, fresh fish or reindeer kebabs and perhaps take a ride on the funfair. It is a good-natured, fun event and is well worth attending if you are in the area at the right time.

Naturally, it is a good idea to book accommodation well in advance if you are planning to visit during either of the events.

**AROUND PAJALA: JUNOSUANDO** Mention the village **Junosuando** to most Swedes and they'll look at you with a blank expression – barely anyone outside Lapland has ever heard of the place, let alone is able to locate it on a map with any certainty. Yet, that is precisely the charm of this remote village, tucked away 55km to the northwest of Pajala along Route 395. True, there may be precious few sights to tick off for the visitor here, but that's not the reason people come here. Instead, it is home to the best **environmentally friendly accommodation** in Swedish Lapland and offers a chance to experience rural village life at first hand. Located right in the centre of the village in Junosuando's former vicarage built in 1928, Aurora Retreat (  0978 300 61; e *info@auroraretreat.se; www.auroraretreat.se; advance booking required*), run by Swede Mikael and Canadian Maya, is a haven of stripped pine, potted plants and gloriously airy rooms and staircases. The emphasis here is on minimal environmental impact: mattresses are of horsehair; sheets and towels of linen or cotton – even the pigments in the paint on the walls are natural. Virtually all the food served here is organic (quite an achievement considering Junosuando's severe climate and remote location) and, in season, local produce is used to reduce the carbon emissions of transportation.

Up to 12 people can be accommodated in four upstairs **rooms**, sharing two bathrooms; groups can rent the entire house. Maya is an accomplished chef and provides **full board** (accommodation, breakfast, lunch and dinner) for 750kr per person per night. Meals are predominantly vegetarian, although wild meat or fish is available and is most likely to be locally produced reindeer, elk or Arctic char.

Aurora Retreat offers a number of **winter activities**, which can be either booked in advance or on arrival, including: a 5-hour visit to a nearby Sámi **reindeer farm** (1,060kr), **cross-country skiing** through the forest on traditional wooden skis (495kr), **dog sled tours** lasting 4–5 hours (1,550kr), and a visit to Santa (200kr per child including a small gift). There's the possibility to try your hand at making traditional northern Swedish flatbread in what was once the former village bakery (3hr; 540kr), or to drop in to a local farm in the nearby village of Kangos where they produce their own *halloumi*-style cheese from cows' milk (250kr).

**Getting to Junosuando** Handily, Junosuando is easy to reach. The village is on the main bus route between Kiruna and Pajala, and makes a perfect stopping-off point should you be looking to break the journey. Buses arrive and depart from the bus station in Junosuando.

**NORTHWEST TO VITTANGI AND THE ELK PARK** From Junosuando it is a straightforward drive of 55km northwest along Route 395 to **Vittangi**, a major transport hub in these parts. All bus services between Junosuando and

Kiruna/Pajala call in here, offering the possibility of connections north to Karesuando, and ultimately into Finland. Although at first sight there's little reason to linger in Vittangi, look out for the 'Älgpark' signs (they begin close to the village's bus station on the one and only main road) and you will come to Swedish Lapland's only **elk park** (⊕ *Jun–Aug daily 10.00–18.00; rest of year call ahead on* ⟍ *070 247 69 06; www.moosefarm.se; 100kr*), just a couple of kilometres further on, run by the amiable Lars Björk.

Lars will show you a short film of local wildlife – everything you see in the film from bears to bean goose was filmed within a 5km radius of the elk park. Then you will see the elk, which live in a large enclosed area of spruce forest; the prospect of munching Lars's bananas (one of their favourite delicacies) seems to lure them into sight every time. Although there are presently only two elk in the farm, this is a rare opportunity to come face to face with the king of the forest and learn more about Scandinavia's largest mammal from Lars, who is an authority on the subject. Incidentally, there are around 350,000 elk in Sweden, of which, 100,000 are shot every year during the hunting season to help keep the population in check.

## MUONIO AND AROUND

From Pajala, Route 99 heads north to the hamlet of Muodoslompolo, from where Route 404 cuts east to the Finnish border and attractive Muonio. Benefitting from its waterside location on the banks of River Muonionjoki, which forms the border with Sweden, Muonio is a delightful, peaceful, little place. True, there's little to see here in terms of attractions, it is more the simple pleasure of being here and wandering around the streets that repays a visit – plus some superb and affordable **cabin accommodation** perched on a hill overlooking the town (see below). However, there are a couple of other reasons for coming here, too: according to local people, Muonio is one of the best places in Finland to see the Northern Lights during winter; and, if you are thinking of going on a **husky safari**, Muonio's proximity to the **Harriniva Holiday Centre**, just 3km south of town, makes it a less touristy alternative to the Centre for somewhere to stay.

**TOURIST INFORMATION** Muonio's tourist office (⟍ *016 533 533;* ⊕ *Mon–Fri 08.00–17.00*) sits squarely beside the town's main road junction at the intersection of Route 79 from Kittilä and Route 21 from Tornio, inside the building marked Kiela. This is where you will find the planetarium (see page 94), and, quite bizzarely, a massage parlour and gym. The office is of limited use as knowledge of English is poor.

## ⌂ WHERE TO STAY

⌂ **Hotelli Jeris** Jerisjärventie 91; ⟍ 016 558 511; e info@hotellijeris.fi; www.hotellijeris.fi. Twenty kilometres southeast of Muonio beside Jerisjärvi Lake; from Muonio take Route 79 back towards Kittilä for 12km & then swing left on Route 957 heading towards Pallastunturi & the hotel is on your right just after the bridge over Jerisjärvi Lake. Popular with French tour groups, this hotel has dbl rooms in the main building & 42 cabins in 2 separate locations: Jeriskylä, on the hill above the main hotel building, & Jerisranta, below the hotel & next to the lake. Although the lakeside cabins are smaller (sleeping up to 4 people), they are

altogether more agreeable & cosier – & less expensive. All cabins have a fully equipped kitchen, TV & sauna, though neither location affords much privacy as the cabins are all rather close together. The dbl rooms have recently been tastefully renovated in Nordic-style, though the bathrooms are still a little dowdy. The hotel boasts a lakeside spa complex including a jacuzzi & 3 saunas (1 is a smoke sauna); a sauna costs €7; entry to the spa & the smoke sauna costs €10. During the summer, the hotel rents out canoes, rowing boats & mountain bikes. *Lakeside cabin $$$$ per night, dbl room $$$$.*

⌂ **Lomamaja Pekonen** Lahenrannantie 10; ℡ 016 532 237; www.lomamajapekonen.fi. For somewhere to stay look no further than this fantastically located year-round hostel & cabin accommodation on the main road which leads into the village from beside the Shell filling station; this road is straight ahead of you when you come to the main junction when approaching from Kittilä. In addition to no-frills dbls, there is a range of well-equipped, comfortable cabins with & without private sauna (the ones at top of the hill enjoy the best view of the lake opposite & are also those with sauna). There are canoes for rent. *Dbl, cabins with/without sauna $$$/$$.*

✕ **WHERE TO EAT AND DRINK** The two places to eat and drink in Muonio are next door to each other beside the Shell station: **Naapuri**, Kosotuskeino 1, is really more a bar than a restaurant, serving plentiful amounts of beer to its well-oiled clientele; **Uncle La Ban**, run by a friendly Palestinian guy who somehow ended up in Muonio, has pizzas for €7–12 (including an excellent reindeer pizza), salmon (€17), steaks (€18,50) and a choice of salads (€8–12).

## WHAT TO SEE AND DO
### Kiela Northern Lights Planetarium (℡ 016 533 533; ⊕ Mon–Fri 08.00–17.00)
Open the same hours as the tourist office, the Kiela Northern Lights Planetarium (€7) shows a 25-minute film on request about the Aurora Borealis. The presentation is a little on the dry side but it leaves no stone unturned in explaining how the phenomenon occurs; a degree in physics will go a long way in helping you make any sense of the explanation.

## AROUND MUONIO: HARRINIVA
### The Harriniva Holiday Centre (℡ 016 530 0300; e info@harriniva.fi; www.harriniva.fi)
The biggest and best husky centre (with around 400 dogs) in Finland, the Harriniva Holiday Centre, 3km south of Muonio along Route 21 towards Tornio, is the place to get your doggie fix. Established in 1973 by husband and wife team, Köpi and Maria Pietkäinen, Harriniva has developed a reputation over the years for well-organised, good-value husky safaris that are hard to beat. During the winter season, 95% of guests here are foreign, predominantly from Britain, France, Germany and Holland, which gives the entire place an enjoyable, cosmopolitan air. Interestingly, room rates are roughly the same whether booked through a travel agent abroad or directly with Harriniva. This means you won't end up paying through the nose if you simply turn up and book a safari on the spot; although you may find that all the dogs are out in the forest on tours if you leave it to the last minute.

⌂ **Where to stay** All accommodation at Harriniva is clean, comfortable and warm. Prices vary according to time of year; high season is mid-December to early January and mid-February to late April. Rates quoted here are all high season prices.

All **double rooms** ($$$$$$) have wooden floors and walls; some have their own sauna ($$$$$$$). **Apartments** ($$$$$$$), sleeping up to 6 people, are of the same high standard as double rooms and include a television, fridge, microwave and airing cupboard. Breakfast is included in the double room and apartment rates. There's a choice of **cabin** accommodation sleeping up to four people, either with kitchenette, sauna, shower and toilet ($$$) or with no facilities ($$). Cabin rates don't include breakfast and don't vary from season to season. Although none of the accommodation has internet access, a wireless network is available for laptop users in the reception area.

*Winter tours* There are various lengths of **husky** safaris available at Harriniva. At the top end of the scale, for example, a **week long tour** with your own dog sleigh team overnighting in log cabins with all food provided costs €1,180. The cabins have wood-burning saunas but no running water or electricity. Although the pleasure of riding across frozen lakes and weaving your way deep through Lapland's snow-covered forests doesn't come cheap, it is not one you are likely to forget in a hurry. A **one-day** excursion (5hr), once again with your own dog team, covering a distance of around 25km costs considerably less at €198.

Alternatively, Harriniva operates **snowmobile** tours: a three-day safari covering up to 100km per day overnighting in log cabins costs €1,190 per person. A **reindeer safari** (3–4hr), which includes a visit to a local reindeer farm, coffee and cake and a tour by reindeer sleigh of 3km, costs €160.

**Summer tours** Between June and September Harriniva specialises in trips on the River Muonio. There are **white-water raft tours** lasting 1½ hours for €25; or more sedate **river adventure tours** of 4–5 hours at €155 per person. **Canoeing** is possible; a trip of 2–3 hours costs €60. The Muonio river is considered one of the best salmon rivers in Finland and from the end of June to late August, **salmon fishing** is in season (€55 for a boat with an outboard motor plus €20 for fishing equipment). Back on dry land **quad bikes** are available for rent at €75 for a 2-hour excursion. Since not all tours operate daily, it is best to check with Harriniva to find out exactly what's available while you are there.

## KAARESUVANTO AND KARESUANDO

From Muonio, it is a mere 87km northwest to the twin settlements of drab Kaaresuvanto in Finland, and considerably more interesting Karesuando in Sweden, which face each other across the Munionjoki river; on the way you will pass through the hamlet of Palojoensuu, which is where Route 93 begins its journey north to Kautokeino and is a useful way of reaching the North Cape.

In Sámi, both places are known as Gárasavvon; you can walk between both countries here by simply crossing the bridge which spans the river, though remember the one hour time difference between Finland and Sweden. Given Kaaresuvanto's complete absence of attractions, you are far better off spending time in Karesuando exploring its connections with revivalist preacher Lars Levi Laestadius, who left his mark on the village after serving as the local minister for 23 years in the mid-1800s.

**TOURIST INFORMATION** Karesuando's tourist office (✆ 0981 202 05; e turistinfo@ karesuando.se; www.karesuando.se; ☉ Jun–Sep 09.00–18.00 daily; rest of year Mon–Fri 09.00–15.00) is in the customs building by the bridge across to Kaaresuvanto.

## 🏠 WHERE TO STAY

🏠 **Hotell Karesuando** ✆ 0981 203 30; e arctic.tours@telia.com; www.arctictours.se. Opposite the youth hostel, offers modern rooms decorated with Sámi colours & motifs; all rooms have a toilet & most have a shower. $$$$/$$$

🏠 **Cabins in Kuonovuopio** ✆ 0981 202 12. If you want to really get away from it all, the cabins in nearby Kuonovuopio, a tiny hamlet home to barely a dozen people, are perfect. Kuonovuopio is not connected to Karesuando by road; in fact, it barely has a dirt track linking it to an even smaller

hamlet, Kummavuopio. Instead, get here by crossing over the bridge into Finland & continuing northwest towards Kilpisjärvi for about 80km where, just before the hamlet of Peera, there's a footbridge back over the river into Sweden & access to Kuonovuopio. A daily bus leaves Kaaresuvanto for Peera at 14.35 (Finnish time). $$

🏕 **Karesuando Camping** ✆ 0981 201 39; www.karesuandokonst.com; ☉ Jun to mid-Sep. A further 5min beyond the youth hostel, this campsite has cabins with & without running water & cooking facilities for $$/$ per night respectively; there's a smoke sauna (60kr).

☂ **Youth hostel** ⚲ 0981 203 30 & 203 70; arctic.tours@telia.com; www.arctictours.se; ⊕

Apr–Sep. For somewhere to stay make this cosy hostel, a 10min walk from the bridge on Pajalavägen (Route 99), your first port of call. *Dbls from* $$; *dorm beds* $.

✕ **WHERE TO EAT AND DRINK** Karesuando is no gastronomic nirvana. For eating and drinking there's the unappealing **Karesuando Lunch and Grill** at the opposite end of the village to the youth hostel on the road out towards Kiruna (Route 45) by the Statoil and OK filling stations, or, more upmarket, the restaurant at **Hotell Karesuando**. A much better plan, though, is to go self-catering and stock up at the ICA supermarket by Statoil.

**THE TOWN** Beyond the tourist office, you will see a simple log cabin, signed **Laestadius pörte** (*always open; free*), which served as the rectory of Karesuando's best known resident, the preacher and botanist **Lars Levi Laestadius**, who lived here from 1826 to 1849. He raised 12 children in Karesuando with his Sámi wife, Brita Cajsa Alstadius. It was from this humble wooden shack, which Laestadius had built in 1828 and is now a listed building, that his revivalist teachings spread across Lapland attracting followers in three countries, prepared to lead a life of abstinence and repentance in accordance with his strict beliefs. Even today, there are many people in Karesuando who loyally adhere to his principles.

The cabin consists of one main room, decorated with pictures of the man and his followers doing their thing, together with a small hallway and larder. During his life, Laestadius did not only take it on himself to rid Lapland of the evils of alcohol abuse and lead its inhabitants on a path of righteousness and purity, but he was a keen botanist. While a student at Uppsala University north of Stockholm, Laestadius undertook his first botanical research trip and, later, was dispatched by the Royal Swedish Academy of Sciences to carry out further studies at either end of the country in Skåne and Lapland. He became an internationally recognised botanist and was even a signed-up member of the leading Edinburgh Botanical Society. It seems fitting, therefore, that a **botanical garden** was opened in his memory in Karesuando in 1989. Attached to the campsite, the garden contains around 300 species of Arctic plants which grow across Lapland, including the rare poppy that carries his name, *papaver laestadium*.

**The Vita Huset Museum** (⊕ *08.00–16.00 Mon–Fri; 30kr*) is along the Pajala road towards the youth hostel and the campsite. You will come across an elegant old white timber building dating from 1888, set back a little from the road, which once served as the residence of the local police. Today it functions as Karesuando's museum, its name translating rather grandly as 'the White House'. Inside, ask the elderly curator to point out the atmospheric black and white photographs from 1944 (they are hidden away in a side room) which show dozens of Finns fleeing the approaching German troops as the end of World War II. In particular look out for the dog-eared photograph of local woman, Olga Raattamaa, who earned herself the nickname, Empress Olga. Many Finns owe their lives to her bravery as she rowed them over the Könkämä river to safety in neutral Sweden and took care of them in her humble living quarters in Kuonovuopio.

**Kaarevaara Mountain** For a breathtaking view of the surrounding tundra, head a couple of kilometres south out of Karesuando on Route 99 towards Pajala and take the right turn signed Kaarevaara. This road then leads to the top of the eponymous mountain (516m). On a clear day you can see all the way to Pältsa mountain (733m) in the far northwest corner of Sweden, a point where Sweden, Norway and

Finland all meet, known as Treriksröset (see page 98). It is the best place for miles around to observe the Midnight Sun as it dips towards the horizon before circling overhead again. According to local Sámi, the nearby spring, *hilkkukaltio*, has special healing qualities and can even cure eye diseases. Ask at the tourist office for directions of how to get to the spring from the car park and the television mast at the top of the mountain.

## KILPISJÄRVI AND TRERIKSRÖSET

From Kaaresuvanto, it is an uneventful drive of 110km along the E8, passing the footbridge to Kuonovuopio (see above), to Kilpisjärvi, at the very end of the thumb-shaped chunk of land that forms Finland's far northwestern frontier. Unless you are heading on to Tromsø in Norway (a further 165km), the real reason to come to this remote location is to see Treriksröset, the three nation cairn, which marks the geographical point where the Nordic nations of Sweden, Finland and Norway all rub shoulders. Incidentally, there's Midnight Sun in this part of Lapland, mainland Finland's most westerly point, from 22 May to 25 July, and, consequently, Polar Night from 25 November to 17 January.

**KILPISJÄRVI** Squeezed between the mountains of Saana (1,029m) and Salmivaara (598m), Kilpisjärvi is a modest little place that is popular with hikers lured here by the prospect of scaling Finland's highest fells – most of them over 1,000m high. There's no real village centre to speak of, instead, a handful of accommodation options and a supermarket are essentially all that's here, dotted along the E8, which runs through the village. The quay for the boat, *M/S Malla*, which sails across Kilpisjärvi lake towards Treriksröset (see below), is at the northern end of the village, below Kilpisjärven Retkeilykeskus and the fire station.

**Tourist information** The Kilpisjärvi visitor centre (*Kilpisjärven Luontotalo*; ☎ 020 564 7990; e *kilpisjarvi@metsa.fi*; ⊙ mid-May to Sep daily 09.00–16.00, closed late May to mid-June) beside the main road at the southern end of the village is a handy place to stock up on maps and the latest hiking information.

### 🏠 Where to stay and eat

🏠 **Lapland Hotel Kilpis on Käsivarrentie** ☎ 016 537 761; e kilpis@laplandhotels.com; www.laplandhotels.com. Modern rooms have fantastic views over the surrounding bare fells. $$$

🏠 **Kilpisjärven Retkeilykeskus** ☎ 016 537 771; e reception@kilpisretkeily.fi; www.kilpisjarvi.info. The tongue-twisting Kilpisjärven Retkeilykeskus at the northern end of the village with cosy en-suite dbl rooms & cabins with toilet & kitchen. *Dbl* $$, cabin $$$.

🏠 **Saananmaja** On Käsivarrentie by the visitor centre; ☎ 016 537 746; e pirjo.pohjanen@luukku.com. Rents out cabins. $$

🏠 **Retkeilykeskus** Kilpisjärventie, Peera; ☎ 016 532 659; e peeran@luukku.com; www.peera.fi; ⊙ late Feb–Sep. About 25km south of Kilpisjärvi, this youth hostel in the village of Peera is a more economical alternative with dorm beds. $

For **eating and drinking** look no further than **Tuulan Kahvila** in a log cabin on Käsivarrentie, which dishes up a wide range of local specialities such as Arctic char as well as a selection of pizzas, burgers and steaks.

### Activities

*Hiking and wilderness flights* Some of the best views of the fells of this part of Lapland can be enjoyed from the top of Saana mountain. Ask at the visitor centre for a map and information about the various **hiking trails** that lead up and around the peak. You're free to climb Saana's northern slope but access to the western slope is restricted from mid-May to August to protect an area of herb-rich forest, which has been the subject of a conservation order since 1988.

Two companies offer **sightseeing flights** from Kilpisjärvi: Heliflite (☏ *016 532 100;* e *contact@heliflite.fi; www.heliflite.fi*) and Polar Lento (☏ *0400 396 087;* e *polar.lento@harriniva.fi; www.harriniva.fi*) operate to various remote destinations in the surrounding wilderness. The flights are useful if you are planning some serious hiking or fancy fishing in some of the mountains tarns but don't want to hike there first. A sightseeing tour of 10 minutes with Heliflite (*late Jul–Sep*) costs €250; the price is per helicopter and for five passengers.

### Moving on from Kilpisjärvi: Tromsø and the Hurtigruten coastal ferry Between June and late September a handy **bus** runs daily from Kilpisjärvi over the border to Tromsø in Norway. It leaves from Kilpisjärven Retkeilykeskus at 18.10 (Finnish time) and arrives into Tromsø at 19.30 (Norwegian time), providing a connection with the southbound Hurtigruten **ferry**, which sails at 01.30.

**TRERIKSRÖSET** The cairn that marks the point where Norway, Sweden and Finland all meet has a somewhat chequered history. The first cairn was erected in 1897 by a team of Norwegians and Russians (Finland was at that time a Grandy Duchy within the Russian empire). The Swedes refused to take part in the ceremony due to an ongoing border dispute with Norway. The original idea of raising stone plaques bearing each country's national emblem was hurriedly ditched, and a simple cairn of stones was erected instead. In 1901 Norway and Sweden kissed and made up and it was decided to cover the cairn in concrete. However, the concrete ran out and there was only enough to cover the top part of the cairn, which, over time was destroyed by the extreme winter weather. A second cairn, still standing today and resembling a none-too-attractive concrete bunker, was built in 1926 and painted yellow. Perhaps a sign of Sweden's self-appointed role as the Nordic nations' big brother, there's much more interest in visiting the cairn among Swedes than Finns, and especially, Norwegians, who would often rather forget that they share a border with a supercilious, patronising, puffed-up neighbour – at least, if their own prejudices are to be believed.

### Getting to Treriksröset There are two options for getting to Treriksröset. Beginning at the car park beside the E8 at the northern end of the village, a **hiking trail** of 11km (one-way), stony in parts, leads west through the alpine meadows and birch forest of **Malla National Park** (Mallan luonnonpuisto), Finland's oldest, established in 1916, home to some of the country's rarest plants including Lapland rhododendron, glacier crowfoot and the gloriously named one-flowered fleabane.

Alternatively, the **boat** M/S Malla (☏ *0400 669 392 or 016 537 783;* ⊕ *late Jun to early Aug daily 10.00, 14.00 & 18.00 Finnish time; 45mins;* €16 *return*) sails from Kilpisjärvi to the old Sámi settlement of Koltaluokta on the northwestern arm of Kilpisjärvi lake. From here there's a 3km path to the cairn itself, which is duckboarded in parts. The boat waits around two hours before sailing back to Kilpisjärvi. Be prepared for mosquitoes! A good combination is to take the boat there and then hike back, thus avoiding having to time your walk to coincide with the boat's sailing schedule.

# 6

# Finnish Lapland: Rovaniemi to the Finnmark Plateau

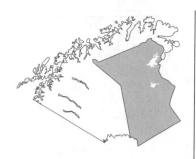

If you are looking for **Santa Claus**, you will find him, most readily, on the Arctic Circle in Finnish Lapland. Over the years, the Finns' well-executed campaign to convince the world that Father Christmas lives in Finnish Lapland appears to have paid off and, during the winter months, the airports here are full of charter flights bringing in children and their parents from all over Europe to see the fat man in the funny red suit. However, Finnish Lapland has much more to offer than just Santa – not least in terms of wildlife. If you haven't yet seen a **reindeer**, the chances are you will here. Birdlife is extremely rich and varied; many species, for example, are attracted to the largest expanse of open water in Lapland, **Inarijärvi Lake**, with its dozens of pineclad islands and skerries.

A land of rounded hills and rolling forests rather than craggy mountains and deep valleys, the terrain of Finnish Lapland may well be less mountainous than in neighbouring Sweden, but it is no less attractive. Tragically, the same cannot be said about the majority of towns and villages, which, as in Norway, were burnt to the ground at the end of World War II. Rebuilding was often uninspired and many settlements, with their graceless platoons of concrete blocks, fail to impress. Two of Lapland's largest and most vibrant **Sámi villages**, though not in Finland itself, are located just over the border on the vast treeless expanses of the Finnmark plateau and more readily accessed from Finnish Lapland than from Norway. The plateau, with its countless mountain tarns and watercourses, is one of the last wilderness areas of northern Lapland: there are no roads, no villages, nor indeed any sign of human influence over an area of several hundred square kilometres.

The undisputed metropolis of Finnish Lapland is **Rovaniemi**, and any visit to this part of the region is not complete without it. Quite unlike any other town in the area, Rovaniemi can not only boast a brash selection of bars and restaurants, but it has also got a couple of respectable shopping centres, a cinema and an excellent museum covering all things Arctic. From Rovaniemi two routes head north: Route 79 leads northwest to the ski resort of **Levi** (near Kittilä), from where the nippy Route 956 strikes off through some gloriously hilly terrain heading for uneventful Enontekiö and ultimately **Kautokeino** over the border in Norway, the site of the great Sámi Easter festival and some quality jewellery and handicrafts. Alternatively, Route 4 (also known as the E75) heads northeast for the gold-panning centre of **Tankavaara** and the unspoilt terrain of the **Urho Kekkonen National Park**, ideal for independent hiking tours. Further north, **Ivalo** is the jumping-off point for bus travel to Murmansk in Russia, whereas enjoyable **Inari**, on the bony shores of Inarijärvi lake, has an excellent Sámi museum and a glorious hiking trail to a remote church out in the wilderness. Beyond here, Route 92 swings

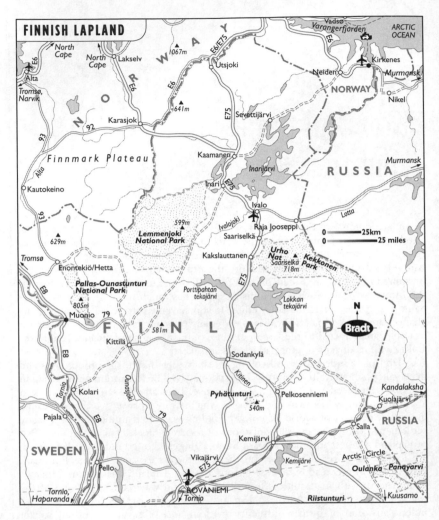

FINNISH LAPLAND

northwest, crossing the border into Norway, and arriving in one of the most significant Sámi villages in Lapland, **Karasjok**, home to the Norwegian Sámi parliament, an informative museum and a **dog-sledding centre**. From either Karasjok or Kautokeino, you are well on your way to the North Cape which is covered on pages 149–52.

## ROVANIEMI

If you believe the tourist office hype, Rovaniemi *is* the capital of Lapland. True, this is the capital of the Finnish province Lappi, and accordingly the centre of all activity and services in the area, but it is not the capital of three-nation indigenous region, known to the outside world as Lapland and the subject of this guidebook. The Finns should be given credit, though, for promoting Lapland and heightening public awareness of its existence. Over the years, the Finnish tourist board has become exceptionally adept at linking Rovaniemi and its location on the Arctic Circle with Lapland and Santa Claus in the popular pysche, with the result that

Rovaniemi receives the lion's share of winter tourists to the whole of Lapland and it is now possible to take a direct charter flight here from airports across Europe, the famous Santa Claus charters. Incidentally, Rovaniemi airport handles around 400,000 passengers every year – not bad for a place that is only Finland's thirteenth largest city. Seemingly, the hordes of tourists who descend on the town in winter don't seem the mind a little artistic licence – the town of Rovaniemi isn't actually on the Arctic Circle itself, although the magic line does slice through the airport to the north of the city.

Rovaniemi may well be the capital of Lappi province, but it couldn't be more different from the rest of Lapland if it tried. Home to the world's northernmost McDonald's, a Hennes and Mauritz store selling the latest European fashions and a town centre square named after the local hard-rock group Lordi, who won the Eurovision Song Contest for Finland in 2006, Rovaniemi is certainly different. Forget any notion of jetting straight into the heart of Lapland and snapping photographs of Sámi in traditional dress leading their reindeer; instead, you are more likely to be snapped by the new speed cameras that line the road out to the Arctic Circle.

**SOME HISTORY** Located at the confluence of two of Finland's major rivers, the Ounasjoki and the Kemi river, the latter providing direct access to the sea, Rovaniemi traces its history back over 8,000 years, when it slowly emerged as a trading centre for hunters and tradesmen who made a living exporting furs from Lapland to the south. However, it wasn't until the 11th and 12th centuries that Rovaniemi was permanently settled and began to grow into the administrative, cultural and commercial centre that it is today.

Sadly, the elegant wooden houses of old Rovaniemi are long gone; the retreating German army began its systematic destruction of the town on 10 October 1944 by burning down a number of old manor houses and the local hospital. Elsewhere in Lapland, the German troops tended to leave churches untouched. Not so in Rovaniemi, and, on 16 October they set light to the town church and its belfry as their parting gesture. During the course of just one week, 25,000 people were evacuated from Rovaniemi to Swedish Lapland and south to Finland's Ostrobothnia province; in total, 90% of Rovaniemi's buildings were laid to waste and all bridges across the River Kemijoki were destroyed.

During spring 1945 the first inhabitants began to return from exile and set about the task of reconstruction. A temporary trestle bridge was built over the rapids at Ounaskoski and railway tracks were even laid on the ice of the frozen river to take trains across to Kemijärvi. In March 1945 it was decreed that the town's layout should be completely redesigned, a task that was assigned to the celebrated Finnish architect, Alvar Aalto, who is responsible for the design of Lappia House as well as Rovaniemi's library and town hall. The main bridge across the Ounasjoki was completed in 1951; it freed people from having to rely on ice roads, ferries and the trestle bridge, which had to be rebuilt every spring.

**GETTING THERE** Rovaniemi's **airport** (airport code RVN) is located about 7km northeast of the town centre along Route 4. A **shuttle bus** runs into town in connection with scheduled flight arrivals. In additional to countless charter companies, Rovaniemi airport is served by Finland's two main carriers, Finnair and Blue1, which operate flights from and to Helsinki. Arriving by **train** or **bus** (both stations are diagonally opposite each other), you will come in southwest of the centre. From either station, take the subway under Valtatie (Route 4) and walk down Hallituskatu, finally taking a left into Rovakatu, which then leads into the town centre; it is a walk of around 30 minutes.

6

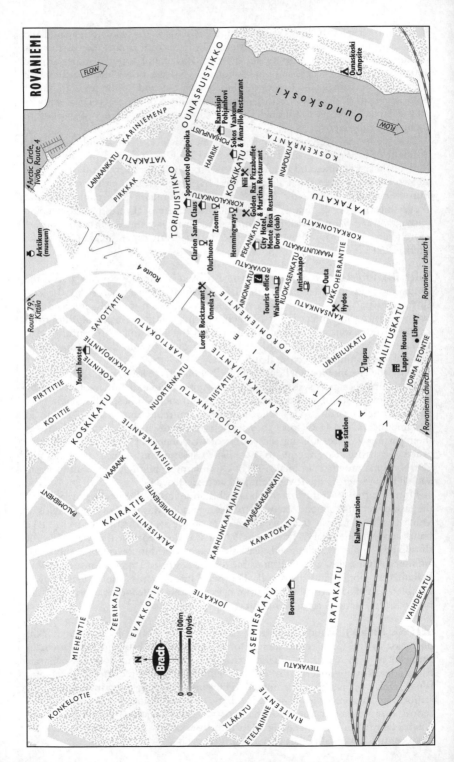

ROVANIEMI

FLOW

Arctic Circle,
Ivalo, Route 4

Ounaskoski

FLOW

Oumaskoski
Campsite

LAINAANKATU
KARINIEMENP

VATAKATU
TORIPUISTIKKO
OUNASPUISTIKKO
PIRKKAK
HARRIK

Rantasipi
Pohjanhovi
Sokos Vaakuna
Niii & Amarillo Restaurant

Arktikum
(museum)

Clarion Santa Claus
Sporthotel Oppipoika

KORKALONKATU
KOSKIKATU
POHJANPUIST

Golden Rax Pizzabuffet

Route 4

Zoomit
Oluthuone

Hemmingways
City Hotel,
Monte Rosa Restaurant,
Doris (club)

VATAKATU

KORKALONKATU
INAPOLKU

PEKANKATU

ROVAKATU
MAAKUNTAKATU

Route 79,
Kittilä

SAVOTTATIE
VARTIOKATU

AINONKATU

Lordis Rocktaurant
Onnela

Tourist office

RUOKASENKATU
KANSANKATU

Antinkaapo
Walentina
Hydos
Outa
UKKOHERRANTIE

Youth hostel

KOKINTIE
TUKKIPOJANTIE

NUORTENKATU

RIISTATIE

POHJOLANKATU

LAPINKÄVIJÄNTIE

PROMENÄENTIE

URHEILUKATU

HAILITUSKATU

Tupsu

PIRTTTIE
KOTITIE

KOSKIKATU

PIISIVALKEANTIE

Lappia House
Library

JORMA ETONTIE

Rovaniemi church

Rovaniemi church

VAARANK
UITTOMIEHENTIE

Bus station

PALOMIEHENT

KAIRATIE
PALKISENTIE

KARHUNKAATAJANTIE
RAJAJÄÄKÄRINKATU

KAARTOKATU

MIEHENTIE
TEERIKATU

EVAKKOTIE
JOKKATIE

ASEMIESKATU

Borealis

Railway station

RATAKATU

N

Bradt

0    100m
0    100yds

KONKELOTIE

YLÄKATU
ETELÄRINNE
RINTENTIE

TIEVAKATU

VAIHDEKATU

**TOURIST INFORMATION** The friendly and well-informed tourist office (☏ *016 346 270; www.rovaniemi.fi/tourism;* ☉*Sep–May Mon–Fri 08.00–17.00, Dec also Sat & Sun 10.00–14.00; Jun–Aug Mon–Fri 08.00–18.00, Sat & Sun 10.00–16.00*) is at Rovakatu 21, opposite the handy Suomalainen Kirjakauppa bookstore, which stocks a useful selection of **maps**. Inside the tourist office there's **internet** access at €2 for 15 minutes, or €2 for unlimited wireless access using your own laptop. There's internet at the library, Jorma Eton tie 6 (☏ *322 2463*), though you will probably have to book a terminal in advance.

For **car hire** all the main players are represented in town within a short walk of each other:

🚗 **Avis** Rovakatu 21;☏ 016 310 524;
e rovaniemi@avis.fi; www.avis.fi
🚗 **Budget** Koskikatu 9;☏ 016 312 266;
e rovaniemi@budget.fi; www.budget.fi

🚗 **Europcar** Pohjanpuistikko 2;☏ 040 306 2870;
e rovaniemi@europcar.fi; www.europcar.fi
🚗 **Hertz** Koskikatu 23;☏ 020 555 2500;
e hertz.rovaniemi@hertz.fi; www.hertz.fi

**WHERE TO STAY** Thanks to the vast number of tourists who pass through Rovaniemi, the town has plenty of accommodation. Although beds are rarely in short supply, it is a good idea to book ahead if you are here in winter, in particular in December, when entire hotels are often booked up by tours groups.

### Guesthouses, youth hostels and camping

🏠 **Borealis** Asemieskatu 1; ☏ 016 342 0130; guesthouse.borealis@co.inet.fi; www.guesthouseborealis.com. This family-run place is extremely handy for the bus & train station, though is a little way from the town centre. Friendly & cosy & the staff are a good source of local information. Rooms are en suite. $$$
🏠 **Rudolf** Koskikatu 41; ☏ 016 321 321; e sales@hotelsantaclaus.fi; www.hotelsantaclaus.fi. Reception for Rovaniemi's youth hostel is at the Clarion Santa Claus Hotel, Korkalonkatu 29. Although a youth hostel, this is not the cheapest place in town to look for a bed. Rooms here are

are on the large side, spotless but plain in the extreme. Dbls $$$, dorm beds $. B/fast served at the Clarion for an additional €8.
🏠 **Outa** Ukkoherrantie 16; ☏ 016 312 474; e mika@guesthouseouta.com; www.guesthouseouta.com. A Rovaniemi stalwart that's been providing simple but clean accommodation to travellers for years. No frills but excellent value. $$
🏕 **Ounaskoski Camping** Jäämerentie 1; ☏ 016 345 304. ☉ late May–Aug. Beautifully situated on the banks of the Ounaskoski rapids across the bridge from the town centre; with sauna & small café. $

### Hotels

🏠 **City** Pekankatu 9; ☏ 330 0111; e hotel@cityhotel.fi; www.cityhotel.fi. Popular with French tour groups, this functional hotel, close to the tourist office, is handy for the city centre. Rooms are a little on the small side & less stylish than elsewhere in town, but rates are accordingly lower. The Monte Rosa Italian restaurant is handily located in the same building & doubles as the hotel's b/fast room. $$$$$
🏠 **Clarion Santa Claus** Korkalonkatu 29; ☏ 016 321 321; e sales@hotelsantaclaus.fi; www.hotelsantaclaus.fi. With well-appointed Nordic-design rooms right in the heart of the town centre, this hotel is hard to beat for style & location, though it doesn't come cheap. $$$$$$
🏠 **Rantasipi Pohjanhovi** Pohjanpuistikko 2; ☏ 016

337 11; e pohjanhovi.rantasipi@restel.fi; www.rantasipi.fi. This legendary place opened in 1936 & soon became renowned throughout Lapland as the place to eat, drink & make merry; Fri evenings saw loggers & lumberjacks from the surrounding forests pour into town to spend their hard-earned wages on booze. Today, things are a little more genteel & rooms, sadly, a little too staid for the money, though it's still a sound choice. $$$$$$.
🏠 **Sokos Vaakuna** Koskikatu 4; ☏ 020 1234 695; e vaakuna.rovaniemi@sok.fi; www.sokoshotels.fi. The recent refit has really brought this place up to scratch. The swanky rooms are big on Nordic minimalist design, though try to avoid those that look directly onto Koskikatu & people's living rooms

on the opposite side of the street. The sauna suite though is disappointingly small. $$$$$$
⌂ **Sporthotel Oppipoika** Korkalankatu 33; ☏ 020 798 4609; e sales@santasport.com; www.santasport.com. Exceptionally good-value hotel in town centre, which boasts a decent-sized swimming pool & an excellent sauna suite. Rooms may be a little plain but for superb value for money look no further than here. $$$

✖ **WHERE TO EAT AND DRINK** There's no shortage of places to eat and drink. In addition to the rash of Tex-Mex places preferred by the locals (seemingly fed up with the likes of local reindeer and elk meat), you will find a couple of places serving up traditional Lapland delicacies – one place even has snow grouse on the menu.

## Cafés and restaurants

✖ **Amarillo** Koskikatu 4. The best of Rovaniemi's Tex-Mex places, the interior here is much cosier than similar places & the food correspondingly better. All your Latin favourites including chicken tortillas or burritos (€9.90), or beef fajitas (€16.90). In addition to the attached bar, there's a pleasant summer terrace, which catches the evening sun & is a great place for a beer.

⊔ **Antinkaapo** Rovakatu 13. ⊕ Closed Sun. For the best selection of gooey cakes in town, look no further than this long-established & justifiably popular café close to the tourist office.

✖ **Golden Rax Pizzabuffet** Koskikatu 11. Upstairs from Martina, this is the place to come if you want to fill up on unlimited supplies of pizza, chicken wings, lasagne & salad. The quality of the pizzas, though, is poor. But at €7.90 for as much as you can eat & drink (soft drinks), it is hard to beat.

✖ **Hydos** Kansankatu 10. One of Lapland's very few Turkish restaurants dishing up Oriental treats such as Iskender kebab with yoghurt & fried potatoes (€9.50), meatballs (€12), vegetable falafel (€11) & a more mainstream selection of pizzas (€6–8). The restaurant is plain & simple but the fare is good & makes a welcome change.

✖ **Lordis Rocktaurant** Koskikatu 25. Inspired by 2006 Finnish Eurovision winners, Lordi, this restaurant-cum-bar features life-size models of the band members & delights diners with a selection of heavy metal music. Gourmet fast food is the aim of the menu: reindeer sausage (€11.90), smoked salmon (€15.90) & roast chicken (€12.90).

✖ **Martina** Koskikatu 11. An Italian-style chain restaurant with salads (€11.90), garlic chicken (€13.70), plus a couple of steak dishes for around €17. Popular with locals.

✖ **Monte Rosa** Pekankatu 9. Inside the City Hotel, this is Rovaniemi's most popular Italian restaurant serving pizzas (€9.90), fajitas (€14.90) & the cheapest selection of Lapland delicacies in town, such as sautéed reindeer (€19.90) & cloudberry crème brûlée (€5.60).

✖ **Nili** Valtakatu 20. *The* place to come if you want to sample northern Finnish delicacies – some of which you won't find on any other menu in the whole of Lapland. With reindeer skin & horns providing the interior décor, this Sámi-inspired restaurant is a real find – the only shame is that the owners are not Sámi themselves, but from Helsinki. Starters include cèpes in sour cream (€7.80); mains feature roast breast of snow grouse with Lappish cheese potatoes (€29.90), smoked whitefish (€18), silverside & saddle of reindeer (€22.50), & even bear meatballs in a creamy game sauce (€33.20).

⊔ **Walentina** Rovakatu 21. ⊕ Closed Sun. Next door to the tourist office, this is another of Rovaniemi's old-style cafés which serves sandwiches & light snacks as well as decent coffee & cakes.

## Bars and clubs

☆ **Doris** Koskikatu 4. Inside the Sokos Vaakuna hotel, it seems strange that any club with such a fuddy-duddy name could attract anyone under the age of 60. But, this place does just that, & is second only to Onnela in popularity.

♀ **Hemmingways** Koskikatu 11. Attracting middle-aged tourists in droves, this snug English-style pub is a good choice for an early evening drink before dinner.

♀ **Lordis** Koskikatu 25. Downstairs from the restaurant, this rock pub is for hardcore heavy metal fans. With chains hanging menacingly over the bar, it's not surprising then that Sun nights here are given over to that strange beast: heavy metal karaoke.

♀ **Oluthuone** Koskikatu 20. A locals' favourite serving the cheapest beer in town. The atmosphere can be correspondingly raucous. There's a big TV screen showing the latest matches.

☆ **Onnela** Koskikatu 25. Mention the name to virtually anyone in Rovaniemi, & it'll send them into raptures. Barely able to contain their delight that this chain club has now opened on the Arctic Circle, locals flock here for disco, rock, '80s & Finnish pop/rock — each available on a different dance floor. Quite simply, the best & largest club in town.

♀ **Tupsu** Hallituskatu 24. Another locals' hang-out, a little distance from the town centre, close to the bus station. It is a good place to come if you are tired of rubbing shoulders with other tourists dressed in the latest cold-weather gear, telling stories of surviving the Arctic chill. Here talk is not only down to earth, but predominantly in Finnish; a breath of fresh air.

♀ **Zoomit** Koskikatu 10. Facing Hemmingways, this brasserie-style watering hole couldn't be more different to its neighbour. Both café bar & pub, it is justifiably popular with Rovaniemi's 20-somethings who come here to chat & pose in the large glass & chrome windows looking out on the town's main drag.

**THE TOWN** Although Rovaniemi is today the main town in Finnish Lapland (and third largest in Lapland as a whole after Luleå and Tromsø) with a population of 58,000, it is not a big place. The town centre is based on a familiar grid pattern and within an hour or so you will have covered most streets of note on foot. In summer the combination of uniform white and grey buildings befuddles your view at every turn making every street look virtually identical, whereas in winter the buildings seemingly become less important and merge effortlessly into a cityscape that is dominated by streets of snow and ice. Due largely to the rebuilding in the 1940s, though, Rovaniemi is not somewhere you are likely to want to linger and is best used as an entry point into Lapland before striking out further north for a more genuine taste of northern Finland. However, while here, make the most of Rovaniemi's attractions, which include the best museum in Lapland and the quintessential Lapland experience on the Arctic Circle featuring the ever popular Mr S Claus.

## WHAT TO SEE AND DO

**Arktikum Museum** (Pohjoisranta 4; *www.arktikum.fi*; ☉ *Jun–Aug daily 10.00–18.00, mid-June to mid-Aug daily till 19.00, rest of year Tue–Sun 10.00–18.00; €10*) Just a ten-minute walk north of the town centre, Rovaniemi's Arktikum is an engaging combination of provincial museum and Arctic Centre that is totally absorbing and quite simply the best museum you will come across for miles around. The building itself is quite remarkable – entered through a giant arched glass atrium – it is built into the surrounding hillside, emerging here and there from beneath piles of stones and rocks.

Inside, you will find an array of considered and intelligently presented exhibitions and displays on all aspects of life in the Arctic. The sections given over to **Sámi life** and culture are the most factual and informative of any museum in Finland: from the poignant photographs and static displays it is clear to see the tremendous impact that modern technology, such as the use of helicopters, snowmobiles and mobile phones, has had on traditional Sámi herding techniques and consequently indigenous culture – it is all explained in a no-nonsense, unsentimental manner. Equally enlightening is the section on contemporary Rovaniemi itself; don't miss the evocative black-and-white video footage of the glory days, before **World War II**, when people from across the Arctic would flood into town, drawn by tales of the high life and good times. Compare that to the scenes of total devastation that followed, barely a couple of years later, with the retreat of the German forces from Lapland and the numbing effects of their scorched earth policy. The two scale models of pre-war and post-war Rovaniemi help to give an idea of just what happened here in 1944 – understandably, the

6

mindless destruction of what was clearly an elegant and prosperous town is not something that is easily forgotten – or forgiven – in these parts.

## Marttiini Old Knife Factory (*www.marttiini.fi;* ⊕ *Mon–Fri 10.00–18.00, Sat 10.00–14.00; also Jun–Aug Sun noon–16.00*) While you are at Arktikum, consider a quick visit next door to the Marttiini Old Knife Factory housed inside a sturdy concrete building designed in functionalist style at Vartiokatu 32. The Finns make some of the best knives in the world, a skill that has stupidly earned them the misguided reputation in the other Nordic countries for always carrying a knife and being more than ready to use it. Be that as it may, when sharpness is everything, this is the place to come to buy a knife from the factory shop on site. There are countless varieties available and prices range from a few euros to several hundred – you can even have the blade engraved with a slogan of your choice.

## Rovaniemi Church (⊕ *09.00–16.00 daily*) Back in the town centre, stroll along Rauhankatu where, at no. 70, you will find Rovaniemi's parish church built in 1950 to replace the church destroyed by the Germans in 1944. Although the structure itself is nothing remarkable, take a step inside to see the massive altar fresco, *Fountain of Life*, created by Lennart Segerstråle. Measuring a whopping 14m in height, it draws on motifs from Lapland's nature and everyday life to portray the conflicting powers of good and evil in the human heart. Ask at the tourist office for details of occasional concerts which are held in the church.

## Lappia House and the library (*Library:* ⊕ *Sep–May Mon–Thu 11.00–20.00, Fri 11.00–17.00, Sat 11.00–16.00; Jun–Aug Mon–Thu 11.00–19.00, Fri 11.00–16.00, Sat 11.00–15.00*) An Alvar Aalto architectural classic at Hallituskatu 11, close to the bus station, Lappia House is one of Rovaniemi's most eye-catching buildings, completed in 1975. This mammoth structure of polished white stone with an arched roof of varying heights resembling a silhouette of Lapland's snow-covered fells, contains the town's theatre, concert hall, and the town library. However, most interestingly for visitors, it is the Lapland section which is really worth exploring, particularly if you are curious to find out any aspect of the region – you will find it on the left of the main entrance. As the largest source of Sámi and other Lapland-related information in the world, you name it, they've got it covered – in several languages.

## The Arctic Circle and the Santa Claus Village Think what you might about a tourist attraction based around the delights of meeting a child-loving old man with a long white beard dressed in a red suit, the **Santa Claus Village** (↘ *016 356 2096; www.santaclausvillage.info;* ⊕ *Sep–May daily 09.00–17.00; Jun–Aug daily 09.00–17.00; free*), one of Finland's top visitor sites 8km northeast of Rovaniemi, is quite within the realms of decency. Located smack bang on the **Arctic Circle**, an imaginary line drawn around the globe at latitude 66° 32' 35' north, it is easily accessible from Rovaniemi along Route 4 or by daily **bus** #8 (*€3.10 single, €5.60 return; 30mins; hourly*), which leaves from the railway station and then calls at several stops in town, each emblazoned with an Arctic Circle/Santa Claus logo. The main attractions of the village are a small collection of gift stores, the Santa Claus post office and office, where you can meet the great man, and a reindeer enclosure. It is possible to fix up a short reindeer or husky sleigh ride here (see below).

Incidentally, the Santa Claus Village and the nearby **Santapark** are not the same thing. In recent years the Santapark, once a set of fairground rides but now a motley collection of ice sculptures, a bakery and an elf school about 1.5km from the village itself, has lost its direction and seems to teeter on the brink of closure from one year to the next; concentrate on the Santa Claus village and you won't go far wrong.

The first thing most people want to do when they arrive here is pose beside the Arctic Circle sign, between the car park and main entrance, and take lots of photographs. Give yourself over to this indulgence and snap away – it is one of the few signs marking the circle, which is labelled in six different languages, though, tellingly, not one of them is Sámi. From here it is a short walk to the main building, Lahjatalo, which goes by the name of the **Santa Claus Gift House**. Inside, on two floors, you will find a number of souvenir shops selling everything from T-shirts to reindeer skins in addition to a couple of cafés serving coffee, cakes and light snacks. The low building with a central tower immediately behind the gift house is where Father Christmas himself hangs out inside the **Santa Claus Office** (⊕ *Sep–May daily 09.00–17.00; Jun–Aug daily 09.00–18.00; Santa fills his already ample stomach & takes a nap 11.00–noon & 15.00–16.00*). Here, if you form an orderly queue, you can enter Santa's grotto and come face to face with the big guy with the beard. Whether you have children in tow or not, it is actually quite a fun thing to do – even if it is only to marvel at how the Finns have pulled off this masterpiece of self-promotion.

Having placed your order for a new Ferrari next Christmas, head out the door to your left across the courtyard to the other building with a tower, the **Santa Claus Post Office**, where you can leave your name and address for the dubious pleasure of receiving a Christmas letter from Santa (€8). If you still haven't had your fill of Santa, you can head off to the **Christmas Exhibition** (*www.santahouse.fi;* ⊕ *08.00–18.00 daily; late Jun to late Aug till 19.00;* €5), in the building immediately behind the post office, where there's more information than you could ever hope to digest about Christmas traditions, Christmas in Finland – and, of course, about Lapland and its most famous inhabitant.

Hidden among the trees behind the Santa Claus Office, you will find a **reindeer enclosure** where, if you've just jetted in, you are likely to get your first sighting of Lapland's best known animal – though only between early December and early January.

## Reindeer and husky sleigh rides

The **Arctic Circle Reindeer Park** just 1.5km from the Santa Claus Village is the place to fix up a short ride on a sleigh pulled by reindeer. The trip covers about 500m and costs €16 per person. You can make bookings through Eräsetti Safaris at the Santa Claus village (↘ *016 362 811, www.erasetti.fi*).

Alternatively, if you fancy dog power, husky sled rides are available at the **Arctic Circle Husky Park** close to the Santa Claus village. Book through Polar Speed Tours (↘ *040 824 7503; www.levi.fi/polarspeed*). Entrance to the husky park itself costs €5, whereas a sleigh ride of 500m is €20 per person; a longer trip of 2km is €34 per person.

## ACTIVITIES AROUND ROVANIEMI: SNOWMOBILE, HUSKY & REINDEER SAFARIS

Given the paucity of attractions in Rovaniemi itself, it makes perfect sense to escape from the town into the surrounding forests as soon as you've had enough of the town's sights, such as they are. Accordingly, there are a whole host of companies specialising in activities ranging from snowmobile safaris – which, incidentally, are much cheaper in Finland than in neighbouring Sweden, in part, due to lower value added tax rates – to trips by reindeer or husky sled and cross-country skiing in winter, or in summer, riverboat and fishing trips. The main operators are listed below with an idea of prices and length of each tour. There are full details on the companies' websites.

## General safaris

**Arctic Safaris** Koskikatu 6, ☏ 020 7868 700; www.arcticsafaris.com. Tours include ice fishing experience (€100), snowshoe hiking (€103) & 9hr husky safari (€263).
**Eräsetti Safaris** Valtakatu 31 & at the Santa Claus villlage, ☏ 016 362 811; www.erasetti.fi. Tours include Northern Lights search by reindeer sled

(€97), reindeer herding safari (€91) & husky excursion (from €114).
**Lapland Safaris** Koskikatu 1, ☏ 016 331 1200; www.laplandsafaris.com. Tours include a visit to a husky farm (€114), reindeer & snowmobile safari (€159), & cross-country skiing (€53).

## Snowmobile specialists

**Enonvene** Napapiirintie 20, ☏ 016 3560 190; www.enonvene.com. From €60 for 1hr.

**Snow & River Adventures** Lentokentäntie, ☏ 016 362 210; www.snowandriver.com

**MOVING ON FROM ROVANIEMI: LAPLAND BUS ROUTES** Look at a transport map of this part of Lapland and you will soon spot that rail lines pretty much expire at Rovaniemi. Northbound travel from here is now by **bus** along two main routes: **northeast**, following Route 4, towards Sodankylä, Ivalo, Inari and Utsjoki. At Utsjoki you can walk over the bridge into Norway to pick up the Nordnorgeekpressen to and from Kirkenes; alternatively, following Route 79, **northwest** to Kittilä, Muonio, Karesuvanto (connections are possible here by again walking across the bridge into Swedish Karesuando), Kilpisjärvi and ultimately Tromsø in Norway. The only way to travel between these two main transport arteries is on an infrequent service that operates between Kittilä and Sodankylä (☏ 0600 930 03 for times), otherwise you have no choice but to backtrack to Rovaniemi and start out again.

**Getting to the North Cape** Rovaniemi is the starting point for the daily summer bus service (*Jun & late Aug; 10hr*) to the North Cape running via Sodakylä, Ivalo, Inari, Karasjok, Lakselv and Honningsvåg (*leaves railway station daily at 11.10 & arrives at North Cape in time to see the Midnight Sun, weather permitting; return journey departs from North Cape at 01.00, arriving back into Rovaniemi at 17.35*). It is a long journey by any measure, but the bus is comfortable and it is a direct service. Detailed timetable information is available at www.eskelisen-lapinlinjat.com or ask at the tourist office in Rovaniemi.

**Getting to Sweden** If you want to head to Sweden from Rovaniemi, be prepared for plenty of changes since there is no direct service. The best idea is to first head for **Haparanda** and **Luleå**, from where you can decide whether you want to head north to **Kiruna** or south to Stockholm; there are train services from Luleå to both places. From Rovaniemi, first take a Finnish train south to Kemi (*times available at www.vr.fi*) and then pick up a bus from immediately outside Kemi train station bound for Tornio or, occasionally, Haparanda in Sweden; some buses from Kemi operate through to Haparanda, while others require you to change in Tornio onto a local service, which then crosses the bridge into Sweden; or, better, walk over the bridge from Tornio to Haparanda yourself. You're now in Sweden and from Haparanda bus station there are then direct Swedish buses to Luleå. From Luleå onwards travel is by train, either northwest to Gällivare, Kiruna and ultimately Narvik in Norway; or all points south to Stockholm. Swedish train times can be found at www.connex.se.

The tourist office in Rovaniemi, bombarded with requests for how to make this journey, have put together the best timings: ask for their *Timetables from Rovaniemi to Sweden and Norway* handout.

# NORTHWEST FROM ROVANIEMI: TOWARDS KAUTOKEINO

From Rovaniemi, Route 79 heads northwest following the course of one of Finnish Lapland's greatest rivers, Ounasjoki; a picturesque, though uneventful, 150km to reach the first town of any significance: Kittilä.

**KITTILÄ** One of Lapland's dullest places, Kittilä has little to recommend it, but it is a useful entry point for this part of Lapland, and, in winter, there are charter flights to Kittilä airport (airport code KTL) from several European cities including London, Birmingham and Manchester. To be clear, nobody flies here to satisfy a burning desire to see Kittilä, a modern, charmless town that was totally destroyed by retreating German forces during World War II and whose reconstruction has been totally uninspired; they are here instead for one of Finland's best ski resorts, **Levi**, just 20km north.

**Where to stay and eat** Should you want to break the long journey north from Rovaniemi and need to stay in Kittilä, you can stay at **Hotel Kittilä** (↘ 016 643 201; e hotelli.kittila@levi.fi; $$$), located beside the main road at Valtatie 49, which is easily spotted thanks to an incongruous, lifesize Spitfire-like plane suspended outside the front door (the owner is a plane buff). Room rates include a buffet breakfast and use of the hotel's sauna and swimming pool. For somewhere to **eat**, the hotel restaurant is your best bet.

Kittilä's **youth hostel** (↘ 016 648 508) and **campsite** can be found at the opposite end of the main road, at Valtatie 5.

**LEVI** Attracting half a million visitors every year, Finns from across the country wax lyrical about Levi, one of Lapland's main ski resorts with 45 slopes and hundreds of kilometres of cross-country ski and snowmobile tracks. Yet outside Finland, Levi remains little known – indeed eight out of ten visitors here are Finnish. Facilities are first class with over two dozen lifts, including a gondola (more are planned in the next couple of years) and après ski that compares favourably to better known resorts in central Europe. To be strictly accurate, Levi refers principally to the mountain here (530m), which is where all the **ski slopes** are to be found, whereas hotels, the tourist office and other facilities actually located in the village of **Sirkka** beside Route 79, but this distinction is lost on most people and the whole place tends to go simply by the name Levi. During the quieter summer months, Levi can be a good place to **hike** the trails, which during the winter are busy with cross-country skiers. A good choice is the Levi Fell circle (upper route), which covers 18.5km and takes in some of the area's best scenery en route; ask at the tourist office for a map of the area.

**Tourist information** Levi straggles over a couple of kilometres alongside Route 79 and you will find the tourist office operated by Levin Matkailu (↘ 016 639 3300; www.levi.fi; ⊕ Sep–May Mon–Fri 09.00–16.30; Jan also Sat & Sun 11.00–17.30; Jun–Aug Mon–Fri 09.00–21.00, Sat & Sun 11.00–16.00) at the northern edge of the village, beside the main road, at Myllyjoentie 2. **Buses** to and from Rovaniemi stop outside Hotelli Levintunturi beside the main road.

**Where to stay and eat** It is best to book your accommodation in Levi as part of a package tour which will include your flight since booking somewhere to stay on arrival will work out much more expensive. However, if you are only here for a couple of nights, the tourist office can usually fix something up from its truly extensive list of overnight options, which include hotel rooms, apartments and log

Finnish Lapland: Rovaniemi to the Finnmark Plateau  NORTHWEST FROM ROVANIEMI: TOWARDS KAUTOKEINO

6

109

cabins. Reckon on paying around €120 per night for a double room during high season (mid-Feb to late Apr, Christmas and New Year); in low season (early May to late Aug and Oct) prices are roughly half. The main **hotels** have similar top-notch rooms and prices:

🏠 **Hullu Poro** ☎ 016 651 0100; www.hulluporo.fi. $$$$$/$$$

🏠 **K5 Levi** ☎ 016 639 1100; www.k5levi.fi; $$$$$/$$$

🏠 **Lapland Sirkantähti** ☎ 016 323 500; www.laplandhotels.com; $$$$$/$$$

🏠 **Levitunturi** ☎ 016 646 301; www.hotellilevitunturi.fi; $$$$$/$$$

Each of the hotels has a good quality restaurant serving local Lapland specialities as well as a range of cheaper burgers, salads and pizzas.

**ENONTEKIÖ/HETTA AND AROUND** From Levi, Route 956 strikes off north heading for Enontekiö/Hetta, a switchback ride through some wonderful fell-land scenery. However, heading for Enontekiö/Hetta is a confusing experience. Road signs reassuringly confirm that you are heading for **Enontekiö**, the name used on all maps of the region. On arrival in this pint-sized village, 37km south of the Norwegian border, you are welcomed into **Hetta**, which, even for the most linguistically challenged visitor, is clearly not at all the same name. The devil is in the detail: Hetta refers to the name of the village, whereas Enontekiö is the name of the surrounding district. Mention the name Hetta, though, to most Finns and they'll look at you blankly (even Finnair which flies here has never heard of the place), since it is better known outside the immediate vicinity by its administrative title, Enontekiö: don't say you haven't been warned.

By any name, Hetta is quite possibly the most unremarkable place in the whole of Lapland – it simply fails to excite the senses. An elongated settlement stretching for several kilometres either side of Route 93, which runs through the centre of the village, the only real reason to stop here is to pick up information about the nearby **Pallas-Yllästunturi National Park**, which couldn't be more different. A glorious mountain plateau of boreal forest and bare fells which begins just south of Hetta and reaches Kittilä in the south, this is one of Finnish Lapland's most enjoyable expanses of unspoilt wilderness (see below). Things are a little more animated at Christmas when the village and its tiny airport buzzes with activity as hundreds of children and their parents head off in search of Santa Claus and another version of the Lapland experience having flown in for the day, predominantly from Britain. Late March is another good time to be here for the annual **Marianpäivä**, or **Saint Mary's Day** celebrations, a traditional Sámi festival when local people would gather to baptise their children, attend wedding ceremonies and bury their dead once the ground had begun to thaw somewhat. Today the festivities include reindeer racing and lasso throwing on Ounasjärvi lake in town as well as a number of art of cultural exhibitions. There's more information from the tourist office (see below) and at www.enontekio.fi.

**Tourist information** From the junction on the western edge of the village (where Route 93 heads north to Kautokeino), it is a further 2km east, along the main road (signed for Sirkka), to the tourist office also known as the Fell Lapland Nature and Culture Centre (☎ 020 546 7950; e tunturi-lappi@metsa.fi; www.outdoors.fi; ⏱ Jun–Sep Mon–Fri 09.00–20.00, Sat & Sun 09.00–17.00; Oct–Feb Mon–Fri 09.00–16.00; Mar–May daily 09.00–17.00). The helpful staff here have maps and information about **hiking** in the Pallas-Yllästunturi National Park and can advise on hiking to Treriksröset, the point where Finland, Norway and Sweden all meet near Kilpisjärvi to the northwest. Inside the centre there's a rather pedestrian

**exhibition** (*same hours as tourist office; €5*) of black and white photographs, which tell the story of the Sámi migrations to the Arctic Ocean which ceased in the 1960s, when changing herding practices rendered the old ways obsolete.

**Where to stay** Street names tend not to be used in Hetta since the place is so very small. We've given directions as appropriate instead.

**Finnhostel Hetta** ✆ 016 521 361; e hetta@laplandhotels.com; www.laplandhotels.com. Attached to Lapland Hotel Hetta, the hostel here has simply furnished en-suite rooms as well as a common room with TV & laundry facilities. $$$$$/$$$

**Lapland Hotel Hetta** ✆ 016 521 361; e hetta@laplandhotels.com; www.laplandhotels.com; $$$$$/$$$. The best hotel in Hetta with smart, well-appointed rooms & also boasts a swimming pool, several saunas & a fitness room beside the main lake.

**Hetan Lomakylä** (18 cabins) ✆ 016 521 521; e info@hetanlomakyla.fi; www.hetanlomakyla.fi. Cabins of varying standards occupying a pleasant location on the shores of Ounasjärvi Lake. $$$

**Galdotieva Fell Centre** (10 cabins) Palojärvi, 31km north of Hetta on Route 93; ✆ 016 528 630; e info@harriniva.fi; www.harriniva.fi. A gloriously remote spot close to the Norwegian border with lakeside log cabins, all with electricity & fridge, though some without shower & toilet (facilities available on site). 4 cabins have their own sauna & those without shower & toilet are excellent value. *With sauna* $$$, *without shower & toilet* $ *per night.*

**Hetan Majatalo** Riekontie 8; ✆ 016 554 0400; e info@hetan-majatalo.fi; www.hetan-majatalo.fi. A good choice with comfortable, modern en-suite rooms with wood panelling $$$. Simpler rooms in the attached guesthouse for $$.

**Where to eat and drink** Your best bet in Hetta is **self-catering** in one of the cabins listed above – provisions can be bought at the village supermarket. Alternatively, Hetan Majatalo and Lapland Hotel Hetta have decent **restaurants**, which specialise in local specialities such as reindeer and charge around €15 for a main dish. If you are self-catering at Galdotieva, you'd be wise to take all provisions with you, though the restaurant at the centre serves lunch and dinner (mains in the range €15–25); breakfast is €7.

**PALLAS-YLLÄSTUNTURI NATIONAL PARK** Finland's third largest national park covering over 1,000km², the Pallas-Yllästunturi National Park was established in 2005 to protect the fell chain in this part of central Lapland. A long, narrow, ribbon-shaped wedge of land stretching from Hetta in the north to roughly Kittilä in the south, the park contains a wide range of unique fell, forest and peatland habitats. Pallas-Yllästunturi is a veritable haven for naturalists: plants such as mountain bearberry, trailing azalea, alpine clubmoss and Lapland diapensia are all well represented. The fauna of the park is equally rich: in spring the snow bunting is among the first migratory birds to arrive, and, in summer, around 150 species of bird can be seen in the park. Of the larger mammals, bear and elk are regular inhabitants of the park, whereas wolverine, lynx and wolf are less frequent visitors.

**Hiking trails** Although there are several trails that wind their way through the park, the best and most easily accessible is the marked 55km long **Hetta-Pallas trail** for which you will need three to four days (summer only). From Hetta, first cross Ounasjärvi lake by boat (ask at the tourist office for the exact starting point) and head south through the pine forest towards the Pyhäkero day shelter. **Wilderness huts** (all open and not requiring reservation) are situated at regular intervals along the trail at Sioskuru, Pahakuru, Hannukuru (where there's a sauna) and Nammalakuru. At the end of the trail, the **Pallastunturi visitor centre** (✆ 020 564 7930; e pallastunturi@metsa.fi; ⏱ 09.00–16.00 daily) is a good place to check onward bus times to Muonio, Kittilä or Rovaniemi. Currently, departures are at 10.05 (*Mon–Fri*) for Kittilä; 13.15 (*Sat only*) for Rovaniemi; and 16.50 (*Mon–Fri*) for Muonio. For accommodation at this end of the trail, there's the comfortable Lapland Hotel Pallas (↖ *016 323 355;* e *pallas@laplandhotels.fi; www.laplandhotels.fi;* $$$$$/$$$) whose predecessor, incidentally, was used by holidaying German officers during World War II until they blew it up in 1944; or Hotelli Jeris (see page 93), which can be reached on the buses to Kittilä and Rovaniemi.

## KAUTOKEINO

Occupying a lonely, isolated spot across the border on Norway's barren Finnmarksvidda plateau, 80km north of Enontekiö/Hetta, it is hard to see quite why Kautokeino (Guovdageaidnu in Sámi) exists where it does. However, the translation of the village's Sámi name, 'halfway point', helps to throw some light on the matter, since the village is located midway between two traditional reindeer grazing areas. Providing ready access to the River Kautokeino, on whose banks the settlement has grown, Kautokeino (the Norwegianised version of the Sámi name) slowly developed into a stopping point on the long migration.

Indeed, it is clear to see how important the village is to Norway's Sámi community: not only is Sámi virtually the only language you will hear on the streets and, therefore, a sign of cultural dominance, but it is the location for the Sámi high school and reindeer herding college, the Sámi university college, the Nordic Sámi Institute, the Norwegian Sámi parliament's language department and the National Sámi theatre – quite a feat for a place which counts a population of barely 2,000 people.

**SOME HISTORY: THE KAUTOKEINO REVOLT** The first ever Sámi uprising took place in Kautokeino in the autumn of 1852, sparked by long-lasting frustration about local living conditions. The Sámi felt a deep sense of exploitation when they considered their unequal relationship with Norwegian traders and their growing dependence on hard liquor (introduced by Norwegian merchants and pioneers from the south).

Following the closure of the land border between Norway and Finland in 1852, which deprived the local Sámi of traditional grazing pastures in Finland and, thus, threatened their traditional livelihood, a group of 35 Sámi Laestadians (see below) marched on the village, murdering a local shopkeeper whom they held responsible for the increasing alcoholism of the local inhabitants. They then burnt down his store and butchered the local policeman when he tried to intervene. The gang beat up the local priest when he tried to prevent the violence. The revivalist preacher, Lars Levi Laestadius, was charged in connection with the incident for whipping the local Sámi into a religious fervour and urging them to wage war on the unrepentant, but the charges against him were later dropped. Of the 33 people who were tried for insurrection, five were sentenced to death. Following the execution in Bossekop (Alta) of two of them, Aslak Hætta and Mons Somby, the authorities confiscated their skulls and sent them to Oslo University as examples of both primitive people and criminals for scientific research; in 1996, following a request from family members, the skulls were traced to a collection held by an institute at Copenhagen University, which then returned them for burial alongside the men's headless bodies in Kåfjord cemetery near Alta. The death sentences on Anders Bær and Lars Hætta were commuted to imprisonment, and in Oslo prison they wrote their memoirs including an account of the revolt, though these were not published until 1958. Lars Hætta translated several books from Norwegian into Sámi while

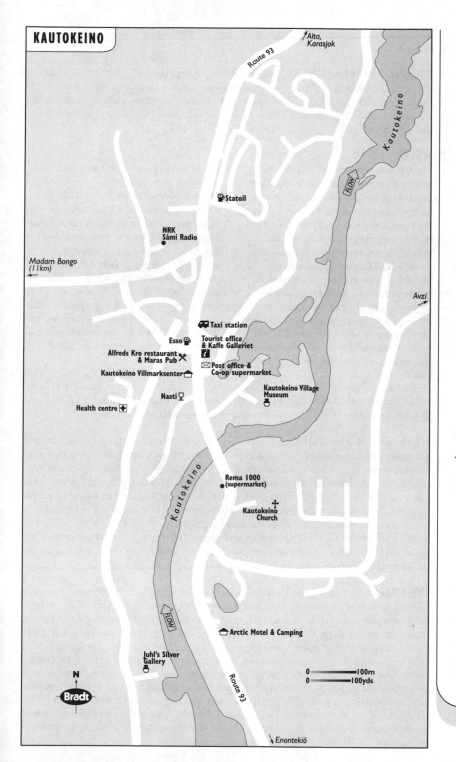

KAUTOKEINO

Route 93

Alta, Karasjok

Kautokeino

FLOW

Statoil

NRK
Sámi Radio

Madam Bongo
(11km)

Avzi

Taxi station

Esso
Tourist office
& Kaffe Galleriet

Alfreds Kro restaurant
& Maras Pub
Post office &
Co-op supermarket

Kautokeino Villmarksenter

Kautokeino Village
Museum

Nasti

Health centre

Kautokeino

Rema 1000
(supermarket)

Kautokeino
Church

FLOW

Arctic Motel & Camping

Juhl's Silver
Gallery

N

Bradt

0 ————— 100m
0 ————— 100yds

Route 93

Enontekiö

in jail, including the Bible, which helped to secure his early release after 15 years behind bars.

**TOURIST INFORMATION** Kautokeino's tourist office (✆ *78 48 65 00;* e *destinasjonkautokeino@trollnet.no; www.kautokeino.no;* ☉ *mid–late Jun 09.00–16.00 daily; Jul to mid-Aug 09.00–18.00 daily*) lurks beside the main road adjacent to the huddle of municipal buildings, which, in a broad sense, could be described as the village centre.

## WHERE TO STAY

🏠 **Kautokeino Villmarksenter** ✆ 78 487 602; e vmsenter@start.no. This less friendly establishment has extremely spartan rooms that take the prize for the smallest bathroom in the whole of Lapland. When approaching from Alta, follow the signs on the main road marked 'Samisk høgskole/Sámi allaskuvla' & then turn immediately left. $$$

🏕 **Arctic Motel & Camping** Suomaluodda 16; ✆ 78 485 400; e samicamp@start.no; www.kauto.no. Accommodation is sparse, though, the best bet in the village is this motel at the southern end of the village, past the church & just over the bridge. They have a good selection of cabins, both with & without running water & kitchen facilities, though they could do with smartening up the grounds a

little by removing some of the debris that's littering the place. From $$.

🏠 **Madam Bongos Fjellstue** ✆ 78 486 160; www.kautokeino.com/bongo. If you don't mind being outside Kautokeino, the marvellously named Madam Bongos Fjellstue, 11km west of the village in the Sámi hamlet of Cunovuoppe, is a great place to stay. Run by local woman, Karen Anna Bongo, there's accommodation both in a *lávvu* (Sámi tent), cabins or regular dbl rooms. She serves up delicious Sámi specialities, such as reindeer meat in onion sauce, around the fire in her *lávvu*. Get here by following the road up past the Villmarksenter & then turn left at the T-junction. *Tents, dbls & cabins* $ *pp.*

A new Thon hotel is planned for Kautokeino to replace the village's previous hotel which burnt down several years ago, though, at the time of writing, building had still to commence. Check www.thonhotels.no for opening details.

**WHERE TO EAT AND DRINK** Eating in Kautokeino throws up few options: there's essentially only a choice between **Kaffe Galleriet** beside the main road, opposite Villmarksenter, which is good for open sandwiches (40kr), coffee and cakes, and, much better, **Alfreds Kro**, Hánnoluohkka 4, behind Villmarksenter, where you can order a main course of meat or fish and then help yourself to the salad buffet (around 90–150kr depending on the main course). For drinking, **Maras pub**, immediately below Alfreds Kro, is a friendly place to meet local people (☉ *daily from 18.00, closed Mon*). More noisy and rowdy is the aptly named Nasti, a bit of a local boozers' hang-out, below Villmarksenter, off the main road at Álttáluodda 16.

**THE VILLAGE** In order to do Kautokeino justice, you really need to spend a couple of days here, meeting people and chatting, to try to get under the skin of the village. Like so many other Sámi settlements, it is not a visually appealing place, strung out rather aimlessly along Route 93, which forms the main street, and if you simply rush in and rush out again, you risk misunderstanding the Sámi community and may leave with the wrong impression. Since there are no sights here, appreciating what Kautokeino has to offer is more to be found in sharing a cup of coffee or a beer with one of the locals and discussing what life is like here, or heading out into the surrounding unsullied countryside and getting in touch with nature. The village is at its most animated during the Easter Festival (see below) though is relatively empty in summer when a third of the population is at the coast tending reindeer.

**The Juhls' Silver Gallery** (\ 78 484 330; www.juhls.no; ⊕ late Jun to early Aug 09.00–21.00 daily; mid-Aug to mid-June 09.00–18.00) While in Kautokeino, make sure to visit the Juhls Silver Gallery, a veritable treasure chest of locally produced top-quality jewellery as well as other handicrafts of Scandinavian design. Established by man and wife team, Frank and Regine Juhl, back in 1959, the gallery has grown over the years and now offers an intriguing insight into their work and its influences over the decades they have lived in Kautokeino since moving here from Denmark and Germany, respectively. Quite remarkably, the couple met in Kautokeino and decided to settle here – at a time when there wasn't even a road to their house and the only access was by boat across the Kautokeino river. Both Regine and Frank developed a keen interest in nomadic cultures, carefully observing the style of dress and personal adornment of the local Sámi, which was to become a key element of their work and design. Although the Sámi had no tradition of silvermaking due to their nomadic lifestyle, they acquired silver chains and brooches through trade and these have now become a key part of their traditional dress on special occasions.

From their hilltop location overlooking Kautokeino, the workshop and showrooms have been extended over the years, and wondering through the complex from room to room is to explore the couple's work decade by decade – exquisitely beautiful silverwork, mosaics and lapidary are on display throughout the site which is made up of low-lying showrooms with pagoda-style sloping rooves designed to reflect the snowdrifts of the tundra. The gallery is an easy place to spend an hour or two simply strolling around and watching the craftspeople at work in the workshop. Free guided tours (15mins) operate throughout the day and there's a small café where you can get free coffee and biscuits. Juhl's Silver Gallery is 2.5km from the centre of Kautokeino, perched on a ridge by the west bank of the river. Follow the signs from the main road opposite Kaffe Galleriet.

### Guovdageainnu Gilisillju: Kautokeino Village Museum (⊕ mid-June to mid-Aug 09.00–19.00 Mon–Sat, noon–19.00 Sun; rest of year Mon–Fri 09.00–15.00; entry is 20kr) The small headland, by the bridge, that forces the Kautokeinoelva river into a sharp righthand bend, is where you will find Kautokeino's diminutive museum, a collection of traditional Sámi timber storehuts as well as a modest exhibition focusing on the cultural history of the Sámi people through a series of old photographs, tools and assorted other knicknacks.

### Kautokeino Church (⊕ Jun to mid-Aug 09.00–21.00 daily) Sitting squatly on a small hillock at the southern end of the village, just over the river, Kautokeino church is visible for miles around and, indeed, draws churchgoers from across the tundra – it is one of the best attended churches in Norway, particularly at Easter. Although a church first stood on this spot as early as the 18th century, the original structure was burnt to the ground by retreating German forces at the end of World War II. Today's church, completed in 1958, is unusually long in shape with a ridge turret above the entrance at its western end, which culminates in an onion-shaped steeple and spire. A roof-covered porch before the main door, supported by vertical and slanted wooden posts, is reminiscent of Sámi building design. The wood-panelled interior is decorated in the traditional Sámi colours blue, green, red and yellow and is lit by the original chandelabra that was rescued from the village's first church.

### Easter Festival Undoubtedly, the best time of year to be in Kautokeino is at Easter when the entire village is consumed by the week-long Easter Festival, a historically traditional event when the local Sámi community celebrated (albeit with snow still on the ground) the end of a long winter and looked forward to the coming of

spring. It was a time for religious festivals and wedding ceremonies. Although today's festival still is an important religious event, it is the time for the **reindeer racing** world cup, a **film festival** focusing on the indigenous people of the Arctic, concerts, theatre performances and the Sámi version of the Eurovision **song contest** when, in addition to the selection of the best song, the best *joik* is chosen. There's more information at www.saami-easterfestival.org.

**MOVING ON FROM KAUTOKEINO** Buses arrive and depart from the Statoil filling station at the northern end of the village on the main road. Plan your journey here carefully since schedules are skeletal at best: services leave for Alta at 04.50 (*Mon, Wed & Fri*); 11.40 (*Mon & Fri*); 14.25 (*Fri*) and 14.40 (*Wed & Sun*). The bus to Karasjok is even less frequent: there's currently just one departure on Friday (17.10) and Sunday (20.20). From Kautokeino, it is 130km to Alta and to Karasjok, and 80km south to Enontekiö in Finland. There is no bus connection across the border into Finland.

## NORTHEAST FROM ROVANIEMI: TOWARDS KARASJOK

The other main road north from Rovaniemi, **Route 4**, heads northeast for a grinding 128km before reaching uneventful **Sodankylä** (Soaðegilli in Sámi), the only place of any significance between Rovaniemi and Kakslauttanen (see below).

**SODANKYLÄ** Sodankylä is not one of Lapland's most interesting or aesthetic towns, but, in addition to a decent Sámi art gallery, there are a few other diversions worthy of your time, notably one of the oldest wooden churches in the whole of region. Sodankylä is reputed to be the coldest place in Finland, indeed, in January, although statistically the average temperature here is a chilling −14C, it is commonly below −30C.

**Tourist information** Sodankylä is effectively strung out along one long main road, Jäämerentie. The tourist office (✆ 016 618 168; e tourist.information@sodankyla.fi; ◷ Jun–Aug Mon–Sat 09.00–17.00; Sep–May Mon–Fri 09.00–17.00) is located with the art museum, beside the old church, at Jäämerentie 3, beside the junction with Kemijärventie. From the bus station, at the opposite end of Jäämerentie, the tourist office is a straightforward walk down the main road of around ten minutes.

**Where to stay** The high season in Sodankylä runs from November to April, when test drivers from Peugeot are in town to put their latest models through their paces in Arctic conditions and during the Midnight Sun Festival in June (see below).

**Sodankylä** Unarintie 15; ✆ 016 617 121; e hotsod@hotmail.com. An uninspiring hotel just behind the bus station with little to recommend it, unless everywhere else is full. $$$$$/$$$$
**Karhu** Lapintie 1; ✆ 020 1620 610; e info@hotel-bearinn.com; www.hotel-bearinn.com. 2 blocks west of Jäämerentie, at the junction with Kasarmintie, modern & comfortable dbl rooms. $$$
**Majatalo Kolme Veljestä** Ivalontie 1; ✆ 611

216; e majatalo.kolmeveljesta@pp.inet.fi; www.majatalokolmeveljesta.fi. Located just beyond the northern end of Jäämerentie, this homely guesthouse has dbls with use of the kitchen & sauna. $$
**Nilimella** Kelukoskentie 5; ✆ 016 612 181; e antti.rintala@naturex-ventures.fi; www.naturex-ventures.fi. Sodankylä's campsite (◷ Jun–Aug) is across the river, diagonally opposite the old church. *Also rents out cabins for* $.

**Where to eat** Make no mistake, Sodankylä is no gourmet's paradise. Choices are limited to the dingy locals' drinking hang-out, **Revontuli** (*Jäämerentie 9*) which dishes up smoked salmon for €12, sauteed reindeer at €15 and pepper steak for €15 as well as an array of pizzas. More pizzas from €6.50 can be found at **Pizza-Paikka à la Riesto**, opposite the bus station (*Jäämerentie 25*). Try to ignore the orange plastic chairs inside **Seita-baari** (*Jäämerentie 20*), because locals swear that the reindeer stew here is the best for miles around.

**The town** Although Sodankylä can trace its history back to the late 17th century when local Sámi gathered here to celebrate key dates in the religious calendar, arriving by reindeer sled in winter and boat in summer, there's just one building still standing to remind today's visitor of times past. The town's fantastically preserved **wooden church**, dating from 1689 and known as *vanha kirkko*, was – unusually – spared the ravages of the retreating German forces during World War II, and today remains totally intact in its original position beautifully located beside the Kitinen river. Built of coarse timber and topped by a shingle roof, this compact church has an exceptionally narrow nave and a bulging pulpit that vies for what precious space there is with the pews. Beneath the floorboards, in the crypt, there's a collection of preserved mummies; if the church warden is around you may be able to coax them to let you down for a nose around. You will find the old church to the east of the tourist office, tucked away in the graveyard beside the town's more modern church, which is totally void of charm and interest.

**Alariesto Art Gallery** (⊕ *11.00–17.00 Mon–Fri; €5*) Just beside the church, you will find one of Lapland's better Sámi art galleries, which contains the naivistic work of local artist, Andreas Alariesto (1900–89) – plenty of brightly coloured, sometimes happy, sometimes sombre scenes of day-to-day Sámi life, with a fair smattering of reindeer and locals in traditional costume. Alariesto described his own work as an attempt to 'chronicle a world that had already passed, one that would fade into oblivion with my death' and his ultimate aim was to preserve the Sámi culture he was part of.

**The Midnight Sun Film Festival** (*www.msfilmfestival.fi*) For one week each year during the middle of June, Sodankylä is overrun with film buffs, drawn here by the latest cinematic offerings of Finland's leading directors on show during the Midnight Sun Film Festival. The brainchild of local film producers, brothers Mika and Aki Kaurismäki, the festival aims to showcase the best of Finnish and European cinema, using the allure of the Midnight Sun to entice people to visit what is otherwise a singularly unattractive town. Appealing primarily to hardened film enthusiasts, the attraction of sitting for hours on end in a darkened cinema while there's 24-hour daylight outside remains a mystery to most other visitors. Naturally, accommodation is at a premium during the festival and if you are planning to visit at this time of year, you'd be wise to book somewhere to stay well in advance. There's more information about the event on the website and at the tourist office.

**TANKAVAARA** About 90km north of Sodankylä, just after the tiny hamlet of **Vuotso**, lies the **Tankavaara Gold Museum and Panning Centre** (⊕ *Jun to mid-Aug 09.00–18.00 daily; mid-Aug to late Sep 09.00–17.00 daily; €7*). This is the place to head for if you fancy trying your hand at prospecting for gold – every year, thousands of people come here to try their luck. The museum is interesting enough, tracing the history of the gold rushes in this part of Lapland, but it is getting your hands wet which is the real fun part of a visit here. Sadly, though, not everyone has the luck of the 11-year-old schoolboy who recently turned up a nugget weighing almost 40g. To pan for gold in the river here costs €3.50 per hour, on top of the museum entrance fee, which then gets you some basic training and all the equipment you need. Naturally, you are allowed to keep any gold you might find. In early August each year, Tankavaara hosts the **Finnish National Goldpanning Championships** when hopefuls from across the country gather here to slosh piles of dirt and stones around.

**Where to stay and eat** Should you want to stay here, there's comfortable hotel accommodation available at **Hotel Korundi** (✆ *016 626 158; www.tankavaara.fi;* $$) or there's a choice of log cabins ($$), which include a small kitchenette. The **Wanha Waskolimies** restaurant on site serves up a tasty selection of Lapland delicacies including reindeer and locally caught salmon.

**KAKSLAUTTANEN** The hotel and igloo village of Kakslauttanen (✆ *016 667 100;* e *hotel@kakslauttanen.fi; www.kakslauttanen.fi*) is a real gem. A good 250km north of Rovaniemi, it is easily the best choice of **log cabin** accommodation in the whole of Finnish Lapland and makes for a great place to spend Christmas (see below). If your heart is set on spending the night in an **igloo** but you resent paying the inflated prices charged by Sweden's Icehotel, you will be delighted to know that it doesn't come any more affordable than here.

Kakslauttanen isn't really a village, it is really little more than an idyllic collection of log cabins and, during the winter season, a gaggle of igloos, beautifully located either side of a small river, directly beside Route 4, where a hole in the ice is kept open for those early morning dips. Kakslauttanen boasts the largest **smoke sauna** in the world with a capacity of around one hundred people. Together with its smaller brother, the sauna is heated using woodsmoke and best entered once the smoke has died down somewhat, generally after an hour or so (€37 per person; minimum seven people in the smaller smoke sauna; minimum 20 people in the larger one).

**Where to stay and eat** Kakslauttanen's 31 log **cabins** (*winter* $$$$$/*summer* $$) are first-class. Not only are they located a respectable distance from each other to allow a little privacy (something which is hard to find in other similar establishments), but they are all built to the same high standards using the truly impressive dead standing pine. Imported from Russia, these rough-hewn tree trunks have a sizeable diameter of over half a metre and conspire to give the whole village (they've been used to build the saunas and the main reception building, as well) a sturdy yet superbly cosy feel. Although the size of each cabin differs (they sleep from two to six people), every one comes equipped with a full kitchen, fireplace and sauna while outside there's a generously-sized terrace, perfect for standing to cool off after a sauna.

Every winter between December and April, the hotel constructs its own more modest version of Sweden's Icehotel. The **igloo village** is composed of one main building of snow and ice (with a floor area of around 850m$^2$) housing nine sleeping rooms, a restaurant, gallery and chapel – the temperature inside here varies between –3°C and –6°C. Next door there are six other smaller, **snow igloos** ($$$$$), which can sleep up to five people. If you choose to sleep in an igloo, you will be provided with a snug gown sleeping bag, woollen socks and a hood to keep you warm.

Kakslauttanen offers the chance to spend the night in a **glass igloo** ($$$$$), specially constructed of thermal glass in the shape of a regular igloo. The glass keeps the interior at normal room temperature and doesn't frost up and, naturally, offers clear views of the night sky, increasing your chances of seeing the aurora borealis (visible between late August and late April). Each glass igloo has a toilet, small shower and electrically operated reclining beds.

In addition to the possibility of preparing meals in the log cabins, **meals** are available in the restaurant in the main reception building. Half board, for example, is €25.

**Activities and airport transfers** Reindeer, husky and snowmobile safaris can all be booked through the hotel. A trip to the reindeer farm in the village of Purnumukka, 20km south of Kakslauttanen, costs €89 per person for a two-hour trip. Alternatively, a husky-sled tour lasting up to two and a half hours costs €112 per person and a snowmobile safari of the same duration is €93 per person. Alternatively, if you are flying directly to this part of Finnish Lapland and arriving at Ivalo **airport**, you can arrange to be met from your plane and driven by snowmobile to Kakslauttanen for €180 per person (minimum four people); a more conventional pickup by car is €22 per person.

**Christmas at Kakslauttanen** On 24 December each year the hotel runs a special package of Christmas events aimed at children. The day kicks off with a sledge ride into the forest where adults receive a glass of Finnish mulled wine, *glögi*, as they sit around a campfire; children are recounted stories of Father Christmas and his reindeer. Then, everyone goes off in search of a Christmas tree, which is then cut down and brought back to the hotel. A Christmas lunch buffet is then served. At 17.00 there's a church service (optional), followed by smorgasbord buffet at 19.00 consisting of a cold, warm and dessert table. The highlight of the day comes at 21.00 when Santa arrives with his reindeer bearing gifts for the children; parents can present their own gifts to Father Christmas so he can give them to their children, but there's a small gift from the hotel to all children under the age of 15. The log cabins are decked out with special Christmas tablecloths and candles to add to the festive spirit.

**URHO KEKKONEN NATIONAL PARK** From Kakslauttanen, a minor road leads east for around 7km to **Kaunispää** hill (546m), which marks the western extent of one of Finland's greatest national parks, Urho Kekkonen, named after the former president, and now one of Europe's last wilderness areas. Measuring a whopping 2,530km$^2$, the park is truly vast and it is therefore essential that you plan any hiking trip here with extreme precision. Maps are essential as the 190km of walking paths are poorly signed; there are cabins dotted throughout the park which can be booked in advance (see below).

**Tourist information and where to stay** The best place to get the latest information about the state of the terrain – mostly upland hills, boggy in parts, and dense forest – is from **Tunturikeskus Kiilopää** (⟍ *670 0700;* e *kiilopaa@suomenlatu.fi; www.kiilopaa.com*), a **youth hostel** and national park information centre, at the end of the road from Kakslauttanen, where staff can advise on booking cabins in the park itself. Open all year round except May and October, the centre has both dorm beds ($), private rooms ($$) and log cabins ($$$$); there's a restaurant and smoke sauna on site.

**SAARISELKÄ** A further 12km north of Kakslauttanen along Route 4, the pleasant, purpose-built holiday village of Saariselkä (*www.saariselka.fi*) proudly bills itself as the most northerly ski resort in the world. It is a modest sort of a place, consisting of just four hotels and two fells, Kaunispää (with chairlift) and Iisakkipää, for downhill skiing, and, hence, is unlikely to be the main reason for your travel to Lapland. Facilities at Levi near Kittilä, for example, Saariselkä's arch rival, are more likely to appeal to those more used to the upmarket ski resorts of central Europe.

6

However, if you are driving by, it is worth making the short detour to the top of **Kaunispää** hill (437m), signed off Route 4 just to the north of Saariselkä, from where there are superb views of the surrounding fell land stretching for 70km or so on a clear day. The Panorama Café at the summit is a fine place to stop for a cup of coffee and a slice of cake to savour the view.

## Where to stay and eat

**Tunturihotelli** 016 681 501; e sales@tunturihotelli.fi; www.tunturihotelli.fi. The best of the hotels offers a range of comfortable dbls, with free access to the hotel's saunas, & apartments sleeping up to 13 people which feature their own sauna. The restaurant in the main building serves up delicious blue cheese & reindeer soup as well as sautéed reindeer with mashed potato for around €20. *Dbls Sun–Wed $$$$, Thu–Sat $$$$$; apts $$$$$$ per night.*

**Activities** Should you decide to stay in Saariselkä, the hotels can arrange a number of activities in addition to skiing, including two-hour **snowmobile safaris** (€85pp *for two people sharing a snowmobile*) and a 1 to 2 hour **husky safari** (€102pp). In summer you can try your hand at **gold panning** in the local rivers (€10pp) or go **river rafting** on the River Juutua, which flows into Inarijärvi lake (€57pp).

**IVALO** Just 23km north of Saariselkä, Ivalo (Avvil in Sámi) conspires to be the dullest place in the whole of Lapland. An ugly and soulless village, strung out aimlessly along the E75, there's only one real reason be here – and that's to leave again on the **bus**, which chugs its way along Route 91 to the Russian border at **Raja-Jooseppi** (53km) before continuing to **Murmansk** in Russia. Although

### GETTING FROM FINNISH LAPLAND TO RUSSIA

Departing from Ivalo's bus station on Piiskuntie (a left turn off the main E75 when driving south through the village, beside the tourist office), a bus leaves at 15.30 on Mon, Wed & Fri for the 300km bumpy ride along Russia's potholed Route P11 to Murmansk; the journey takes six and a half hours. Tickets are available from the bus station (€50 one-way). It is best to get a Russian visa before you leave home since they are not available at the border. If you don't have one, the tourist office in Inari can help you get one from the Russian Embassy in Helsinki. The return service operates three times weekly (*Mon, Wed & Fri*), leaving the bus station in Murmansk at 08.30, arriving in Ivalo at 14.00; remember Russian time is one hour ahead of that in Finland. Connections are available to and from Rovaniemi; see www.goldline.fi for more details.

It is also possible to reach Russia from Kemijärvi, a small town 85km northeast of Rovaniemi, which is on the Finnish rail network (*www.vr.fi*). From here a twice-weekly bus (*Mon & Thu*) departs at 15.30 and runs via Salla and the border at Kelloselkä to Kandalaksha (Kantalahti in Finnish) on the White Sea, a distance of 270km, arriving at 21.55 Russian time. The return service operates twice-weekly (*Mon & Thu*), leaving Kandalaksha at 08.00, arriving into Kemijärvi at 12.20 Finnish time; for more details see www.goldline.fi. Once again visas must be obtained in advance. A single ticket from Kemijärvi to Kandalaksha costs €35.

With advance planning it is possible to make a round-trip from Lapland to Russia, leaving from Ivalo and returning back into Kemijärvi (or vice versa) and travelling between Murmansk and Kandalaksha by train (Murmansk to Saint Petersburg trains call at Kandalaksha several times daily).

For information about how to get to Russia from Norwegian Lapland, see page 159.

there are a couple of hotels and extremely basic eateries dotted along the main road (see below), Ivalo is not somewhere you are likely to want to linger. However, as you pass through the village, it is worth making a stop at Lapland Shop (also known as Lahjatalo Ivalo in Finnish) on the main road, Ivalontie, just before the Lauran Grilli restaurant. Thanks to Ivalo's location well off the beaten tourist trail, it is a good place to pick up Sámi **souvenirs**, in particular reindeer skins (from €45), at considerably lower prices than in more touristy locations.

**Tourist information and where to stay** Ivalo's tourist office at the junction of Piiskuntie and Ivalontie is frankly of limited use. Open only restricted hours in summer, it is a better idea to save all your questions for the helpful office in Inari.

Should you find yourself in the unenviable position of having to spend the night in Ivalo, your best bet is the riverside **Hotel Ivalo** (✆ *016 688 111;* e *hotelivalo@hotelivalo.fi; www.hotelivalo.fi; $$$$*), Ivalontie 34, on the outskirts of town just past the Shell station.

**✗ Where to eat** When it comes to finding something to eat, choices are limited to the greasy spoon **Anjan Pizza** on the main road close to the Shell station with a range of unappetising pizzas from €6.50, and the even less palatable **Lauran Grilli** opposite, which dishes up an identical range of pizzas from €6 and burgers starting at €4.20. The best place for lunch is **Veken Pubi** (⊕ *11.00 and 17.00 Mon–Fri*), next door to Anjan Pizza, which serves a set buffet meal for €7; beware, though, it is the local boozers' hang-out and may not appeal to those of a nervous disposition. From Ivalo, it is 288km south to Rovaniemi and 39km north to Inari.

## INARI

A short drive of 39km northwest from Ivalo, Inari is to Finland what Karasjok is to Norway. Home to Sámediggi, the Finnish Sámi parliament, Inari (Anár in Sámi) is the centre of Sámi culture in Finland. Although other Sámi groups and Finns have moved into the region for various reasons (people were resettled in Inari, for instance, when Finland lost the Petsamo region to the Soviet Union in 1944), the Sámi have historically always lived in the same place, around the rocky shores of Inarijärvi lake (Anárjávri in Sámi), and today constitute a distinct ethnic group within the Sámi community as a whole, with their own traditional costume and language. However, Inari Sámi is threatened with extinction since its speakers total barely 325, many of whom are elderly or middle-aged; there are currently fewer than 20 schoolchildren who have this branch of Sámi as their native language.

Although Inari is a pretty enough place to wander around for an hour or so, there are several reasons that make it an ideal stop on the long haul between Rovaniemi and the North Cape: the best Sámi museum in the whole of Lapland is here; an enjoyable hiking route out to a wilderness church starts from just off the main street; and boat trips on the steely waters of the lake are available during the summer months.

**TOURIST INFORMATION** Clustered around the mouth of the Juutuanjoki river where it flows into Lake Inari, the village is little more than one elongated main road, Inarintie, which runs over a distance of a kilometre or so. The helpful tourist office (✆ *016 661 666;* e *inari.info@sarriselka.fi; www.inarilapland.or;* ⊕ *Jun–Aug 09.00–19.00 daily; rest of year Mon–Fri 10.00–17.00*), Inarintie 38, goes by the name of Inari Info and has masses of information about the surrounding area as well as advice about

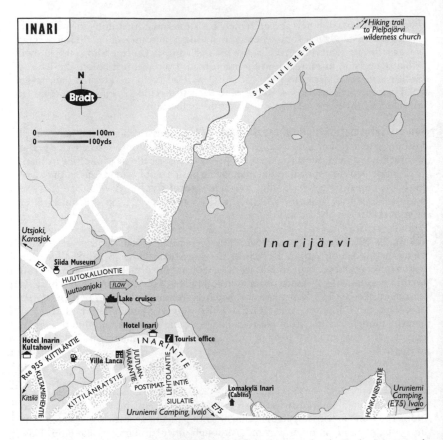

**INARI**

N

**Bradt**

0 ▬▬▬▬100m
0 ▬▬▬▬100yds

Hiking trail
to Pielpajärvi
wilderness church

SARVINIEMEEN

*Inarijärvi*

Utsjoki,
Karasjok

E75

Siida Museum
HUUTOKALLIONTIE
Juutuanjoki  FLOW
Lake cruises

Hotel Inari

Hotel Inarin
Kultahovi

Rte 955 KITTILÄNTIE
KULTAHOVIENTIE

Kittilä

Villa Lanca

KITTILÄNRATSTIE

JUUTUAN
VAARANTIE

INARI NTIE
LEHTOLANTIE

POSTIMAT.  INTIE

SIULATIE

Uruniemi Camping, Ivalo

E75

Tourist office

Lomakylä Inari
(Cabins)

HONKANIEMENTIE

Uruniemi
Camping,
(E75) Ivalo

how to obtain a Russian visa, should you be planning to take the Ivalo–Murmansk bus (see page 120). They can fix up a fishing licence (€20) if you fancy trying your hand at catching trout in the lake. There's **internet** access inside the tourist office at €2 for 15 minutes. All **buses** use the tourist office as their main stop in the village.

##  WHERE TO STAY AND EAT
**Hotels** Inari has two hotels:

🏠 **Hotel Inarin Kultahovi** Saaikoskentie 2; ☎ 016 671 221; ℮ inarin.kultahovi @ co.inet.fi; www.saariselka.fi/kultahovi. Modern, decent rooms (some with river views) & the best evening restaurant in the village serving up traditional Arctic dishes as well as more mainstream staples such as pork chops at reasonable prices. $$$$
🏠 **Hotel Inari** Inarintie 40; ☎ 016 671 026; ℮ info @ hotelliinari.fi; www.hotelliinari.fi. Newly renovated & next to the tourist office, which

functions as the village's youth hostel renting out simpler, though perfectly adequate rooms ($) as well as plusher, en suite rooms ($$$$). If you want to meet local people, the restaurant here is the place to come; known as the 'living room of the village', it attracts diners & drinkers, though the former are greatly outnumbered by the latter, particularly on Fri & Sat nights, when things can get especially loud & drunken. $$$$$

## Cabins and camping

🏠 **Lomakylä Inari** Inarintie 26; ☎ 016 671 108; e info@lomakyla-inari.fi; www.lomakyla-inari.fi. Alternatively, top-notch waterfront cabins are available at this sedate holiday village. $$$$ 🏠 **Villa Lanca** ☎ 040 748 0984; www.villalanca.fi. A handful of tastefully decorated dbl rooms are rented out here along with a lakeside cabin. $$$ ⛺ **Uruniemi Camping** ☎ 016 671 331; e petti.kangasniemi@uruniemi.inet.fi; www.uruniemi.com. The village campsite also offers cabins which are a little smaller & more basic. $$

Undoubtedly the best place to **eat** is the Siida museum's restaurant, **Sarrit**, which serves up a variety of different reindeer dishes (all €16), such as smoked reindeer in blue cheese sauce, as well as freshly caught trout from the lake with hollandaise sauce and boiled potatoes (€17); the restaurant keeps the same hours as the museum (see below).

**THE VILLAGE** Inari is not the sort of place where you hurtle from one sight to another, ticking them off as you go; there aren't any. Instead, prepare to learn more about the Sámi lands you are travelling through and the intimate relationship between indigenous man and nature at the **Siida Museum** (*www.siida.fi*; ☉ *Jun–Sep 09.00–20.00 daily; rest of year Tue–Sun 10.00–17.00; €8*), beside the main road and on the banks of Inarijärvi, one of the best museums in Finland and Inari's main attraction. Although the Sámi community in Finland is considerably smaller than that in Norway, the professional, contemporary approach to the museum's contents and layout is sure to impress and there are clear lessons to learn for other museums elsewhere in the region.

From the entrance hall, a sloping walkway leads visitors to the main exhibition area on the first floor. Here, in a modest-sized room, an easy-to-understand timeline runs the circumference of the room recounting Sámi history from prehistoric times to the present day, placing events in Lapland alongside their chronological counterparts elsewhere in the world: for instance, while Che Guevara and Ayatollah Khomeini were at large in the 1970s, the Sámi were rejoicing at the completion of their new road to Sevettijärvi. The key theme of the museum, though, is nature and, as you step into the main exhibition space, it is as if you are suddenly immersed in the wilds of Lapland's fells. A series of floor-to-ceiling photographs measuring a whopping 10m wide by 5m high span the room, conjuring up resonant images of Lapland's landscapes and seasons. The sound of birdsong, the howl of the wind and the gentle trickle of mountain streams, played from surround speakers in the ceiling, add to the sensation of being out in nature and at the mercy of the elements: from displays on the variegated flowers that carpet the Lapland fells in spring to the fascinating lifecycle of the brown bear, the exhibition leaves no stone unturned and is a real treat for the senses.

Although a number of smaller sections are worth a quick glance, namely, those on religion, reindeer husbandry and the resettlement of the Skolt Sámi who fled from Petsamo to Inari after the end of World War II, you should continue your visit outside where, during the summer months, you can wander at leisure around a whole host of traditional wooden Sámi homes and outbuildings which survived the war years only to fall into neglect and disrepair. Moved to the museum in the early 1960s, the dwellings form a key part of local Sámi culture, both from reindeer-herding Sámi and the fishing community of Inarijärvi, and cover a 7 hectare (17 acre) site behind the museum building.

Other than the Siida museum, there's little else to detain you in the village itself, though, before you drive on, be sure to have a look inside the row of handicraft stores you will find on the main road opposite the tourist office, in particular Sápmi Duodji (☺ *daily Jun–Aug 09.00–20.00; rest of year Tue–Sat 10.00–17.00*) which has a wide range of tasteful souvenirs.

**Activities: hiking and lake cruises** Beginning from Sarviniementie (see map page 122), a short stroll of 2.5km will take you the beginning of the worthwhile **hiking trail** (4.5km one way) north to the **Pielpajärvi wilderness church**, built beside Lake Inari in the 1750s and now abandoned. The path negotiates an area of old-growth pine forest on its way to the church and climbs to a modest height of 141m; although it is a straightforward hike to the church, take extra care if it is wet as the path (indicated by yellow marks on the trees) can be extremely slippery. To return it is simply a question of retracing your steps, or continuing southeast from the church for a further 2.5km, to reach the inlet, Pielpavuono, and the landing stage for the summer boat that plys the waters of the lake. Check departure times before setting out at the tourist office (or call the telephone numbers listed below) if you intend to return by boat.

Just over the bridge from the museum you will find a small harbour from where the vessel makes two-hour **lake cruises** (✆ *0400 879 203 &* ✆ *0400 295 731;* ☺ *Jun to mid-Sep 1–2 daily;* €*15*) around the island-studded Inarijärvi, calling in at Pielpavuonio to pick up hikers from the wilderness church. Alternatively, fishing trips are available at a cost of €40–60 depending on the number of participants.

In winter, exhilirating **snowmobile tours** across the lake can be booked from Villa Lanca (see above), opposite the tourist office, for around €115 per person.

**NORTH FROM INARI: UTSJOKI** From Inari there's a choice of routes north: Route 92 cuts northwest for the Norwegian border and Karasjok (see below), whereas Route 4 continues north to Utsjoki (Ohcejohka in Sámi), which holds the title of the northernmost municipality in the European Union. Indeed, when Finland joined the EU in 1995, Utsjoki felt so neglected by Helsinki, let alone Brussels, that there were calls for the district to cede from Finland and join Norway across the Tana river and outside the Union. This is the only area in Finland where Sámi are in the majority and, hence, throughout the village you will hear various Sámi dialects in use, rather than Finnish, as the lingua franca. Although there's little to see in Utsjoki itself, the surrounding scenery more than compensates: the tiny settlement is dominated by the holy fell known as Áiligas (342m), a Germanic loanword referring to the sacred, which was once a place of sacrifice to the reindeer spirits, *seiddi*.

**Hiking trails** The main reason to come to Utsjoki is to go hiking. During the summer months, there's an enjoyable 10km marked trail to **Mantojärvi Lake**, south of the village, where there's a church and a few old timber cabins which once served as overnight places to stay for people who'd travelled here to attend church. The path starts at Utsjoki before climbing in order to later descend towards the lake.

Another more challenging marked trail (64km long) begins at Kenespahta, 20km south of Utsjoki, and leads through the Kevo canyon inside the **Keno Nature Reserve** (Kevon luonnonpuisto), which is sandwiched between Routes 4 and 92 southwest of Utsjoki, terminating at Sulaoja, 10km east of Karigasniemi. There's only one overnight cabin on the trail so you must have your own tent with you. Ask at the hotel (see below) for details of the precise routes.

**Getting there** Utsjoki lies at the confluence of the rivers Utsjoki and Tana. Route 4 runs south through the village towards Inari and doubles as the main street. You will find virtually all the services Utsjoki has to offer on this road.

🏠 **Where to stay** At the northern end of the village, just before the bridge to Norway, a right turn leads to the village's main place to stay, **Hotel Luossajohka** (↘ *016 321 2100;* e *info@luossajohka.fi; www.luossajohka.fi; $$$$*), which has a choice of cosy double rooms overlooking the River Tana. The hotel can fix up **salmon fishing** in the river and has a summer sauna on the shore. Alternatively, back on the main road, **Camping Lapinkylä** (↘ *016 677 396*) has cabins (*$$*).

✗ **Where to eat and drink** The best place to eat in the village is at the **hotel restaurant**, which serves up local specialities such as freshly caught fish from the River Tana. Opposite the campsite, there's an unnamed **café** – look out for the Finnish sign *Kahvila Käsitöitä*, meaning 'café, handicrafts' (⊕ *Mon–Fri 09.00–17.00*), which serves light snacks. **Gaissane** is a bar and café, opposite the Shell station and the post office near the bridge, which has lunch (⊕ *Mon–Fri 11.00–15.00*) as well as pizzas (*15.00–21.00 Wed–Fri & 18.00–21.00 on Sat*). As most of these places are only open in summer, it is definitely worth ringing ahead out of season to see exactly what is open – if anything. In addition to the above, there are two **supermarkets** selling provisions and two fuel stations, where, incidentally, both petrol and diesel are considerably cheaper than across the border in Norway.

### Moving on from Utsjoki
A daily **bus** runs from Utsjoki at 12.05 to Inari and Ivalo, arriving at 14.10 and 14.50 respectively. In the opposite direction, by crossing into Norway on foot over the Tana bridge, it is possible to pick up a Norwegian bus to either Karasjok or Kirkenes. Services operate in both directions on Monday, Wednesday, Friday and Sunday. Timings are approximate: for Kirkenes the bus reaches the bridge at about 14.00 (*Mon & Wed*) or 16.00 (*Fri & Sun*); for Karasjok the bus comes at around 11.00.

### NORTHWEST FROM INARI: KARASJOK
Leaving Inari, Route 92 forges a lonely way along the eastern stretches of the **Finnmarksvidda plateau**. As you finally descend the barren, windswept heights of the plateau, passing the border settlement of Karigasniemi, the pine and birch trees very slowly start to reappear and a lone television transmitter can be spotted in the distance – sure signs that civilisation is not far away. Nestling in a wooded river valley and better known to the local indigenous population as Karasjok. **Karasjok** is Norway's Sámi capital, home to 3,000 people, seat of the Sámi parliament, base for NRK's Sámi Radio and the true heartland of the Sámi language. As you wander around the streets and pop in and out of the handful of shops here, you will quickly hear that Sámi is the dominant tongue (eight out of ten people speak it), recognisable, even to the untrained ear, by its soft guttural nature and total lack of sing-song tones so prevalent in Norwegian. To attend church on Sundays, in particular, and for other important occasions, such as meetings or Sámi holidays, local people don their *gákti*, or, traditional costume, nowadays a sign of pride and belonging. Unlike many other villages further north, the Sámi here are in the majority and there's a real sense of a thriving community living comfortably within the Norwegian state rather than struggling to assert their identity against it.

### Getting there
Karasjok sits around a kink in the river and is an important crossroads in this part of Norwegian Lapland. It comprises three main roads: the E6, Porsangerveien, which enters the village from Lakselv (74km) to the north, transmuting into Kautokeinoveien (Route 92), beyond the main roundabout, and continuing west towards Kautokeino (130km); Tanaveien, the continuation of the E6 northeast towards Tana Bru (182km), which heads down the hill from the main roundabout towards the main shopping area and another roundabout; from where,

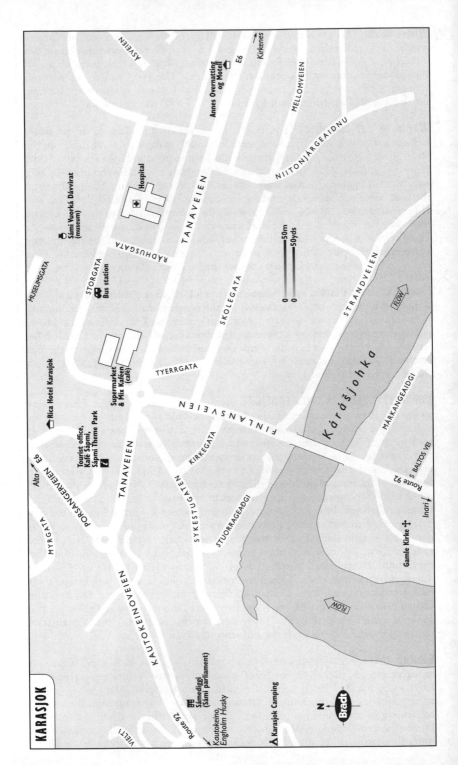

KARASJOK

Bradt

Finlandsveien, Route 92, crosses the river and heads southeast for the Finnish border at Karigasniemi (18km) and on to Inari (116km). Incidentally, Karasjok is the coldest place in Norway: during a particularly severe cold snap in January 1999, the mercury plummeted to a mind-boggling –51.2°C.

**Tourist information** The tourist office (↘ *78 46 88 02;* e *post@karasjokinfo.no; www.karasjokinfo.no;* ⊕ *Jun–mid-Aug 09.00–19.00 daily; mid to late Aug 09.00–16.00 daily; rest of year Mon–Fri 09.00–16.00*) is beside the gaggle of handicraft stores and workshops at Porsangerveien 1, adjacent to the Rica hotel (see below).

**Where to stay** For somewhere to stay choices are limited to **Engholm Husky** (see below); the modern pile **Rica Hotel Karasjok** (↘ *78 46 74 00;* e *rica.hotel.karasjok@rica.no; www.rica.no;* $$$$$$/$$$$$), Porsangerveien 1; the cheap and cheerful **Annes Overnatting og Motell** (↘ *78 46 64 32;* $$$$), Tanaveien 31, heading out towards Kirkenes; and all-year **Karasjok Camping** (↘ *78 46 61 35;* e *halonen@online.no*), which has cabins ($$), 1km or so after the Sámediggi and off the Kautokeino road.

**Where to eat and drink** When it comes to eating, your best bet is the upmarket restaurant inside the **Rica hotel**, which serves up top-notch Arctic delicacies such as fillet of reindeer with lingonberries (315kr), garlic roast monkfish (250kr) and bacon and leek gratinated salmon (249kr). For lighter meals, there are two choices: **Kafé Sápmi** in the same building as the tourist office, which serves snacks and sandwiches, or, the **Mix Kafeen** (free internet access), at Storgatan 1 (down the hill from the roundabout outside the Sápmi theme park and behind the Co-op supermarket), which closes at 17.00 (⊕ *Sat 15.00; closed Sun*).

**The village** Karasjok's attractions are subtle. While there's a certain pleasure to be gained in walking the streets and watching local people go about their daily lives, taking in one or both of the village's museums will give you a deeper understanding of Sámi life. It is best to start with **Sápmi** (*www.sapmi.no; same hours as the tourist office; 100kr*), a sort of multimedia Sámi theme park, which aims to provide visitors with an insight into local culture and history, predominantly through a creatively produced film show. Housed in the same building as the tourist office, the Stálubákti (Sámi for 'mountain spirit') magic **theatre** is the main attraction: in a specially created cinema complete with artificial northern lights in the ceiling, this slick presentation introduces visitors to recent technological and global changes that have affected the Sámi way of life (the use of snowmobiles and helicopters, for example, in reindeer husbandry) as well as providing a fascinating insight into the ancient myths and beliefs that have shaped their community. Immediately outside the cinema, you will find examples of traditional Sámi dwellings: the *siida* (Sámi camp or settlement) consisting of a summertime *lávvu* (tent) and the more substantial winter *goahti* (turfhut). A elderly local Sámi couple are on hand in the summer months to demonstrate their daily chores and there's even a couple of resident reindeer who seem resigned to being used for lassoo practice.

**Sámi Vuorká Dávvirat: Sámi Museum** (*also signed in Norwegian: De Samiske Samlinger; www.samimuseum.com;* ⊕ *Mar–Oct 09.00–15.00 daily; Nov–Feb Mon–Fri 09.00–15.00; 75kr*) Sadly, Karasjok's other museum, the Sámi Vuorká Dávvirat located on the other side of the Rica hotel at Mari Boine geaidnu 17, is not a patch on Sápmi (nor for that matter, the Siida museum just over the border in Inari in Finland). However, if traditional costumes are your thing, you are in luck; the museum is stuffed full of them. From ornately decorated wedding costumes to red-and-blue

Sunday best, they are all here, neatly hung in glass cabinets for your delight and delectation. The English-language labelling is at pains to point out that the *gákti* varies even within a particular region, though, to be honest, the significance is likely to be lost on the uninitiated. More interestingly, the wearing of traditional costume was already becoming less common in the 1920s when men in Karasjok began donning Western-style hats in preference to more traditional Sámi headgear. Although the museum displays a series of old wooden tools, bowls and axes, there's little reason to linger. Immediately outside, you will find a collection of traditional Sámi wooden buildings as well as a series of pits in the ground used to hunt wild reindeer between 2900 and 800 BC.

**Sámediggi: the Sámi parliament** (*Sametinget in Norwegian;* ↘ *78 47 40 00;* ⊕ *Mon–Fri 09.00–15.30*) More engaging is the Sámediggi just beyond the roundabout on Kautokeinoveien, the world's first indigenous parliament opened in 1989, housed in a striking building in the form of a semi-circle with wooden façades and triangular points in the form of a Sámi *lávvu*. In addition to gawping at the building's unusual construction, the main reason to venture here is to browse through the impressive number of English-language books held in the parliament's extensive library, seemingly everything from information on how to milk a reindeer to a children's school atlas in Sámi is on the shelves. There's a handy **café** to the right of the library, which, itself, is located behind the reception desk.

**Gamle kirke: the Old Church** The only other sight to speak of in Karasjok is the Gamle kirke (Old Church), on the south side of the river, about 100m over the bridge off Route 92 towards Finland. Located on a wide plain near the bend in the river, this evocative wooden structure with hipped roof, turret and steeple, dating from 1807, was the only building left standing in the village after World War II and is consequently the oldest church in Norwegian Lapland. The Gamle kirke soon proved too small, though, for the needs of an expanding village and in 1974 a modern church was built on the steep slope to the north of the river.

**Activities from Karasjok** After your fill of culture, Karasjok makes a good base from which to explore the unspoilt nature in this corner of Norwegian Lapland. One of the best places to arrange activities in the vicinity is **Engholm Husky** (↘ *78 46 71 66 & 91 58 66 25;* e *post@engholm.no; www.engholm.no*), a husky farm and adventure centre 7km west of Karasjok, on the Kautokeino road (Route 92). Run by the enterprising Swede, Sven Engholm, who moved here from his native Malmö, 2,000km to the south, in the early 1980s, this riverside retreat offers just about any activity you'd care to mention. In winter Sven runs self-drive **dog sled tours** ranging from one to ten days or, alternatively, the chance to ride as a passenger on a dog sled. Departure dates for the tours vary, as do prices (*day tours from 1,100kr*), but full details are available on the Engholm website. Other options include cross-country **skiing**, or the rare opportunity to follow a Sámi family with their **reindeer** on their spring migration to the Arctic Ocean – once again, full details are available online. In summer, there's **horseriding** or **trekking** with huskies who will carry your pack. Pickups are available from Karasjok (75kr) as well as from nearby airports.

Staying here is a real treat. Hand built and decorated by Sven, stay in snug two to three berth **cabins** (\$\$ *per cabin plus 200kr pp*); showers and toilets are in a separate building where breakfast is served. Between June and August Engholm Husky is the official **youth hostel** for Karasjok; reserve a dorm bed and you will get a bed (\$) in one of the cabins sharing with up to four others.

In addition to a sauna and free wireless internet, the site includes a traditional Sámi turfhut, offering the chance to sit on reindeer skins around an open fire and enjoy an Arctic dinner (advance reservation required).

**Moving on from Karasjok** Karasjok lies on the Hammerfest–Kirkenes bus route: there are four buses every week to Kirkenes (*Mon, Wed, Fri & Sun*), and a daily service to Hammerfest via Lakselv and Skaidi (change here for Alta). If you are planning to take the bus to Kautokeino, it needs careful planning: there's just one service on Fri and another on Sun. Karasjok is connected to Finland by a daily bus which runs via Inari, Ivalo and Sodankylä to Rovaniemi. The bus station is on Storgata, behind the Co-op supermarket off Tanaveien.

*Scots pine*

*Globe at the North Cape*

# 7

# Norwegian Lapland: Tromsø to Kirkenes

A highly indented coastline of barren, tundra fells backed by monumental fjords, towering snow-capped mountains and rocky, windswept islands, makes Norwegian Lapland one of the most scenically rewarding places to travel in the whole of Europe. Quite unlike the densely forested heartlands of Swedish and Finnish Lapland where spruce and pine trees dominate the landscape, these coastal lands at the top of Europe, buffeted by the Arctic winds, are either completely void of trees or slavishly support a few dwarf species that have become specially adapted to the ferocious climate. It is a place where snow storms and blizzards sweeping in off the Arctic Ocean can persist for days during the long, dark winter, yet equally a land of exquisite beauty in spring and summer when the delicate flowers of the Arctic burst forth, profiting from the relentless 24-hour daylight of the **Midnight Sun**. The unforgiving geography of Norwegian Lapland is at its most awe-inspiring in the west, where the mountain chain reaches dizzying heights of 1,700m. Further east, the landscapes become less agitated, slowly falling away, to be replaced with plateaux of grey, weatherbeaten rocks which slip effortlessly into the steely waters of the Arctic Ocean. Travel here is as rewarding as it is circuitous; often the quickest, shortest and most enjoyable way between two points is by boat, and it is with complete justification that the Hurtigruten **coastal ferry**, which plies the waters off the coast of Norwegian Lapland, claims to be the most beautiful sea voyage in the world.

Handsome **Tromsø** with its streets of old timber houses and 360° views of serrated peaks and mountaintops is well worth visiting. Linked directly to Sweden by air and Finland by bus, it is an easy place to reach from elsewhere in Lapland. The town trades on its links with the Arctic and boasts a couple of excellent themed museums, in addition to an eclectic bar and restaurant scene – unusual for somewhere so far north. To the east, **Alta**'s prehistoric **rock carvings** are exceptional, making the pint-sized town a worthwhile stop on the long journey to the **North Cape**, *the* destination in Norwegian Lapland. This remote, windswept headland at the very top of Europe has been big on the tourist trail for years. Souvenirs that bear that magic name and logo are much sought after and carry particular prestige – come here and be sure to buy the T-shirt to prove it.

From Europe's most northerly point, everywhere naturally lies south, albeit rather unsatisfyingly. However, take heart, another last place awaits: **Kirkenes**. A grubby former mining town hard on the border with Russia, Kirkenes is the end of the road. You're now as far east as Istanbul in Turkey and your nearest neighbour of any significance is Murmansk. Kirkenes's attraction is its proximity to Russia: there are daily buses and planes across the border as well as boat trips down the river which forms the border between Russia and Norway. Be sure to have arranged your visa in advance if you fancy popping over to see the Russian Bear.

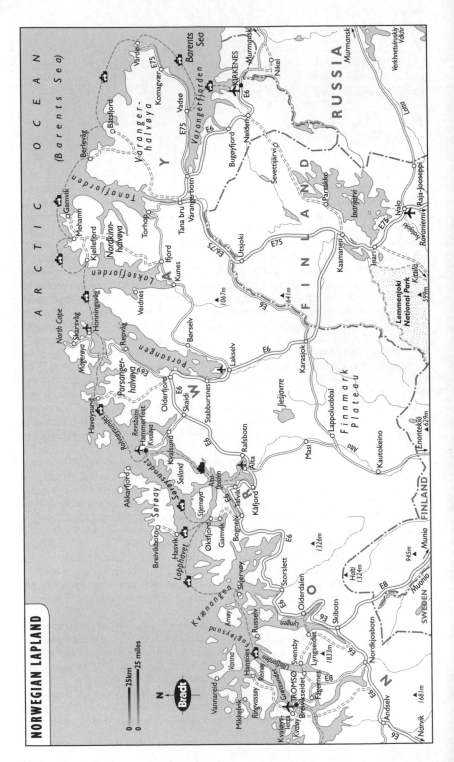

# NORWEGIAN LAPLAND

The 'Gateway to the Arctic' as the city thrills in billing itself, Tromsø is one of the undisputed highlights of Norwegian Lapland. Although geographically well out on a limb, it is worth making a special effort to get there to enjoy some rare urban sophistication, the like of which you won't find for miles around. Once known, quite ridiculously, as the Paris of the North, Tromsø can, nevertheless, boast a sophisticated café and restaurant culture, top hotels and several big name stores; it has a couple of superb museums which will no doubt whet your appetite to learn more about the Arctic and maybe even to go there. A new flight between London Stansted and Tromsø (see Getting There, below), which will operate twice-weekly all year round, looks set to introduce Tromsø to the outside world and make direct access to Lapland much easier.

With a population of 65,000, Tromsø is the second biggest town in Lapland, but if you talk to locals you will soon discover that they don't consider themselves to live in Lapland (despite the embarrassing fact that the town uses a reindeer as its emblem). For the record, Tromsø is the capital of Troms, a Norwegian province which is further north than both Sweden's Lappland and Finland's Lappi, two administrative regions, which, for people who live there, most definitely *are* part of Lapland. For most Norwegians living here, Norwegian Lapland doesn't begin until they cross the provincial border into Finnmark (the region which includes Alta, Karasjok, Kautokeino and all points east to Kirkenes). Most visitors seem happy to let the Norwegians fight it out among themselves, since, as far as they are concerned, everything above the Arctic Circle is Lapland – Swedish, Finnish or Norwegian.

**SOME HISTORY** Tromsø first enters the history books in 1252 when the northernmost church in the world was constructed here, in order to secure the surrounding coastal areas for Norway. Indeed, until the late 18th century, Tromsø consisted of little more than a church, its vicarage and several outlying farms and simple dwellings. In 1794, with a population of barely 80 souls, Tromsø was granted town status in an attempt to promote free trade across the north. Freed from restrictive trade practices previously imposed by Bergen and Trondheim, who, until then, had held a monopoly on trade with the north, the town began to prosper.

Despite suffering a naval attack by the British in 1812 during the Napoleonic Wars, the town continued to grow, largely due to the lucrative hunting of whales, seals and walrus off Spitsbergen which began in 1820; the harbour was often full of British, Dutch, German and Russian ships drawn here by the rich pickings in the Arctic Ocean and, by 1850, Tromsø had overtaken Hammerfest in the rush to harvest the waters of the north. Tromsø's links with the Arctic took a new turn in the early 20th century when expeditions to the North by Roald Amundsen, Fridtjof Nansen and Umberto Nobile departed from here. Indeed, it was from Tromsø that Amundsen set off by seaplane in search of his missing Italian competitor, Nobile, and other members of the Italia Expedition in 1928; Nobile returned, Amundsen did not. There is a statue in his memory erected in Tromsø harbour.

In May 1940, Tromsø served as the capital of free Norway for several weeks, welcoming the king and the Norwegian government, who fled here from Oslo as the resistance in the south showed signs of collapse. However, on 7 June 1940 they were forced to flee to England, continuing their fight against Germany in exile and urging the Norwegian people to resist the occupying forces in broadcasts on the BBC. Unlike many other places in the north of Norway, Tromsø escaped the

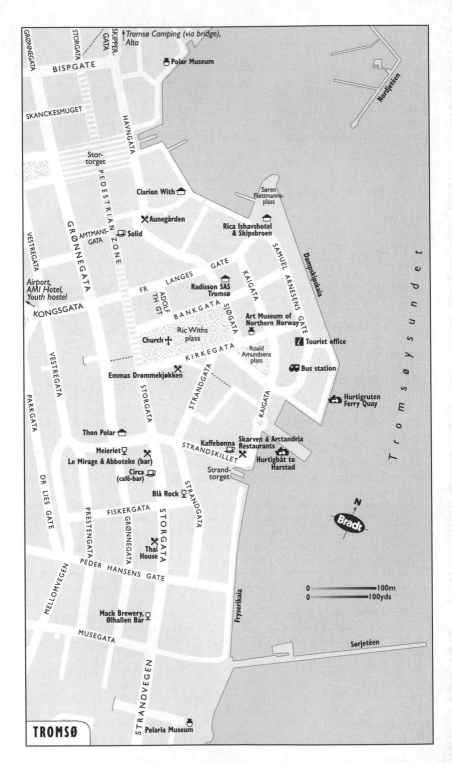

TROMSØ

scorched earth policy of the retreating German forces, which laid vast stretches of Lapland to waste. The post-war years were good to Tromsø: in 1964 the airport was opened transforming communications with this part of the country in one stroke and in 1972 the university was founded with specialist departments of Sámi studies and marine biology. Today the town is not only a service centre for the surrounding fishing and agricultural settlements but it is the new home of the Norwegian Polar Institute and is even hoping to host the Winter Olympics in 2018.

**GETTING THERE** Handling over half a million passengers every year, Tromsø **airport** (airport code TOS) is an excellent way of reaching this part of Lapland. There are now direct year-round flights with Norwegian (www.norwegian.no) from London Stansted to Tromsø on Saturdays and Tuesdays, thus avoiding the necessity to change planes to reach Lapland. There are direct **flights** from Oslo with SAS and Norwegian as well as from Kiruna and Luleå in Sweden with Barents Airlink. The Norwegian airline Widerøe operates to Tromsø from various smaller airports across the north of Norway including Alta, Andenes (Vesterålen Islands), Hammerfest, Kirkenes, Narvik and Stokmarknes (Vesterålen Islands). The flight to and from Kirkenes, for example, is well worth considering since it will save a one-way drive of 800km. Regular shuttle buses (45kr) run into town from the airport, terminating at the Rica Ishavshotel by the harbour; a taxi from the airport costs 130kr. Coming from the south, the Hurtigruten **ferry** arrives at the quay in the town centre at 14.30; from the north it docks at 23.45. The Hurtigbåt **express passenger boat** from Harstad arrives 100m from the tourist office at an adjacent quay. All **buses** stop outside the tourist office, close to the ferry quay.

**TOURIST INFORMATION** The tourist office (↘ 77 61 00 00; *www.destinasjontromso.no;* ☺ *Sep–late May Mon–Fri 09.00–16.00, Sat 10.00–14.00; late May to Aug Mon–Fri 08.30–18.00, Sat & Sun 10.00–17.00*), Kirkegata 2, is a two-minute walk from the ferry quay.

   **Free internet** is available at the library on Grønnegata, though there's often a queue and you may need to book a slot. Otherwise, there are terminals at Mejeriet café at Grønnegata 37–39 and at Darklight at Stortorget 1 – all three places are in the centre of town.

**WHERE TO STAY** Hotel accommodation in Norwegian Lapland can be expensive and of relatively poor quality. Hotels, particularly in the smaller towns, are sometimes rather old 1960s buildings and consequently rather tired. Not so in Tromsø. Here, a cluster of great new hotels right on the harbourside, means there's plenty of choice and standards are universally high. In short, if you are going to splurge and treat yourself, do it here.

🏠 **Radisson SAS Tromsø** Sjøgata 7; ↘ 77 60 00 00; e reservations.tromso@radissonsas.com; www.radissonsas.com. Undergoing renovation at the time of writing, this hotel is one of the tallest buildings in town & looks set to get even bigger. Offering all the creature comforts associated with a leading chain – plush rooms, tasteful décor, free high-speed internet – as well as a truly amazing sauna suite with fabulous views over the harbour from the saunas themselves. $$$$$$$/$$$$$
🏠 **Rica Ishavshotel** Fredrik Langesgata 2; ↘ 77 66 64 00; e rica.ishavshotel@rica.no; www.rica.no.

The best hotel in town enjoying a wonderful harbourside location. Built to resemble the funnel & upper decks of a ship, this extravagant hotel is all chrome, glass & wood both inside & out. Rooms are generously proportioned, tastefully carpeted & contain nice touches of woodwork. Ask for one overlooking the harbour & it is hard to think of anywhere you'd rather be. The sumptuous b/fast buffet is one of the best you will find. There's free wireless internet access for all guests with their own laptop. $$$$$$$/$$$$$
🏠 **Clarion With** Sjøgata 35–37; ↘ 77 66 42 00;

℮ booking@with.no; www.with.no. Elegance comes at a price in this chi-chi harbourfront hotel built on land reclaimed from the sea. Old-world charm meets modern Scandinavian design, here, in a perfect location right on the quayside. $$$$$$/$$$$

⌂ **Viking** Grønnegata 18–20; ☎ 77 64 77 30; ℮ booking@viking-hotell.no; www.viking-hotell.no. This hotel has recently smartened up its act with newly renovated Nordic-style rooms & state-of-the-art bathrooms. Accommodation is a little on the cramped side but prices are reasonable for the quality on offer. $$$$$

⌂ **AMI** Skolegata 24; ☎ 77 62 10 00; ℮ email@amihotel.no; www.amihotel.no. A pleasant mid-range hotel with comfortable, though simply furnished rooms, overlooking the town from a hilly location several blocks up behind the harbour. $$$/$$

⌂ **Thon Polar** Grønnegata 45; ☎ 77 75 17 00;

℮ polar@thonhotels.no; www.thonhotels.no. Smart budget rooms from this chain, which, at its best (like here) offers good value for money. The building occupies 2 buildings opposite each other right in the heart of the centre. A sensible choice. $$$

Δ **Tromsø Camping** (approximately 50 cabins plus camping) Tromsdalen; ☎ 77 63 80 37; ℮ post@tromsocamping.no; www.tromsocamping.no. ⊕ Open all year. Camping & a choice of cabins of varying sizes & standards. $$ *for a 2-bed cabin with hotplate but no bathroom.*

⌂ **Tromsø Vandrarhjem** Åsgårdveien 9; ☎ 77 65 76 28; ℮ tromso.hostel@vandrerhjem.no; www.vandrerhjem.no/tromso. Extremely basic hostel which operates summertime only (⊕ mid-June to mid-Aug). Accommodation is in 2- to 4-berth rooms. Take bus #26 towards Giæverbukta & get off at the stop called Åsgårdveien (about 15min). Use of communal kitchen. *Dorm bed* $; *dbl* $$.

## ✗ WHERE TO EAT AND DRINK

Throughout Scandinavia, the distinction between cafés, bars and restaurants is rarely clear cut. With a relatively small customer base, most places tend to offer a bit of everything in order to make enough money to survive and, quite unknown in many other countries, to pay their staff respectable wages. In Tromsø, things are a little different due to the size of the town. However, most of the cafés and bars listed below also serve food.

## ✗ Restaurants

✗ **Arctandria** Strandtorget 1. High-class Arctic specialities in this elegant restaurant (upstairs from Skarven): try the starter of reindeer carpaccio (95kr), which is truly spectacular. If your conscience allows, there's also whale steak with vegetables, almond potatoes & cranberries for 215kr.

✗ **Aunegården** Sjøgata 29. Housed in a listed timber building in the centre, the cuisine is a cross between Norwegian & Mediterranean. Lunch salads from 124kr, soup 79kr, chicken pasta 135kr, & broccoli & cauliflower gratin 127kr. For dinner there's goulash soup for 95kr, fish pasta 145kr or fillet of pork marinated in maple syrup & mustard 172kr. The homemade cakes are legendary.

✗ **Emmas Drømmekjøkken** Kirkegata 8. ⊕ Closed Sun. Recognised by France's Chaîne des Rotisseurs in

2006, the exceptional cuisine here is Tromsø's finest. Fish mains from 272kr, for example, loin of cod in soya & lime sauce with baked garlic; & meat mains from 269kr, such as fried schnitzel or fillet of venison (325kr). The tarte tatin is to die for (128kr). If you fancy pushing the boat out there's a 3-course set menu of Arctic specialities for 750kr.

✗ **Skarven** Strandtorget 1. Downstairs from Arctandria, this modern brasserie offers an exceptionally good value lunch salad buffet (89kr) as well as soups (89kr) & a delicious fish stew (89kr). The prices are exceptionally good, the food excellent.

✗ **Thai House** Storgata 22. ⊕ from 15.00 daily. All your (expensive) Thai favourites from 190kr.

## Cafés and bars

♀ **Abboteke** Storgata 42. Tromsø's best (though not the cheapest) selection of cocktails, whiskies & brandies. It is a fun, easy-going (& rather cramped) place with music – predominantly 1960s & 1970s soul & jazz – attracting Tromsø's movers & shakers.

♀ **Blå Rock** Strandgata 14–16. The place for

rock'n'roll. Signed pictures (& guitars) on the walls from greats like Elvis, the Rolling Stones & even R.E.M. The largest selection of different beers in town. Also serves burgers.

♀ **Circa** Storgata 36. A chilled café-bar popular with the city's students offering occasional live music, when the place really buzzes.

⫸ **Kaffebønna** Strandtorget 1. Alongside the Skarven complex of restaurants, this specialist coffee shop is where you will find Tromsø's best coffee & a mouth-watering selection of cakes & pastries.

⫸ **Le Mirage** Storgata 42. A classic Mediterranean-style café serving up a variety of light dishes as well as more substantial evening fare such as *filet mignon* in pepper sauce for 168kr.

⫸ **Meieriet** Grønnegata 37–39. The largest & most popular café open from b/fast until the early hours of the morning when it mutates more into a bar than a café. Internet available.

♀ **Skarven Bar** Strandtorget 1. One of the best watering holes in town, especially when the sun's shining, when people drape themselves over the outdoor terrace taking the rays. Soft music & an altogether agreeable place for a quiet drink & chat.

♀ **Skipsbroen** Fredrik Langesgata 2. Inside the Rica Ishavshotel, this bar occupies the glass tower designed to look like a ship's funnel at the seaward end of the Rica building. With floor-to-ceiling windows it offers great views of the harbour. Drinks, though, are pricey.

⫸ **Solid** Storgata 73. Perfectly located on Tromsø's main pedestrian street, this place is a café by day serving food until 18.00: tuna or Greek salad for 92kr & pasta dishes for 96kr; by evening it is a bar with the cheapest shorts in town (35–66kr).

♀ **Ølhallen** Storgata 4. ⏰ 09.00–17.00. Closed Sun. This noisy beer hall is a Tromsø institution, attracting the city's hardened drinkers from early in the morning. It may not be the most genteel place for a drink but it certainly shows a darker side to Tromsø's (& northern Scandinavia's) character.

**THE CITY** It is a pleasure to wander around the streets and harbour area in Tromsø. Since the city was relatively untouched by World War II, there are plenty of old timber buildings, painted a mêlée of reds, greens and yellows, to please the eye – and, quite unusually, for a town in Lapland, there's life in the streets in the evening. Although the city has a sizeable population, the centre is not big and is easily negotiated on foot. In fact, you can walk from one side of the central shopping area to the other in just over a quarter of an hour. It is a good idea to start your wandering down by the harbour, which is where most of the main hotels are located; from here you can head inland to take in the main pedestrian street before continuing west to one of the town's most enjoyable museums, Polaria. In the town centre, the main sight is the **domkirke**, Tromsø cathedral, built in 1861, which dominates the surrounding streets from its imposing position in Stortorget off Kirkegata; for what it is worth, this is the northernmost Protestant cathedral in the world. The construction of the handsome timber structure was part funded by the town's merchants who had grown rich on the trapping trade in the Arctic.

## Polarmuseet: the Polar Museum
(*Søndre Tollbugate 11; www.polarmuseum.no*; ⏰ *daily mid-June to mid-Aug 10.00–19.00; mid-Aug to Sep & March to mid-June 11.00–17.00; Oct–Feb 11.00–15.00; 50kr*) Enjoying a prime location on the harbourfront, Tromsø's Polarmuseet is housed in a former customs warehouse dating from 1830 and contains some of the most fascinating exhibits you will find in Lapland. It is fitting that Tromsø has an entire museum dedicated to its links with the Arctic, since the town owes much of its prosperity today to the hunters and trappers who based themselves here during the first half of the 19th century. Indeed, the museum kicks off with an exhibition about trapping in the Arctic; beside the rather unsavoury mock display of a stuffed reindeer being slaughtered, there's information about the early Spitsbergen expeditions whose main target over a 25-year period was walruses. The hunts were ended when walrus numbers in Spitsbergen began to plummet. In the 20th century the focus turned to polar bears and Arctic foxes; the latter were trapped on the inhospitable Norwegian island of Jan Mayen, the former on Spitsbergen. Sealing from ships was a common practice and began in Norway in the mid-1800s (it continued for around a hundred years) when seal skins were used to make shoes and rope and their blubber was boiled down to produce lighting and heating oil. Incidentally, a similar practice using pilot

whale blubber was once commonplace in the Faroe Islands. Room 2 on the ground floor is given over to the tough life of trappers and hunters who lived on Svalbard in the 17th and 18th centuries. Although **Svalbard** (Spitsbergen) was known during medieval times and appears in the Icelandic sagas by its understated Norse name, Svalbard (literally 'cold coast'), the islands were discovered by Dutch explorer, Willem Barentz, in 1596 who sailed here in search of the Northeast Passage to China. His crew gave the islands their more common name, Spitsbergen, meaning 'pointed mountains'. Finds from Barentz's camp from the time, such as knives, gunpowder measures and an oil lamp, are on display. More remarkable, however, are the artefacts from a Russian trapping station in the west coast settlement of Russekeila, probably dating from the 1700s, including boatbuilding tools, a frame for drying socks and even a clay pipe.

Upstairs, one of the greatest explorers the world has ever known, **Roald Amundsen** (1872–1928), is given pride of place. After dropping out of university where he was studying medicine, Amundsen did everything possible to improve his qualifications as a polar explorer, first joining a sealing trip in the Arctic and then participating in an expedition to map the magnetic South Pole. It was during this voyage that he decided to lead an expedition to the **North Pole** through the Northwest Passage. Indeed, after buying the former sealing ship, *Gjøa*, in Tromsø in 1901, he sailed from Oslo (then called Christiania) to the North Pole where he would spend two years collecting data. On arrival in Nome in Alaska in 1906 the *Gjøa* became the first vessel to sail through the Northwest Passage. However, it is Amundsen's race against Britain's Captain Robert Scott to reach the **South Pole** that really earned him international fame. He and four of his men reached the Pole on 14 December 1911, over a month ahead of Scott's expedition, who died on their way back to base camp. Among a glorious selection of Amundsen's thermal underwear and other polar necessities, a series of evocative black and white photographs of the men and their expedition really bring the exhibition to life; the expressions on their faces clearly show the hardship they endured.

Amundsen's next goal was to reach the North Pole by air. In May 1926 he flew the airship, *Norge*, with an international crew of 16 members from Ny Ålesund in Spitsbergen across the Arctic Ocean and the North Pole, dropping the Norwegian, American and Italian flags at the Pole as they crossed to Alaska. Roald Amundsen had now planted the Norwegian flag on both Poles and sailed both the Northwest and Northeast Passage. Just two years later when news reached Amundsen that one of his former crew members, Italian Umberto Nobile, had crashed while returning from the North Pole in the airship, *Italia*, Amundsen set out from Tromsø in the flying boat, *Latham*, to search for the missing explorer. Tragically, although Nobile and eight of his men returned to safety, radio contact with Amundsen was soon lost and he and his crew were never seen again.

Another Norwegian legend, at least in Tromsø, is honoured upstairs: Henry Rudi, known to his friends as 'the polar bear king'. Henry spent his first winter on Svalbard in 1908, when he managed to kill no fewer than 90 polar bears. That was just the start of his dubious career, and over a 40-year period he was responsible for the deaths of 713 polar bears in Spitsbergen, Greenland and the Norwegian Arctic island of Bjørnøya. Admired across the country for his bravery, Rudi was awarded the king's medal of honour for his work in the Arctic. He died in 1970.

**Polaria Museum** (*Hjalmar Johansgata 12; www.polaria.no;* ⊕ *mid-May to mid-Aug 10.00–19.00 daily; mid-Aug to mid-May noon–17.00 daily; 90kr*) At the opposite end of town, the Polaria museum is an easy stroll of 10 minutes or so from the town centre; simply follow Storgata west past the Mack brewery (see below). Dedicated to the pristine nature of the Arctic, the museum's key exhibit is the absorbing

15-minute panoramic film of the flora and fauna of Spitsbergen. The film was mostly shot from the air by helicopter and when viewed on the five giant 180° surround-screens in the specially constructed cinema inside the museum, you get a dizzying sense that you are there, skimming across the tundra, banking hard round every mountain top, but it is the bearded seals in the museum's aquarium that really steal the show. You can get up close to them by walking through a glass tunnel which slices through their watery habitat. Several smaller tanks contain examples of much of the marine life of the Arctic – everything from cod to starfish.

## Macks ølbryggeri: the Mack brewery (*www.mack.no; tours: Mon–Thu 13.00; Jun–Aug also 15.00; 130kr*) You guessed it, yet another 'northernmost in the world' boast. This time the title goes to Macks ølbryggeri, the Mack brewery, established by local bigwig, Ludvig Mack, in 1877, and which still today operates as a family-run concern. The beer of choice across the whole of Norwegian Lapland, Mack really has established itself as a market leader over the years and, in an attempt to maintain its position, is constantly reinventing labels and slogans, championing its spurious links to the Arctic and the polar bear. Think what you will, it seems to work. Enjoyable tours of the brewery include a valuable half-litre of the golden nectar and a less than gorgeous badge.

## Nordnorsk kunstmuseum: the Art Museum of Northern Norway (*Sjøgata 1; www.museumsnett.no/nordnorsk-kunstmuseum;* ☉ *late Jun to late Aug Mon–Fri noon–18.00, Sat & Sun noon–17.00; late Aug to late Jun Tue–Fri 10.00–17.00, Sat & Sun noon–17.00; free*) A ten-minute walk back along Storgata, turning south into Kirkegata, will bring you to Tromsø's worthwhile Nordnorsk kunstmuseum. With northern Norway as the dominant theme, the museum hosts permanent and temporary exhibits of paintings and sculptures from the early 19th century to the present day. Though the museum's permanent collection is not especially large, it is buoyed up by frequent loans from other museums. All the big names in the world of northern Norwegian art are here though: Axel Revold, Willi Midelfart and Kjeld Gabriel Langfeld, to name but a few. Particularly pleasing is *Morgen* by Revold (1927), which portrays a naked boy lying by the fjord, dreamily gazing out over the awe-inspiring nature of his homeland. Look out, too, for *Laestadius Teaching the Laplanders* by François-Auguste Biard (1798–1882) for an artistic impression of the fur-clad revivalist preacher, Lars Levi Laestadius, and his work in Lapland, which is enough to put the fear of God into anyone.

**MOVING ON FROM TROMSØ** The Hurtigruten leaves from the quay beside the Rica hotel. Departure times are: 18.30 northbound for Hammerfest (arrival 05.15), Honningsvåg (arrival 11.45) for the North Cape, and Kirkenes, a total journey of 40 hours or so; southbound the Hurtigruten leaves at the unsociable hour of 01.30 for Harstad (arrival 08.00) and the Vesterålen and Lofoten islands. Incidentally, the Rica Ishavshotel has unofficially agreed to store luggage during the day free of charge for passengers leaving on the 01.30 departure. If you have a drink in the hotel while waiting for the boat, you will see it arrive outside and can make a last minute dash without waiting outside in the cold. The Hurtigbåt express passenger boats leave for Harstad three or four times daily (*Mon–Fri*) and twice daily at the weekend. The quay is adjacent to the Hurtigruten.

Bus #800 leaves the bus station outside the tourist office for **Narvik**, a four-hour journey (*several times daily: 06.20 Mon–Fri, 10.30 & 16.00 daily, & 20.20 Sun*). The Nord-Norgeekpressen, service #805, departs for **Alta** daily at 16.00, arriving at 22.30.

Between June and late September there is a daily bus to **Finland** departing at 07.30 and running via Kilpisjärvi (10.55 Finnish time), Muonio (13.55), Kittilä (15.25) and Rovaniemi (17.45).

**Heading east by road** Take one look at a road map of this part of Norway, and you will soon realise how difficult road transport can be. If you are heading east from Tromsø by car for Alta and destinations beyond, you will save yourself a drive of around 120km by using two car ferries to help you cross the fjords of Ullsfjorden and Lyngen, which, inconveniently, get in the way of all road journeys east, forcing the main highway, the E8, into a lengthy detour. Although it is no faster to take the ferries, and works out more expensive, it is more than worth it because the ferries not only break up a very long journey but they afford views of some of the most dramatic mountains in northern Norway. First, head out of Tromsø on the **E8** (synonomous with the E6 at this point) and then turn left at Fagernes onto **Route 91** heading for the first ferry from **Breivikeidet** to **Svensby**; departures are roughly hourly and take 20 minutes; car and driver 73kr. Once in Svensby continue on Route 91 heading east for the next ferry from **Lyngseidet** to **Olderdalen**; once again this ferry sails roughly hourly and is timed to connect with the arrival of the previous ferry into Svensby, giving you enough time to drive between the two; the crossing is 40 minutes and costs 102kr for a car and driver. From Olderdalen, continue by the E6 northeast to Alta, a distance of around 230km.

**Flights to Spitsbergen and all points east** Other than Oslo, Tromsø is the only place in Norway with direct flights to Spitsbergen. SAS operates regular services to the capital, Longyearbyen; full details about the islands and how to get there are contained in *Spitsbergen: the Bradt Travel Guide* by Andreas Umbreit, which is the definitive source of information on the Norwegian Arctic. Even if you are not detouring to Spitsbergen, it is well worth considering flying to destinations east of Tromsø since distances are comparable with similar journeys you might undertake to cross entire countries in central Europe, for example, Tromsø to Alta alone is 405km. The plucky Norwegian airline Widerøe (*www.wideroe.no*) operates to some extremely remote airstrips across the north of the country and has some attractively competitive fares if booked in advance.

## ALTA

Despite its dramatic setting at the head of the eponymous fjord, Alta is not one of Norwegian Lapland's most attractive towns. Post-war reconstruction has done the place few aesthetic favours and today Alta consists of a rash of ugly concrete blocks which loom either side of the main E6 as it weaves through the settlement over a distance of 2 or 3km. If there is a town centre it is the gaggle of ten or so streets which lie south of the E6 called **Alta Sentrum**. Here you will find Alta's pedestrianised shopping street, Markedsgata, lined with shops, restaurants and a couple of hotels as well as the main shopping centre, Alta Storsenter. From Alta Sentrum it is roughly 1.5km southwest along the main road, known as Altaveien, to the town's only other area of note, **Bossekop**. Equally architecturally challenged, this diminutive area of suburban streets was once home to Dutch whalers who settled here in the 17th century and gave the district its distinctly un-Norwegian name. Today, it is the location of the town's summer tourist office, a handy supermarket and a couple more hotels.

As drab as Alta itself may be, it does have a couple of saving graces. Indeed, one attraction is of world-class: the most extensive area of **prehistoric rock carvings** in northern Europe dating from between 6,000 and 2,000 years ago are to be found just outside the town centre. Now added to the UNESCO World Heritage List, the 5,000 carvings known as petroglyphs were carved into the coastal rocks at the head of Altafjorden by the area's first settlers and depict, among other things, the hunting of reindeer, elk and bear during the Stone Age. Alta is the location for

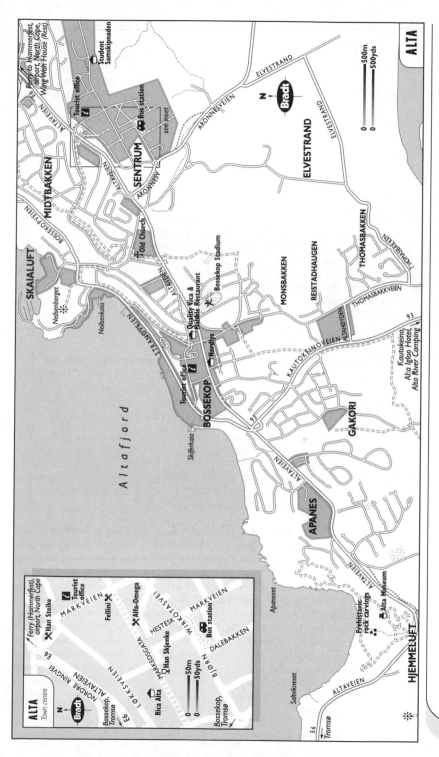

ALTA

**Ferry to Hammerfest, airport, North Cape, Wing Wah House (Rest)**

Student Samskipnaden

Tourist office

Bus station

see inset

SENTRUM

ALTAVEIEN

AROMNESV

ARONNESVEIEN

ELVESTRAND

ELVESTRAND

ELVESTRAND

ELVESTRAND

N

MIDTBAKKEN

BOSSEKOPVEIEN

Old Church

SKAIALUFT

Neilsenberget

Neilsenkaia

STRANDVEIEN

ALTAVEIEN

Quality Rica & Halide Restaurant

Bossekop Stadium

Nordlys

Tourist office

BOSSEKOP

Skiferkaia

A l t a f j o r d

KAUTOKEINOVEIEN

93

93

MONSBAKKEN

REISTADHAUGEN

THOMASBAKKEN

THOMASBAKKVEIEN

ALTAHØYDEN

THOMASBAKKEN

ELVESTRAND

**Kautokeino, Alfa Igloo Hotel, Alta River Camping**

GAKORI

93

ALTAVEIEN

APANES

ALTAVEIEN

Apaneset

Saltvikneset

ALTAVEIEN

Prehistoric rock carvings

Alta Museum

HJEMMELUFT

ALTAVEIEN

Tromsø

E6

N

500m
500yds

0
0

**ALTA**

---

**ALTA**
*Town centre*

Brack

N

NORDRE RINGVEI

ALTAVEIEN

E6

**Bossekop, Tromsø**

Han Steilke

Tourist office

MARKVEIEN

Fellini

Alfa-Omega

LØKSVEIEN

MARKEDSGATA

HESTESKOVEIEN

WIRKOTSVEI

Han Skjenke

BJØRN

Rica Alta

MARKVEIEN

Bus station

DALEBAKKEN

50m
50yds

0
0

**Bossekop, Tromsø**

141

another of Lapland's icehotels, the **Alta Igloo Hotel**, a smaller and altogether more agreeable version of the more commercialised Jukkasjärvi original in Sweden, which makes a highly unusual overnight accommodation choice in winter (see below).

**GETTING THERE** Alta is a major transport hub for this part of western Finnmark and sooner or later you are likely to wind up here. Direct **buses** run to Alta west from Tromsø, south from Kautokeino and east from Karasjok and Kirkenes. There are buses to and from Honningsvåg (change here for the North Cape) and Hammerfest to the north. All services call at the bus station between Markveien and Dalebakken in Alta Sentrum and buses to the east make a stop at the airport. Alta **airport** (code ALF) is useful for flights to and from Oslo with SAS and Norwegian as well as regional services to Tromsø, Kirkenes and a good few other smaller airstrips with Widerøe.

Although it is possible to **walk** from the airport into town (a distance of around 4km) by simply following the main E6 up the hill, there are a couple of buses that run into town: the town bus (Bybuss is displayed as the destination) runs roughly once an hour along the main road outside the airport or there are intermittent long-distance buses which call in at the airport; departure times are posted up inside the terminal building. There's a year-round passenger-only **ferry** between Alta and Hammerfest. Alta is 240km from the North Cape, 571km from Kirkenes and 405km from Tromsø.

**TOURIST INFORMATION** Alta has two tourist offices:

**Z** **Main year-round office** Parksenteret shopping centre in Alta Sentrum; ℑ 78 44 95 54; e infoalta@via.no; www.altatours.no; ⊕Mon–Fri 08.30–16.30, Sat 10.00–14.00
**Z** **Summer-only office** ℑ 78 44 50 50; email &

website as above; ⊕ Jun–Aug Mon–Fri 09.00–20.00, Sat & Sun 10.00–17.00. Located in the Bossekop shopping centre near the Co-op supermarket. This office offers internet access at a price of 25kr for 30mins.

Both offices are run by friendly, knowledgeable staff who can help out with booking accommodation and bus times.

**WHERE TO STAY** Alta has a choice of several central hotels as well as a number of campsites; it is worth booking ahead in summer when the town fills up with people breaking the long journey up to the North Cape.

🏠 **Alta Igloo Hotel** Alta Friluftspark; ℑ 78 43 33 78; e safari@alta-friluftspark.no; www.alta-igloo-hotel.no. Made entirely of snow & ice, the rooms here are just 6m² & contain nothing but a mattress, which sits on a wooden frame above a block of snow. Come here for the experience, not a good night's sleep. $$$$$$$.
🏠 **Quality Vica** Fogdebakken 6; ℑ 78 48 22 22; e booking@vica.no; www.vica.no. This homely hotel has the feel of a mountain lodge despite its location in Bossekop. The wood panelling & wallpaper is a little worn in places but this is still the pick of Alta's hotels offering a hearty b/fast. Free internet access. $$$$$$/$$$$
🏠 **Nordlys** Bekkefaret 3; ℑ 78 45 72 00; e e-post@nordlyshotell.no; www.nordlyshotell.no.

From the outside this place in Bossekop can't decide whether it belongs to 1970s suburbia or is actually a row of wooden pine chalets. The garish mix of styles, however, is outweighed by the rooms, which are comfortable & spacious. $$$$$
🏠 **Rica Alta** Løkkeveien 61; ℑ 78 48 27 00; e rica.hotel.alta@rica.no; www.rica.no. A vast, ugly, white hulk of a building, which looks too much like the architect's original plastic model for comfort. Inside rooms have an impersonal chain feel with wooden floors & Nordic décor. The central location helps outweigh the lack of charm. $$$$$/$$$$
🏠 **Student Samskipnaden** Follumsvei 33; ℑ 78 45 05 25; e firmapost@sif.hifm.no; www.sif.hifm.no. Cheap & cheerful accommodation

in student halls of residence available all year round. $$

Å **Alta River Camping** Steinfossen 5; ℄ 78 43 43 53; e post@alta-river-camping.no; http://alta-river-camping.no. The best of the town's campsites located 4km south of town beside the river on Route 93 towards Kautokeino. Cabins available. Open all year. $$

## ✖ WHERE TO EAT AND DRINK

✖ **Alfa-Omega** Markedsgata 14–16. Centrally located on Alta's main pedestrian street this is both bar (on the left as you enter) & restaurant. A limited Mediterranean-inspired menu such as tapas (267kr) or beef with rösti potatoes in a thyme sauce (239kr). Several salads available (139kr).

✖ **Fellini** Upstairs inside the Parksentret shopping centre with a hard-to-find entrance on Markedsgata. The cheapest Italian restaurant in town with pizzas from 85kr (the medium size is plenty big enough), pan pizzas for 119kr, kebabs from 85kr & burgers for 70kr. Grill dishes such as beef with gorgonzola sauce (154kr) are available.

✖ **Haldde** Fogdebakken 6. Upmarket cuisine in this restaurant inside the Vica hotel with an emphasis on Arctic specialities such as fillet of reindeer, whale steak & cloudberry dessert as well as several fish dishes. Reckon on 170–329kr for a main course.

♀ **Han Skjenke** Markedsgata. A newly opened bar in the same squat building as the Subway sandwich on the main drag store, which looks set to become *the* place to imbibe in Alta. Small & intimate.

✖ **Han Steike** Tasteful American-style grill restaurant with slate walls & wooden floors serving an array of good-value meat & fishy treats: rack of lamb (149kr), spare ribs (236kr) & grilled salmon (199kr).

✖ **Wing Wah House** Skoleveien 1. Cosy Chinese restaurant that does takeaway, serving all your favourites, such as spring rolls (59kr), satay beef (125kr) & chicken with peanuts (125kr) at very reasonable prices.

**THE TOWN** Alta town centre is not going to hold your attention for long, but while you are here it is worth strolling up and down the pedestrianised centre and having a look around the two shopping centres in Alta Sentrum: Parksenteret and Alta Storsenter. Inside both, you will find an impressively large array of shops for a town with a population of barely 15,000 people, including an outlet of Vinmonopolet and a bookshop selling local maps inside the larger Alta Storsenter. If you are here in winter, keep an eye out for the well-executed ice sculptures that adorn the central shopping area; anything from pop stars to snowmen can make an appearance.

**Alta Museum** (*www.alta.museum.no;* ⏱ *May & Sep 09.00–18.00 daily; Jun–Aug 08.00–21.00 daily; Oct–Apr Mon–Fri 09.00–15.00, Sat & Sun 11.00–16.00; Oct–Apr 40kr, May–Sep 80kr*) Once you've had your fill of Alta's commercial delights, it is a good idea to head straight for Alta museum right beside the main E6 on the western edge of town in an area known as Hjemmeluft (Jiepmaluokta in Sámi), about 1.5km west of the junction with Route 93 to Kautokeino. After paying your entrance fee, forsake the museum's more mundane interior exhibitions and head immediately outside to see the star attractions, the **prehistoric rock carvings**, which are located in two main areas immediately behind the museum building. Wooden walkways have been constructed to save the carvings from the rigours of thousands of pounding feet and it is imperative you do not stray from the path; allow 45 minutes or so to see the main area (to the left of the museum when looking out over the fjord). When combined with the second area of carvings to the right, you will need about two hours in total; the walking paths run for a total length of around 3km.

Amazingly the petroglyphs were not discovered until the early 1970s; they'd simply lain hidden under layers of mud since their creation up to 6,000 years ago. Painstaking restoration work was carried out on some of the carvings and today around 20% have been repainted using the same red colour as the originals to give an impression of how they were intended to be seen. Hammers and chisels made of rock or horn were used to make the carvings, which portray any number of different Stone Age subjects: the hunting of wild animals such as elk and reindeer, catching birds, fishing, skin boats, weapons, people in procession, dancing and magical symbols to name but a few.

The 5,000 carvings are found in five different locations around Altafjorden (the museum area is just one of the five). It is thought they had more than one purpose: some were clearly made to worship gods or to relate ancient myths whereas others were aimed at placating the spirit of totem animals or ensuring fertility and prosperity. Today experts regard the carvings as an attempt by our ancient ancestors to immortalise their surroundings and express their ritualistic view of the world in what we now regard as art. The rock carvings are only visible between May and late September or early October (depending on the weather) since once the first snows of winter have fallen the carvings remain covered until the spring thaw.

Inside the museum, a series of exhibitions tell the history of Alta and the surrounding region of Finnmark. It is safe to forgo the rather tedious displays on hunting and fishing and home in instead on a fascinating story hidden away in the museum's far left-hand corner: a black and white photograph of protestors holding a banner reading '*La elva leve*' ('Let the river live') is a poignant reminder of the bitter conflict that was fought out here in the early 1980s over the future of the **Alta river**.

Other photographs and newspaper articles relate the history of the **Alta Dispute**, when local Sámi activists took on the might of the Norwegian state over plans to dam the River Alta-Kautokeino to produce hydroelectric power. Their efforts attracted international attention and marked a turning point in Sámi-state relations. Demonstrations were held at the dam construction site nearby Stilla as well as in Oslo where five young Sámi staged a hunger strike outside parliament bringing work on the dam to a standstill. Matters came to a head in 1981 when 600 Norwegian police forcefully removed 1,100 peaceful protestors from the construction site. During the course of the Alta Dispute the Sámi learned how to work with the media and influence public opinion, which, certainly in the north of Norway, was strongly against the dam. However, construction work continued unabated and the River Alta was finally dammed in 1987. The Norwegian government set up two committees to investigate the issue of Sámi rights in the light of the protests whose findings paved the pay for the setting-up of the Norwegian Sámi parliament, Sámediggi, in Karasjok and the recognition of the Sámi as an indigenous people in the Norwegian constitution in 1988.

Before heading downstairs, take a look at the remarkable display of medieval altarpiece sculptures on display around the corner: the figure of Norway's patron saint, Saint Olav, was carved around 1490 in northern Germany and is a sign of the prosperity of Finnmark during the late medieval period when exports of dried fish to the rest of Europe brought much revenue to this part of Lapland.

More contemporary history is recounted downstairs, though sadly with little English labelling. Be sure, though, to catch the moving black and white film (in Norwegian only) about the forced evacuation of the local population by the Germans in the latter stages of World War II and the devastation caused by the scorched earth policy that ensued. There's a small display about the British attacks on the German battleship, *Tirpitz*, first by submarine in the autumn of 1943 and then by air in April 1944; both occurred while she was at anchor in Altafjorden. As Germany's largest naval vessel, the *Tirpitz* was a serious threat to the Allied supply convoys operating out of Murmansk and with local intelligence the British managed to mount an air raid which put the ship out of operation for several months.

Incidentally, there's a small **café** inside the museum serving simple snacks and sandwiches.

**Alta Igloo Hotel** (✆ 78 43 33 78; e *info@ice-alta.no*; *www.ice-alta.no*) Even if you don't want to spend the night in subzero temperatures tucked up inside an igloo, it is worth making the 20km trip south from Alta to see the Alta Igloo Hotel. To get here take Route 93 towards Kautokeino and follow signs for Alta Friluftspark. Built every year between Christmas and New Year, the igloo hotel stands proudly beside the banks of Alta river until it melts in early April. It is considerably smaller and more intimate than its world-famous bigger brother, Icehotel, in Jukkasjärvi in Sweden (see pages 5–6), though you'd be forgiven if you thought the Norwegians had simply copied the Swedish model. Like the Icehotel, the Alta Igloo Hotel has a chapel, an ice bar and plenty of ice sculptures to adorn the interior. The theme of the sculptures and interior décor changes from year to year but there is always a vast ice swan in the entrance hall to welcome visitors who pay 100kr for the pleasure of setting foot inside the igloo. The Old Norse meaning of *alta* is 'swan'.

Should you decide you want to stay here in one of the 28 rooms (or one of the two suites, which are slightly larger and contain ice sculptures), you will be provided with a thermal sleeping bag and plenty of blankets. There's a cosy lounge with television, where you can relax in the warmth or, alternatively, enjoy an outdoor jacuzzi under the stars before repairing to your own freezebox for the night; the average temperature inside the igloo is –4°C to –7°C. A night here costs 1,975kr per room and includes transfer to and from Alta, dinner, sauna and breakfast the next morning. The sauna, showers, toilets and lounge are in the more conventional service building next door, which is fully heated. The hotel can arrange four-hour **snowmobile tours** (whether you are staying here or not) including lunch or dinner at a cost of 1,250kr per person per snowmobile (2,100kr for two people sharing a snowmobile).

## HONNINGSVÅG AND AROUND

From Alta, the E6 continues its relentless journey north, first threading its way around the head of Altafjorden before climbing and clipping across a barren upland plateau. Bear in mind that sections of this stretch of the E6 can be ferociously windy and are prone to snowdrifts in winter, which can close the road. The red and white barriers along the road are lowered if driving conditions become too hazardous. If this happens, you have no choice but to wait for a snow plough and then drive in convoy behind the plough as it reopens the route for vehicles. Once up on the plateau (385m) and now a full 86km out of Alta, you will finally come to the first settlement of any significance: **Skaidi**. However, this diminutive hamlet is little more than a crossroads and is more strategic to bus travellers than car drivers since it is sometimes necessary, depending on schedules, to change buses here when travelling to and from Hammerfest, 57km to the northwest.

The next section of the road between Skaidi and **Olderfjord**, which occupies a glorious poistion on the west bank of the mighty **Porsangerfjorden** (an inlet of the Arctic Ocean edged by bare, rounded hills), can be equally hard going – the wind up here can be alarmingly fierce at the summit (437m). Some 23km later, things get markedly easier once you drop down into Olderfjord and embark on Europe's northernmost road, the E69, which leads all the way to the North Cape via an impressive array of tunnels. Clinging precariously to the shores of the fjord the road veers around gnarled headlands of shattered rock where it can, and where it can't, it plunges into the hillside inside a tunnel; the first of these is Skarvbergtunnelen (length 2,980m). If the automatic door at the entrance is closed, drive up to the blue sign and wait for the door to rise.

**REPVÅG** The next tunnel, Sortviktunnelen (length 496m), is a mere babe in comparison, and you are now well on the way for the turning to the right for **Repvåg**, a pretty little fishing station, huddled around a wharf, which teeters on stilts on a narrow neck of land that juts out defiantly into Porsangerfjorden. The handful of wooden buildings here, all painted in traditional red and sporting white window frames, were spared the ravages of the departing German troops after World War II and remained standing, in contrast to nearby Honningsvåg, for example, which was burnt to the ground. Inside, much of the decoration and furnishing is made of driftwood or features bits and bobs from the fishing industry. Consequently, this is one of the premier places to stay around Honningsvåg and offers a chance to experience life on the coast of northern Norway a little off the beaten track. Incidentally, although Repvåg is now linked to the E69 by a 2km byroad, in the 1970s it was once a busy harbour with ferries shuttling back and forth carrying all road traffic bound for Honningsvåg and the North Cape, albeit before the days of the North Cape tunnel (see below), which now links the mainland with Norway's northernmost island, Magerøya, doing away with the need for a ferry connection.

**Where to stay and eat** Accommodation at the **Repvåg Fjordhotell og Rorbusenter** (✆ 78 47 54 40; e post@repvag-fjordhotell.no; www.repvag-fjordhotell.no) is available in the main hotel building ($$$) as well as in a number of traditional fisherman's cottages, *rorbuer* ($$), right on the wharf. Rooms are simple but snug and a night spent here is sure to please; the view of the fjord and the surrounding islands is unusual. The hotel **restaurant** specialises in locally caught fresh fish; during the summer months the fjord is brimming with coalfish, whereas in autumn and winter cod and haddock are attracted into its sheltered waters. It is possible to make your own way out on to the fjord by renting one of the three small **boats** the hotel has available. Alternatively, there's a nature **trail** which begins right outside the hotel's front door and leads through an area of reindeer pasture.

**HONNINGSVÅG** A marvel of modern engineering (have your credit card ready) now stands ahead of you: **Nordkapptunnelen**. Opened in June 1999, the tunnel replaced the stomach-churning ferry, which once bobbed across the sound from Kåfjord to Honningsvåg and, in officialese at least, goes by the bizarre name of Fatima: *fastlandsforbindelsen til Magerøya* (the mainland connection to Magerøya). This 6.8km long submarine tunnel reaches a depth below water of 212m as it traverses the sound – though using it is a pleasure which doesn't come cheap for locals and visitors alike. It currently costs 145kr per vehicle and driver; each extra passenger pays 47kr (children 24kr). Unlike many other tunnels where the fee is levied in one direction only, the Nordkapptunnelen authorities charge you in *both* directions. It is estimated the charge will remain in place until around 2014, so there is nothing for it but to wince and hand over your money; cyclists go free, although the 7km ride through the tunnel in near darkness is not a pleasant one. Cash and credit cards are accepted – pay at the toll booth in each direction.

Blinking in the daylight as you emerge from the tunnel, it is not long before you are plunged into yet another two tunnels: Sarnestunnelen (length 190m) and then Honningvågstunnelen (length 4,440m). Finally, at the T-junction on the approach to Honningsvåg, take a right (left goes to the North Cape) and drive into the northernmost village in the world: the 71st parallel of latitude slices ignominiously through the Shell filling station on your right-hand side.

**Getting there** Buses stop first outside the waterside tourist office on Fiskeriveien, below the Rica hotel on the main road, before continuing around the harbour and terminating at Rådhuset, above Honningsvåg's other two hotels. Arriving by the Hurtigruten coastal **ferry**, you will dock 100m to the east at the dedicated Hurtigrutekai. The ship arrives daily here from the south at 11.45 and departs again for all points north at 15.15, allowing passengers time to make a trip by bus to the North Cape; it departs daily southbound at 06.15.

**Tourist information** The tourist office (⟍ *78 47 70 30;* e *info@northcape.no; www.northcape.no;* ⊕ *mid-Jun to mid-Aug Mon–Fri 08.30–20.00, Sat & Sun noon–20.00; rest of year Mon–Fri 08.30–16.00*) is on Fiskeriveien, below the Rica hotel on the main road. Tourist office staff here are friendly and knowledgeable and can help with accommodation, tours to the North Cape and making sense of northern Norway's complicated bus routes and times.

**Internet** access is available at several locations: the tourist office charges 23kr for 15 minutes and Bryggerie' at Nordkappgata 1 has access all year round. The library, Klubbveien 1, has free access though its opening hours are limited (⊕ *Mon & Fri 10.00–14.00, Tue, Wed & Thu 15.00–19.00*).

## Where to stay

**Honningsvåg Brygge** Vågen I A, Honningsvåg; ⟍ 78 47 64 64; e post@hvg.brugge.no; www.hvg.brygge.no. ⊕ Jun–Aug only. Without a doubt, the most charming hotel in the village. This group of former wooden warehouses has been tastefully converted & occupies a prime location on a couple of jetties at the head of the harbour. Rooms are a little on the small side but worth it for the location. Some rooms overlook the neighbouring hotel so ask for one with a view of the harbour. $$$$$

**Rica Bryggen** Vågen I, Honningsvåg; ⟍ 78 47 28 88; e rica.bryggen.hotel@rica.no; www.rica.no. The better of the 2 Ricas in town though not as charming as its neighbour, the Honningsvåg Brygge. With concrete walls rather than timber, it loses out on the charm stakes – though its modern rooms are decent enough. It has superb views from its wharf location out over the harbour, however. $$$$$

**Rica Honningsvåg** Storgatan 4, Honningsvåg; ⟍ 78 47 23 33; e rica.hotel.honningsvag@rica.no; www.rica.no. The first hotel you reach as you come into town & the most dowdy. Crying out for renovation, this white concrete carbuncle may be open all year but its rooms are plain in the extreme. This is the only hotel to have a sauna. $$$$$/$$$

**Árran Nordkapp** Kamøyvær; ⟍ 78 47 51 29; e post@arran.as; www.arran.as. Located in the fishing village of Kamøyvær, 9km north of

Honningsvåg on the North Cape road, this Sámi-run family hotel offers no-nonsense modern rooms with just a hint of Sámi design. $$$$

**Havstua** Kamøyvær; ⟍ 78 47 51 50; e post@havstua.no; www.havstua.no. Occupying the former fishing station right on the jetty, these characterful old timber buildings have been converted into a series of tasteful twin & sgl rooms with an old-world feel. $$$$

**Ⓧ Nordkapp Camping NAF** Skipsfjorden; ⟍ 78 47 33 77; e post@nordkappcamping.no; www.nordkappcamping.no. ⊕ Jun to mid-Sep. The closest campsite to Honningsvåg located 8km north in Skipsfjorden. *Dbls* $$, *cabins with kitchenette* $$, *bungalows with fitted kitchen* $$$$ & *camping* $.

**Repvåg Fjordhotell og Rorbusenter** Repvåg; ⟍ 78 47 54 40; e post@repvag-fjordhotell.no; www.repvag-fjordhotell.no. In the hamlet of Repvåg, 50km south of Honningsvåg off the E69. Charming wooden rooms & fisherman's cottages beside the fjord (see above). $$$/$$

**North Cape Cabins** Skipsfjorden; ⟍ 78 47 37 45 & mobile 91 71 19 64; e post@northcapecabins.no; www.northcapecabins.no. These 3 little wooden cabins in Skipsfjorden, 7.5km north of Honningsvåg on the way to the North Cape, are idyllic. Each sleeping 2, they are located right beside the fjord with sweeping views. They are right beside the road & vehicle noise can disturb the peace. $$

## ✗ Where to eat and drink

✗ **Bryggerie'** Nordkappgata 1. Diagonally opposite the Rica Honningsvåg Hotel & a firm favourite with the locals who come to sample the place's own brew. Pizzas cost 99kr.

✗ **Corner** Fiskerveien 2A. Hidden away below the Rica Honningsvåg Hotel & behind the tourist office, this cosy place has a wide menu ranging from fried halibut to cajun chicken. Reckon on 100–200kr for a main course.

♀ **Nøden** Larsjoda 1B. Immediately opposite the Rica Honningsvåg Hotel & a little up the hill to the left. This is Honningsvåg's only pub – decked out in traditional British style. A note by the exit begs late night revellers to refrain from shouting & making noise when leaving in order to keep the peace with the neighbours.

✗ **Sjøhuset** Vågen 1A; ☎ 78 47 64 64. ① Summer only. Inside the Honningsvåg Brygge Hotel at the harbour. This popular seafood restaurant serves up the freshest & tastiest fish you can imagine with superlative views over harbour & the vessels that landed the catch you are eating. Reckon on at least 250kr per main course & reservations are recommended.

**The village** Honningsvåg, 240km from Alta, is a strangely likeable sort of place. There's a pluckiness about the village that appeals – not least because its exposed location on the edge of one of Norway's most inhospitable islands, Magerøya, actually suggests that it really ought not to be here. Indeed, nearby Hammerfest, has robbed Honningsvåg of the title of northernmost town in the world despite various attempts by local worthies to have their village upgraded and reclassified; having said that, Honningsvåg is no metropolis. The heart of the village is its harbour, a U-shaped affair, around which a couple of parallel roads fit neatly. It is here that you will find most things you need: hotels, restaurants and shops. The place is at its most picturesque at the head of the harbour where a couple of hotels appear to perch somewhat precariously on three stilted wharves.

**Nordkappmuseet: the North Cape Museum** (① *Jun to mid-Aug Mon–Sat 10.00–19.00, Sun noon–19.00; rest of year Mon–Fri noon–16.00; 35kr*) Once you've made a circuit of the harbour and peered at the various comings and goings down by the Hurtigruten quay, there's really little else to occupy your time and you should head for the Nordkappmuseet museum in the same building as the tourist office which holds an evocative exhibition about the reconstruction of the village immediately after World War II. As the German forces retreated during the winter of 1944 they burnt the whole of Honningsvåg to the ground. Black and white photographs show only the church left standing; it became a focal point for the reconstruction effort and was even used as a bakery at one time. Barracks were hurriedly erected to house former inhabitants as they returned after the forced evacuation.

The museum has a mini-display about local birdlife, including the Gjesværstappan islands off Magerøya's northwest coast, which are home to one of Norway's largest puffin colonies – and an event that has left leading wildlife experts baffled. Quite inexplicably the birds return to the islands, after spending the winter out at sea, on the same day every year, 14 April, and at the same time during the late afternoon. In total the islands are home to around three million nesting birds including gannets, Arctic skuas, cormorants and white-tailed eagles. Upstairs, on a small mezzanine floor, staff have mounted a display about the North Cape and its magnetic attraction to countless visitors from across the world over the years. Long though the journey to Europe's most northerly point may be, it was even more arduous before the road opened to the Cape in 1956. Then visitors, including the Norwegian king, Oscar II, came ashore in Hornvika bay, just to the east, and faced a steep climb up the cliff to reach the North Cape plateau (307m). This royal visit did much to finally put the North Cape on the tourist map.

Here, at the end of the world, my longing also comes to an end, and I return home satisfied.

*Francesco Negri, first tourist to reach the North Cape in 1664,*
*after a two-year journey from Italy.*

The Sámi call Norway's northernmost island Máhkarávju or 'steep, barren coast', which has been Norwegianised into today's **Magerøya** and is home to around 3,500 people, three-quarters of whom live in Honningsvåg. As the E69 threads its way north towards the Cape, the island certainly lives up to its name as vistas of bare, windswept rock and tundra unfold at every turn. This Arctic landscape is Norwegian Lapland at its most elemental: a high treeless plateau edged by distant frost-shattered peaks and a coast that has been gnawed into countless craggy inlets by the unforgiving might of the Arctic Ocean. Seeking shelter from the ferocious storms, which sweep in from the sea with merciless regularity, the island's few settlements huddle at the head of fjords which slice deep into the heart of the land.

The English sea captain, Richard Chancellor, brought the North Cape to prominence. Searching for the northeast passage between the Atlantic and the Pacific, he sailed his ship, *Edward Bonaventure,* along this stretch of coastline in 1553 and used the North Cape cliff (307m) as a navigational landmark; its sheer face reaching up from the sea was certainly easy to spot. Although Chancellor failed to reach his destination, China, sea charts of northern Europe soon began to feature his name for the northermost point in Europe, the North Cape, and the rest is history. However, the belief that the North Cape is the furthest extremity of Europe is one of the greatest geographical gaffes of all time. The gently sloping promontory, **Knivskjellodden**, just to the west of the Cape, is the true top of Europe since it stretches 1,500m further north than the cliff. Content not to let the truth get in the way of a good story, the Norwegian tourist authorities promote the North Cape (Nordkapp in Norwegian) as Europe's most northerly point with all their might – and succeed: 200,000 people make the considerable journey here every year and pay handsomely for the pleasure (see below).

Once you finally reach the North Cape, it is worth taking stock of just where you are on the globe: at 71° 10′ 21″ of latitude you are considerably closer to the North Pole than you are to London, for example, and the Norwegian capital, Oslo, is a staggering 1,420km to the south. As a sign of how far north you are, there's **Midnight Sun** at the Cape from 11 May to 31 July and **Polar Night** from 18 November to 24 January each year. There's certainly a tremendous sense of achievement in having made the journey to the very end of Europe, but at the same time, as Francesco Negri pointed out in his journal, *Viaggio Settentrionale* (see quotation above), it is also where curiosity reaches completion and the realisation sets in that you have an extremely long trip ahead of you – there's over 650km to go just to reach the Arctic Circle.

## GETTING THERE

**In summer** Between early June and late August two Norwegian **buses** (#330) make the daily trip from Honningsvåg to the North Cape (45mins) leaving at 10.45 and 21.30; the morning departure runs from late May to early September. The same buses then return at 13.15 and 00.15 (quarter past midnight). Once again, the afternoon bus operates from late May to early September. If you take the second departure you can spend two hours at the Cape (between 22.15 and 00.15) in order to see the Midnight Sun. The single ticket price from Honningsvåg to the North Cape is 90kr. For more details see www.ffr.no.

Coming from the west, it is possible to connect on to the Honningsvåg–North

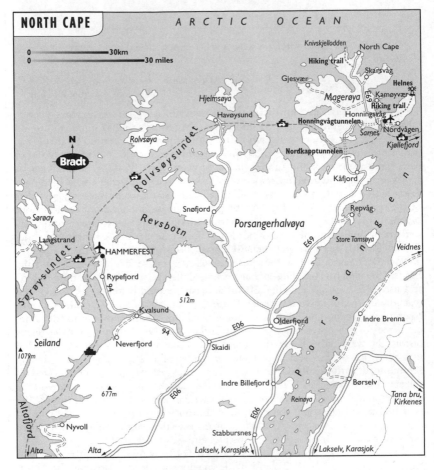

Cape service by leaving Alta at 06.45 (*not Sun*) and again at 14.20 (*Mon–Thu*), 14.45 (*Sat*) or 15.00 (*Fri & Sun*). Coming from Kirkenes and points to the east including Karasjok, there's a daily bus from Kirkenes at 08.05 (*not Tue & Thu*) which connects in Olderfjord with the Alta–Honningsvåg service (departure 17.20). Change again in Honningsvåg for the North Cape bus.

The fixed rate for a **taxi** from Honningsvåg to the Cape and back is 900kr for up to four people. You can book a taxi at the tourist office.

Between June and late August a popular Finnish bus operates to the North Cape from **Rovaniemi** railway station (departure 11.10) – a mammoth journey of 650km taking ten hours. Although local journeys between either Karasjok or Honningsvåg and the North Cape are not allowed, you can board the bus at other points on its way to the North Cape, and you can take the service south from the Cape (it leaves daily at 01.00) and ride it as far as you like: it runs via Lakselv, Inari, Ivalo and Sodankylä back to Rovaniemi arriving at 17.35. Once again, you cannot make a local journey between the North Cape and Honningsvåg or Karasjok. Note also that this bus waits for four hours in Honningsvåg before leaving again (at 17.30) – when, bizarrely, you *can* board the bus for all points to Rovaniemi (though still not Karasjok!). There's more information at www.eskelisen-lapinlinjat.com.

When deciphering the Finnish timetable, it can be useful to know that *pysähtyy* *vain matkustajien **jättämistä** varten* means 'alighting passengers only'and *pysähtyy vain matkustajien **ottamista** varten* means 'boarding passengers only'.

**In winter** It is not possible to drive to the North Cape in your own vehicle when there is no snow on the ground, roughly between October and early May, though the exact period varies from year to year (check with the Honningsvåg tourist office for the latest information). Although the road may appear open, the last 13km section of the E69 between the junction for Skarsvåg and the North Cape is not ploughed; a barrier bars the road. To visit the North Cape during this time you must take the organised tour, which runs in connection with the arrival of the northbound Hurtigruten boat, leaving Honningsvåg at 11.45. Coaches with snow chains then run up to the North Cape, closely following a snow plough, which opens the last section of the road for them to pass – quite something to experience. They then spend about an hour and a half at the Cape before returning back to Honningsvåg for the ship's departure at 15.15. This trip costs 695kr (including North Cape admission) and can be booked through the tourist office.

**NORDKAPPHALLEN: NORTH CAPE HALL** (*www.visitnorthcape.no;* ⊕ *early to mid-May noon–16.00 daily; mid-May to mid-Jun noon–13.00; mid-Jun to end Jul 09.00–14.00; Aug 09.00–midnight; Sep to mid-Oct noon–15.30; mid-Oct to April 12.30–14.00; 195kr*) A commerical pleasuredome designed to relieve you of as many kroner as possible in a short space of time. The hall, cut into the rock of the Cape, is not without its critics either, who claim it is grossly overpriced and has destroyed the natural environment. Be that as it may, it would be churlish not to go inside having made the journey here. The main building is divided into two sections, which are linked by an underground tunnel. As you enter from the car park, you will find a souvenir shop selling seemingly everything your heart could ever desire, emblazoned with the Nordkapp logo; a small café serving coffee and waffles; the Kompasset café and restaurant, offering superb views of the Arctic Ocean through its floor-to-ceiling windows and some of the most expensive à la carte dishes anywhere in Norway; and a post office proudly franking cards and letters with the '9764 Nordkapp' postmark.

Take the stairs or lift down to sub-level three and you will find the impressive Supervideograf **cinema**, which shows a regular free film about the North Cape and Magerøya in all seasons. Ignoring the tacky model of a bird cliff, complete with taped squaks and quacks, beside the cinema entrance, make your way along the underground tunnel towards the edge of the cliff. A potted history of the Cape is presented in a couple of glass display cabinets along the tunnel before you reach a chapel and more surreally a small museum, which commemorates the visit of King Chulalongkom of Siam to the North Cape in 1907 – he was so ill on arrival that he had to be carried up the cliff in Hornvika by stretcher. Don't despair, there's one final chance to spend more money before you finally reach a viewing window onto the sea below: the cavernous Grotten bar, where hapless tourists are encouraged to splash out on caviar and champagne to celebrate their trip to the Cape.

Back in the main section of the building, below the post office and the souvenir shop, you will find the exit to the outside viewing area (the wind out here can be particularly strong) and the location for the much-photographed steel globe, which has come to symbolise the North Cape. As you stare out to sea, you are looking at the scene of one of the northernmost naval encounters in history: the **Battle of the North Cape**. In heavy seas and a mounting snowstorm, the German battleship, *Scharnhorst*, sailed from her base in Altafjorden in December 1943 to intercept Allied convoys supplying Murmansk, but was fired on by Britain's Royal Navy, capsizing and sinking off the Cape with the loss of over 1,900 lives.

**HIKING TO KNIVSKJELLODDEN** Should you thirst for last places not have been quenched by Nordkapphallen and its tourist paraphernalia, you might want to escape the crowds and **hike** to the real northernmost point of Europe, Knivskjellodden. The start of the 16km (return) trail is signed from the E69 about 6km before the North Cape Hall and heads off towards the northwest. Don't underestimate how fast the weather can change out here on the plateau and before embarking on the hike you should make sure you are properly equipped; allow about six hours to make the return hike from the road. Perhaps in response to their critics, the hall's operators, the Rica hotel chain, urge visitors not to build cairns since they damage the soil and vegetation, and not to drive their vehicles off the roads provided.

**HAMMERFEST** If you tired of northernmost superlatives in Tromsø, it is time to brace yourself because there are more to come in Hammerfest, an unkempt, industrial place that is overtly proud of its self-declared role in life: the northernmost town in the world. At a latitude of 70.7° north, Hammerfest pips nearby Honningsvåg to the post in terms of population size at over 9,000. When so much tourist hype is at stake, size really does matter and, according to the powers that be, with over 6,000 inhabitants you can call yourself a town. But this title is not only disputed by Honningsvåg, but also by Longyearbyen in Spitsbergen and the Alaskan town of Barrow. Frankly, on the ground, the title means very little and, whatever the truth, you are unlikely to want to linger here since pushing on to the North Cape is likely to be at the top of your agenda if you've made it to such a northerly latitude.

**Some history** Named after its superb anchorage (*hamran* was the name of a group of rocks, now lost to landfill, which boats were once fastened to, hence the placename element *fest*), throughout its history, Hammerfest has always been an important ice-free base for trapping and fishing in the waters of the Arctic. The hunting of whales, seals, walruses and polar bears was the mainstay of the local economy for several centuries. Hunters and trappers rarely settled here permanently and by 1699 there were only three married couples, a priest and a merchant eking out a living here. In 1809, during the Napoleonic Wars, Britain attacked the settlement from two warships offshore, causing the inhabitants to flee with their possessions. The British ships spent eight days in port, giving the sailors plenty of time to loot the church's donation box and silver. In 1890 Hammefest fell victim to another disaster: a fire, which began in the bakery, ripped through the tiny town destroying half the houses. Germany's Kaiser Wilhelm II was the biggest single donor of aid to help with the reconstruction; incongruously, he was a keen sailor and often called in at Hammerfest on board his yacht.

One of Hammerfest's other boasts is that it was the first town to install electric street lighting after two local merchants had been thrilled by a demonstration of the new-fangled invention at a trade fair in Paris. As the German army retreated in 1944, they burnt Hammerfest to the ground. With the help of the Marshall plan, reconstruction began and today there is no building in Hammerfest that is more than 65 years old except the church, which remained standing. The recent artificial enlargement of the island of Melkøya, just outside the harbour, and the construction of a gas terminal there has brought new prosperity to the town. Creating new jobs to replace those lost from the fish processing sector, the plant will handle exports from Norway's gas fields in the Arctic Ocean.

**Getting there and tourist information** Steaming into Hammerfest on a Hurtigruten ship with the horn blaring is infinitely the best way to arrive, seeing the town as generations of sailors have, banking steeply up the hillsides behind the harbour. However, arriving from the south, it is a pleasure that unfolds rather blearily at 05.15 as the ship puts in from Tromsø. Southbound arrivals from Honningsvåg are more sensibly timed at 11.15. The quay is located on the eastern side of the harbour. Hurtigbåt **express passenger boats** from Alta dock just around the corner, off Sjøgata. Hammerfest's **bus** station, if, indeed, the ill-defined gravelly area outside the **tourist office** (❟ *78 41 31 00;* e *info@hammerfest-turist.no; www.hammerfest-turist.no;* ⊕ *mid-Jun to mid-Aug Mon–Fri 09.00–18.00, Sat & Sun 10.30–13.30; rest of year Mon–Fri 09.00–15.00, Sat & Sun 10.30–13.30*), at Havnegata 3, can be called such, is located between the two quays.

**Internet** access can be found in the Gjenreisningsmuseet at Kirkegata 21, a 5 minutes uphill walk from the town centre east along Kirkegata.

## Where to stay

🏠 **Rica Hammerfest** Sørøygata 15; ❟ 78 41 13 33; e rica.hotel.hammerfest@rica.no; www.rica.no. An attractive waterfront setting for this redbrick hotel just east of the tourist office. Chain hotel rooms decorated in pan-Scandinavian style. Smart, comfortable & expensive. ⑤⑤⑤⑤⑤/⑤⑤⑤⑤

🏠 **Thon Hammerfest** Strandgata 2–4; ❟ 78 42 96 00; e hammerfest@thonhotels.no; www.thonhotels.no. A battered old place crying out for renovation. Insist on a room overlooking the harbour, rather than the ones known as 'cabins', which are little more than overheated rabbit hutches with a view of the inner courtyard brick wall opposite. ⑤⑤⑤⑤⑤/⑤⑤⑤⑤

🏠 **Sentrum** Storgata 3; ❟ 78 42 87 70; e sentrum-htl@fikas.no. Newly opened hotel in the centre of town with pleasant, modern-style rooms that are good value for money. ⑤⑤⑤⑤⑤

🏠 **Skytterhuset** Skytterveien 24; ❟ 78 41 15 11; www.skytterhuset.no. It is the location rather than the rooms which make this motel-style place worth considering. Perched on the hill above town, the views are superb, the rooms sadly are not: cheaply furnished & decorated with little taste. Get here by following Skolebakken up the hill; it begins on the western side of the harbour off the main Strandgata. ⑤⑤⑤⑤/⑤⑤⑤

🅰 **Storvattnet NAF Camping** (7 cabins) Storvannsveien 103; ❟ 78 41 10 10. ⊕ Jun–Aug. Cabins & camping. You can get here on foot by following Skolebakken, or by taxi from town for around 100kr. *Cabins* ⑤⑤

## Where to eat and drink

✕ **Dinner Restaurant** Strandgata 22. Thankfully the Chinese food on offer is a little more imaginative than the name of the restaurant. Known for its large portions; main courses hover around 150kr. Dinner only.

🍸 **Kaikanten** Sjøgata 19. Doubling as pub & café, there are light snacks on offer such as chicken pasta (92kr), sandwiches (from 78kr) & baked potatoes (68kr).

✕ **Mama Rosa** Strandgata 53. A cheap & cheerful Italian restaurant with medium-sized pizzas for 120kr, a large variety of steaks at 165–185kr, as well as kebabs from 99kr, burgers 75kr, & salads for 90kr.

✕ **Mikkelgammen** Salen hill. Take the steps which lead up from Strandgata & follow the zigzag path up the hill. A fabulous Sámi restaurant inside a traditional *gamme* made of turf roof & walls. Inside, the décor draws on indigenous designs for inspiration & is of wood & stone. The place for Arctic specialities, especially reindeer in as many different ways as you can imagine. Recommended.

✕ **Skansen Mat og Vinstue** Sørøygata 15. Inside the Rica hotel, this is Hammerfest's most upmarket restaurant, an intimate little place with gorgeous sea views. It specialises in freshly caught fish – though mains are a little steep at around 300kr.

**The town** Hammerfest is little more than one main street, Strandgata, running parallel to the sea, with two or three side roads branching off perpendicular. Within this small grid, you will find virtually everything Hammerfest has to offer: a small shopping centre, a market where you can pick up Sámi knick-knacks in summer and one or two other souvenir shops aimed at Hurtigruten passengers who hurtle around town for an hour and a half, seemingly visiting every store in sight, while the ferry is docked.

**Isbjørnklubben: the Polar Bear Society** (⊕ *same hours as the tourist office, see page 153; 40kr*) The town's main attraction is the diminutive museum-cum-society, Isbjørnklubben, which is located in the same building as the tourist office at Hamnegata 3, down by the Hurtigruten quay. Established in 1963 to provide brave visitors who had ventured to the northernmost town in the world with a certificate of their achievement, the society today doles out the said diploma, dutifully signed by the Mayor of Hammerfest, membership cards, a polar bear badge made of silver and assorted other bits and bobs of questionable worth; life membership costs 160kr. Thankfully, membership of what must surely be one of the most peculiar societies on the planet is not obligatory and it is a much better idea simply to wander around the museum taking in the exhibits. The history of Hammerfest is told in a series of annotated black and white photographs, which clearly show just how significant the hunting of polar bears, in particular, has been in Hammerfest over the centuries. Should you have a predilection for animals of the Arctic, then you are in luck: you name it, everything from a polar bear to an arctic fox, it is stuffed and on display here.

**Gjenreisningsmuseet: the Museum of Reconstruction** (*Kirkegata 21;* ⊕ *mid-Jun to mid-Aug Mon–Fri 09.00–16.00, Sat & Sun 10.00–14.00; rest of year 11.00–14.00 daily; 50kr*) Much more engaging, albeit a bit of a mouthful, Gjenreisningsmuseet is a gripping account of the dramatic events of World War II in this part of Europe and the forced evacuation of 50,000 people from Hammerfest and other towns in the east of Norwegian Lapland. As Nazi troops fled the advancing Russian forces, the German commander in Lapland, General Lothar Rendulic, implemented a scorched earth policy, under which virtually every building in Norwegian (and Finnish) Lapland was burnt to the ground.

After the war, Rendulic was was convicted of war crimes and sentenced to 20 years' imprisonment though his sentence was later reduced to ten years – something the local population, many of whom were forced to spend the Arctic winter of 1944–45 in caves after losing their homes and livelihoods as a direct result of his decision, was at a loss to comprehend. In the immediate post-war period, the Norwegian government tried and failed to control the return of people to the north; locals ignored the authorities and returned to begin the reconstruction of their homes. Counting more than 11,000 photographs as part of its collection, the museum has a small auditorium where a moving film about the war and its effects is shown at regular intervals.

**MOVING ON FROM HAMMERFEST** The Hurtigruten **ferry** sails northbound from Hammerfest at 06.45 arriving in Honningsvåg five hours later in readiness for excursions to the North Cape (see pages 149–52). Southbound departures are at 12.45 with arrival in Tromsø 11 hours later. From Hammerfest **bus** #215 leaves at 07.10 (*Mon–Fri*), 15.05 (*Mon–Thu*) and 15.40 (*Fri & Sun*) for Karasjok, a journey of over four hours. There is a connection from Karasjok to Kirkenes on Monday, Wednesday, Friday and Sunday. Service #209 leaves at the same times for Honningsvåg. Bus #205 departs for Alta at 08.10 (*Mon–Fri*), 10.15 (*Sat only*), 11.15 (*Mon–Fri*), 16.15 (*Mon–Thu*) and 16.35 (*Fri & Sun*); The Hurtigbåt **express passenger boat** leaves at 11.30 (*Fri only*); 15.00 (*Sun only*); 16.30 (*Mon–Fri*) and 21.00 (*Sun only*) for Alta.

From Hammerfest, it is 142km to Alta; 180km to Honningsvåg; 208km to the North Cape; and 541km to Kirkenes.

With streetnames in both Norwegian and Russian, rusting Russian ships in the harbour and Murmansk's nouveau riche trotting around town doing their shopping, Kirkenes is quite unlike any other town in Lapland. A grubby port at the very end of the E6 and the Hurtigruten line, the place may be hard to like, but it does have a certain hardbitten charm. That's just as well since it is a long way to come just to visit another Norwegian town with its familiar grid of modern anodyne streets. Once here, it is worth taking stock of just how far you've travelled – Kirkenes is as far east as Istanbul and Cairo, Oslo is a mind-boggling 2,480km away, whereas Murmansk is barely 243km, a mere stone's throw in these parts. Indeed, it is the town's proximity to Russia that helps keep the economy ticking over – local politicians are constantly dreaming up new initiatives to enhance all forms of cross-border co-operation in the Barents Sea region.

Kirkenes is named after the church (*kirke*), which was built in 1862 on the headland (*nes* meaning 'point' or 'headland' and cognate with English *ness* in placenames such as Skegness) where the town currently stands; previously the area had been known by the less than holy name of Pisselvnes (piss river headland).

During World War II, Kirkenes paid a high price for its proximity to Murmansk, the only ice-free port in the European part of the Soviet Union, which regularly received supplies and goods from the United States and Britain across the Arctic Ocean to help support Moscow. The Germans posted 30,000 troops in Kirkenes in an attempt to take Murmansk. Sadly, much of the town, including the church, was destroyed during World War II, as Kirkenes's iron ore mines became a target for Soviet carpet bombing. Indeed, the town was second only to Malta in number of air attacks. Following 320 air raids and the German's scorched earth policy, only 13 houses remained standing.

During the Cold War, relations between Norway and Russia were sometimes strained and the border between the two countries close to Kirkenes was a place of tension; on several occasions soldiers and tanks lined up on either side of the border in a show of force. Today, as a member of the European Union's Schengen agreement, Norway maintains an active military base at Høybuktmoen, west of the town, and is obliged to guard the border with Russia. Since there is passport-free travel throughout the Nordic countries, the agreement effectively makes the Norwegian–Russian border the outer frontier of the European Union, at least in terms of immigration.

**GETTING THERE** Arriving by **bus**, you will be dropped outside Kirkenes Senter, a modest shopping complex in the town centre one block inland from the harbour, which effectively serves as the bus station. Hurtigruten **ferries** terminate at the dedicated quay about 1km east of the centre from where a local bus runs into town. The **airport**, 11km west of Kirkenes, is connected to town by a shuttle bus (70kr; 20mins), which runs in connection with flight arrivals; a taxi into the centre costs 225kr.

**TOURIST INFORMATION** Kirkenes tourist office (℡ 79 99 25 44; e *info@kirkenesinfo.no*; *www.kirkenesinfo.no*; ⊕ *Jun–Aug 08.30–18.00 daily; Sep–May Mon–Fri 08.30–16.00*) couldn't be more central, located in the main square at Presteveien 1, a walk of around 500m from the bus station. For information about Russian visas and getting to Murmansk, see *Getting to Russia: Kirkenes to Murmansk* page 159.

Incidentally, despite Kirkenes's extreme location, further east than Finland, the town keeps Norwegian time, rather than Finnish time.

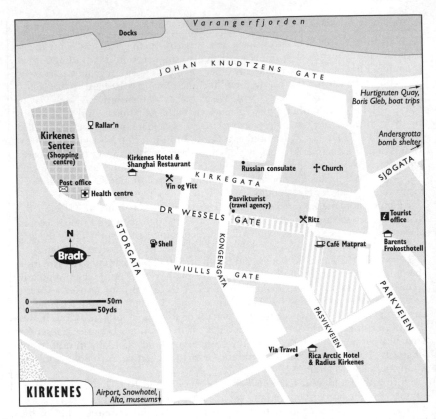

KIRKENES | Airport, Snowhotel, Alta, museums↓

## WHERE TO STAY

**Snowhotel** Førstevannslia; ☎ 78 97 05 40;
e info@radius-kirkenes.com;
www.kirkenessnowhotel.com. Open from Christmas to
Apr, this impressive snow structure lies beside the
Førstevann Lake & offers igloo accommodation in
rooms of snow & ice (see below). $$$$$$$$
**Rica Arctic** Kongensgate 1; ☎ 78 99 59 00; e
rica.arctic.hotel@rica.no; www.rica.no. The best that
Kirkenes has to offer with comfortable, modern
rooms, a swimming pool & sauna. Luxury at the
end of the road, though, doesn't come cheap.
$$$$$$$/$$$$$
**Kirkenes** Doktor Wessels gate 3; ☎ 78 99 21
68; e post@kirkeneshotell.no;
www.kirkeneshotell.no. An odd complex that

combines a hotel with a Chinese restaurant & a
disco. Rooms are fine if uninspiring. Prices are
100kr less at the w/end as compensation for the
din from the disco in the basement. $$$$$
**Barents Frokosthotell** Presteveien 3; ☎ 78 99
32 99; e gcelsius@frisurf.no. A soulless modern
block next door to the tourist office with rather
dreary, though affordable rooms. *Dbls* $$$$ *with
private bathroom,* $$$ *with shared facilities.*
**Kirkenes Camping** Maggadalen; ☎ 78 99 80 28;
e post@kirkenescamping.no;
www.kirkenescamping.no. Located 7km from town in
Maggadalen. ⊕ Jun–Aug. 2- to 4-berth cabins as
well as camping. *Cabins* $$.

## WHERE TO EAT AND DRINK

**Café Matprat** Doktor Wessels gate 18. A no-
nonsense daytime fast food place with burgers
(from 74kr), omelettes (79kr), chicken nuggets
(89kr) & fried chicken (99kr).
**Rallar'n** Storgate 1. The most lively pub in

Kirkenes opposite the main entrance to the
shopping centre attracting a mix of locals, sailors &
tourists.
**Rica Arctic** Kongensgate 1. The best restaurant
in town belongs to the Rica Arctic & has a cheaper

selection of game dishes than Vin og Vilt: reindeer fillet (286kr), fried trout (213kr) & chicken breast (218kr). Ask about their early diner special (before 19.00) with daily changing main courses (149kr). ✖ **Ritz** Doktor Wessels gate 17. Forget any resemblence to its famous namesake, though, this is Kirkeness's best pizzeria with large deep pan-pizzas hovering around 200kr. The best deal is a flat crust *cappriciosa* (89kr). Also takeaway. ✖ **Shanghai** Doktor Wessels gate 3. ⊕ from 15.00

Mon–Thu, from 14.00 Fri–Sun. Inside the Kirkenes hotel, the usual range of Chinese dishes with starters from 50kr & mains from 175kr. ✖ **Vin og Vilt** Doktor Wessels gate 5. ⊕ From 18.00. Closed Sun. An expense-account place specialising in local game. Prices are too high, however: wild duck breast with forest mushrooms, for example, is an extortionate 400kr. Otherwise, reindeer fillet for 325kr or fillet of hare at 365kr.

**THE TOWN** Thanks to the unholy alliance of Soviet bombs and German fires during World War II, Kirkenes town centre is a frightfully drab place to explore: rows of modern concrete blocks befuddle the view at every turn. Instead, head down to the **dockside** on Johan Knudtzens gate for your first impressions of Norway's most remote town. Here, lined up against the quay, a contingent of Murmansk's most battered ships and freighters waits patiently to unload its cargo – and to be repaired. Behind the adjacent Kirkenes Senter shopping complex, the sight of ships hoisted up in the dry dock of the shipyard confirms Kirkenes's role as a strategic port for the Barents Sea area. The quay is usually busy with Russian sailors weaving to and fro, returning to their vessels after sampling the delights of Kirkenes's various watering holes and marauding the town centre searching desperately for anything affordable to take home. Having seen the docks, there's precious little else to hold your attention in town bar the museums.

## What to see and do
### Grenseland and Saviomuseet: the Borderland and Savio Museum (⊕ *both museums mid-Aug to May 10.00–15.30 daily; Jun to mid-Aug 10.00–18.00 daily; 40kr*) From the town centre, a 15-minute walk south along Storgata, which becomes Solheimsveien, will bring you to the lake, Førstevann. Here, at Førstevannslia, by the water's edge, you will find Kirkenes's main museum complex containing the Grenselandmuseet, devoted to the history and nature of the border country hereabouts, and Saviomuseet, which displays the work of local Sámi artist, John Savio.

Exhibitions on the ground floor, including a series of evocative black and white photographs, give a detailed account of events during World War II in the border area including the air raids on Kirkenes and the Murmansk shipping convoys that supplied aid to Russia. Upstairs there's a brief account of the River Pasvikelva, which forms the border with Russia, and about the people who live along its course.

Back on the ground floor, the area of the museum known as Saviomuseet is dedicated to the short life of John Savio (1902–38) from Bugøyfjord, northwest of Kirkenes. At the age of 18 he attended art college in the Norwegian capital, Christiania (now Oslo) and received instruction from leading contemporary painter, Axel Revold. Although the museum mostly displays Savio's sculptures, he also produced a number of paintings that draw on the power of nature and Sámi themes for inspiration. Savio studied art in Paris where his work was exhibited, but he contracted tuberculosis in 1920; the disease returned later and tragically claimed his life at the age of 36.

### The Andersgrotta bomb shelter For a further taste of what life was like in Kirkenes during World War II, check out Andersgrotta, a huge cave hidden away inside the hillside just to the east of the town centre on Christer Aankersgate, which served

as a bomb shelter from 1941 to 1944. In addition to a short tour, a video is shown detailing the 320 air raids directed at Kirkenes – a fate the town shares only with Dresden and Malta, both totally destroyed by air attacks, too. The shelter is open daily on request by contacting Radius Kirkenes at Kongensgate 1 (↘ 78 97 05 40) inside the Rica Arctic hotel; the half-hour tour costs 100kr.

## Boris Gleb: boat trip to the Russian border
Sailing from the quay off Fyllingsveien to the east of the town centre (take Presteveien east out of town and then turn left into Soldatveien), this enjoyable 2½ hour boat trip runs down the River Pasvikelva to the Russian enclave of Boris Gleb, named after two Russian Orthodox saints. The village is unusual in that it lies on the western bank of the river, which otherwise belongs entirely to Norway; the eastern bank is in Russia. Because of its historical links, the village was awarded to Russia when the border was finally formalised in an agreement between Russia and Sweden in 1826. Boris Gleb has even belonged to Finland; from 1920 to 1944 it formed part of Finland's newly acquired Petsamo district until Soviet post-war reparations called for its return to the Soviet Union.

Annoyingly, because of visa restrictions, the boat doesn't dock in Boris Gleb but does sail close enough to see a glimpse of Kirkenes's nearest neighbour. Boris Gleb is the location for the only border crossing between Norway and Russia; the Norwegian border post is at Storskog; Boris Gleb marks the Russian side of the border and start of the journey to Murmansk via Nikel. Incidentally, the timber **church** you see here today was built in the late 1800s and has been recently restored – it is now the only church in Boris Gleb. However, until 1944, there were two churches here: an original, erected in 1565, which served as a place of worship for the local Skolt Sámi until it was destroyed in World War II, once stood alongside today's structure.

**Departures** are daily from June to early September at 10.00 and 15.00 (790kr); there are departures at 18.00 and 21.00 for a minimum of four passengers. Book with Barents Safari at Fjellveien 28 (↘ 90 19 05 94; e *hhatle@online.no; www.barentssafari.no*).

## Kirkenes Snowhotel
Not to be outdone by Lapland's other icehotels, Kirkenes now has its very own **snowhotel**, which opens just before Christmas and operates until late April. Built just behind the museum complex beside the Førstevann lake, the hotel consists of a series of igloo-style rooms of snow and ice and a sauna. A room for two people costs 3,700kr and includes dinner, breakfast and sauna. Bookings can be made with Radius Kirkenes at Kongensgate 1 (↘ 78 97 05 40; e *info@radius-kirkenes.com; www.radius-kirkenes.com*) at the Rica Arctic hotel. While this snowhotel compares favourably with all the other spinoffs of the Jukkasjärvi original, Kirkenes is at a disadvantage in terms of attracting visitors because it is so far away. If you are here though in connection with a Hurtigruten cruise, it is certainly worth calling by for a look (if not spending the night here); it is open to day visitors 11.00–14.00.

## GETTING TO RUSSIA: KIRKENES TO MURMANSK
Given the bureaucratic hoops you have to jump through to visit Russia, it is easier (and much cheaper) to arrange a **Russian visa** before you leave your home country. However, if you decide at the last minute you want to go to Russia, it is possible to get a visa in Kirkenes from the **Russian Consulate**, which operates a same-day service – for an extra fee of 800kr (there's an additional fee for non-Norwegian passport holders). Although you can apply in person, it is probably best to go through an **agent** such as Pasvik Travel, which can then fix up a bus ticket to Murmansk (and accommodation if

required) all at the same time. Visa prices depend on how long you want to stay in Russia: a three-day visa, for example, costs 675kr if applied for at least 16 days before departure. Express fees of up to 800kr are levied for applications lodged within this period.

## Getting a Russian visa

**Russian Consulate** Rådhusplassen 2; ✆ 78 99 37 37; e genkons@online.no; www.kirkenes.rusembassy.org

**Pasvikturist** Doktor Wessels gate 9; ✆ 78 99 50 80; e firmapost@pasvikturist.no; www.pasvikturist.no

**Radius Kirkenes** Kongensgate 1 inside the Rica Arctic; ✆ 78 97 05 40; e info@radius-kirkenes.com; www.radius-kirkenes.com

**Via Travel** Kongensgate 1–3; ✆ 78 99 19 81; www.ferieverden.no/kirkenes

**Visumformidlingen** Fjellveien 44; ✆ 78 99 11 81; e mathed-p@online.no; www.visumformidlingen.no

**Buses and flights to Murmansk** There are daily **buses** between Kirkenes and Murmansk. Leaving from outside the Europris store in the town centre, a bus leaves every day at 15.00, arriving in Murmansk five hours later after travelling via Nikel. Another bus departs from outside the Rica Arctic hotel at 14.00 (*Mon–Fri*), 15.00 (*Sat*) and 16.00 (*Sun*). A single ticket costs 300kr. For the return journey, the buses leave from the Norwegian Consulate in Murmansk at 07.00 (*daily*) and at noon (*Sun only*) from the Polyarnye Zory hotel. If you leave for Murmansk from Kirkenes, it is possible to return to Finnish Lapland by catching a return bus from Murmansk to Ivalo, or, more adventurously, taking a Russian train south to Kandalaksha on the White Sea and, from there, a bus to Kemijärvi in Finland which travels via Salla (see page 120). As we went to press, a new **flight** operarted by Widerøe (*www.wideroe.no*) was set to start between Kirkenes and Murmansk. See the airline's website for the latest information or ask at the tourist office.

**MOVING ON FROM KIRKENES** In addition to the buses to Murmansk mentioned above, a **bus** leaves from outside the Kirkenes Senter shopping complex at 08.05 (*Mon, Wed, Fri & Sun*) for **Karasjok**, arriving at 22.00. At approximately 11.00 it passes the bridge across the River Tana to **Utsjoki** in Finland. The bus pulls into the layby beside the bridge, still on the Norwegian side of the border, rather than crossing the bridge and driving into Finland. By alighting here you can walk over the bridge yourself and pick up a daily Finnish bus south at 12.05 to Inari and Ivalo; remember that Finland is one hour ahead of Norway. Annoyingly, you will probably arrive too late to make the connection in Utsjoki the same day. From Kirkenes it is 324km to Karasjok and 211km to Utsjoki, from where it is a further 165km to Ivalo.

*Reindeer*

# Appendix I

## LANGUAGE

Lapland has four official languages: Finnish, Norwegian, Sámi and Swedish. However, Sámi is not widely spoken, known by just 17,000 people of Lapland's 900,000 strong population. Other than road signs in Sámi, you're unlikely to come into contact with the language and we have therefore excluded it from the vocabulary lists below. All Sámi are bilingual and many also speak English; there's more information about Sámi in the sections *People* (page 13–14) and *Language* (pages 13–14 and 166–7).

**NORWEGIAN AND SWEDISH** The Germanic languages Norwegian and Swedish are mutually comprehensible. Thanks to their common history through Old Norse, the languages have not greatly diverged from each other and share a common word base and grammar. Anyone with a knowledge of German should recognise a whole host of words. With a little practice English mother-tongue speakers should also be able to pick out a number of similarities: for example, *båten sprang läck och sjönk till botten* means 'the boat sprang a leak and sank to the bottom', and *han har en skruv lös* means 'he's got a screw loose'. The task is easier for speakers of northern English or Scottish dialects who will spot even more familiar words: *slänga ut* ('sling out'), *flytta* ('flit') and *leka* (Yorkshire dialect 'lake' meaning 'play') are just three examples. English is widely spoken and understood in Norwegian and Swedish Lapland.

**Pronunciation** Pronunciation in Swedish and Norwegian is tricky. Both languages are tonal and getting the tone wrong can change the meaning of a word. For example, Swedish *femton*, with stress on *fem-*, means 'fifteen', with equal stress as *fem ton* it means 'five tons'. The resulting up and down rhythm produces the hurdy-gurdy sounds you're no doubt familiar with. Although it takes considerable practice to get the tones right, native speakers will usually understand what you're trying to say. In both languages vowels are normally long when followed by a single consonant, short when a double consonant follows. Unusual sounds are highlighted below.

| Letter | English equivalent |
| --- | --- |
| Ä | like English 'eh' |
| Å | like English 'oh' |
| EI, EJ | like English 'ay' |
| J, DJ, GJ, HJ, LJ | as English 'y' |
| G (before e, i, y, ä, ö) | as English 'y' |
| HV (Nor) | as English 'v' |
| K (before e, i, j, ö) | similar to English 'sh' |
| Ø (Nor) Ö (Swe) | like English 'err' |
| RS | as English 'sh' |
| S | always 's', never 'z' |
| SJ, SKJ, STJ | similar to English 'sh' |
| TJ | similar to English 'sh' |

**FINNISH** Finnish is quite different from Swedish and Norwegian. It is not related to either, nor, indeed, to many other languages in Europe. Part of the Finno-Ugric (as opposed to Indo-European) language group, its closest relatives are Sámi, Estonian and, much more distantly, Hungarian. As a result there are very few words you will recognise. Take, for example, *pysähtyy vain matkustajien ottamista varten*, which means 'boarding passengers only'. See what I mean. Its grammatical structure is the stuff of nightmares with 15 cases alone to grapple with. Instead of prepositions, Finnish employs a complex system of suffixes – something which is further complicated by obligatory vowel harmony. Despite that, it's worth learning a few words of Finnish since English is not widely spoken in Finnish Lapland and you'll make things considerably easier for yourself. However, beyond the most simple of phrases, you will need a lifetime to make any real inroads.

**Pronunciation** In Finnish, words are pronounced exactly as they are written with the stress falling on the first syllable. In the case of a compound noun, stress falls on each part of the word. Double consonants are both pronounced and double vowels lengthen the sound accordingly. Unusual sounds are highlighted below.

| Letter | English equivalent |
|---|---|
| Ä | like English 'eh' |
| Å | like English 'oh' |
| J | as English 'y' |
| Ö | like English 'err' |
| S | always 's', never 'z' |
| U | like English 'oo' |
| Y | as in French 'eu' |

## ESSENTIAL VOCABULARY

### BASICS

| English | Finnish | Norwegian | Swedish |
|---|---|---|---|
| Good morning | *huomenta* | *god morgen* | *godmorgon* |
| Good afternoon | *päivää* | *goddag* | *goddag* |
| Good evening | *hyvää iltaa* | *god kveld* | *god afton* |
| Hello | *moi* | *hei* | *hej* |
| Goodbye | *hei hei* | *adjø* | *hejdå* |
| My name is | *minun nimi on* | *jeg heter* | *jag heter* |
| I am from | *olen ... (-sta)* | *jeg er fra* | *jag kommer från* |
| England | *Englannista* | *England* | *England* |
| America | *Amerikasta* | *Amerika* | *Amerika* |
| Australia | *Australiasta* | *Australia* | *Australien* |
| How are you? | *mitä kuuluu* | *hvordan har du det?* | *hur går det?* |
| Pleased to meet you | *hauska tavata* | *hyggelig å treffe deg* | *trevligt att träffas* |
| Thank you | *kiitos* | *takk* | *tack* |
| Cheers | *kippis* | *skål* | *skål* |
| Yes | *kyllä* | *ja* | *ja* |
| No | *ei* | *nei* | *nej* |
| I don't understand | *en ymmärrä* | *jeg forstår ikke* | *jag förstår inte* |
| Do you speak English? | *puhutko englantia?* | *snakker du engelsk?* | *talar du engelska?* |

### QUESTIONS

| How? | *miten?* | *hvordan?* | *hur?* |
|---|---|---|---|
| What? | *mikä?* | *hva?* | *vad?* |
| Where? | *missä?* | *hvor?* | *var?* |

| Which? | kumpi? | hvilken? | vilken? |
|---|---|---|---|
| When? | million? | når? | när? |
| Who? | kuka? | hvem? | vem? |
| How much? | paljonko? | hvor mye? | hur mycket? |

## NUMBERS

| | | | |
|---|---|---|---|
| 1 | yksi | en | xett |
| 2 | kaksi | to | två |
| 3 | kolme | tre | tre |
| 4 | neljä | fire | fyra |
| 5 | viisi | fem | fem |
| 6 | kuusi | seks | sex |
| 7 | seitsemän | sju | sju |
| 8 | kahdeksan | åtte | åtta |
| 9 | yhdeksän | ni | nio |
| 10 | kymmenen | ti | tio |
| 11 | yksitoista | elleve | elva |
| 12 | kaksitoista | tolv | tolv |
| 13 | kolmetoista | tretten | tretton |
| 14 | neljätoista | fjorten | fjorton |
| 15 | viisitoista | femten | femton |
| 16 | kuusitoista | seksten | sexton |
| 17 | seitsemäntoista | sytten | sjutton |
| 18 | kahdeksantoista | atten | arton |
| 19 | yhdeksäntoista | nitten | nitton |
| 20 | kaksikymmentä | tjue | tjugo |
| 21 | kaksikymmentäykri | tjueen | tjugoett |
| 30 | kolmekymmentä | tretti | trettio |
| 40 | neljäkymmentä | førti | fyrtio |
| 50 | viisikymmentä | femti | femtio |
| 60 | kuusikymmentä | seksti | sextio |
| 70 | seitsemänkymmentä | sytti | sjuttio |
| 80 | kahdeksankymmentä | åtti | åttio |
| 90 | yhdeksänkymmentä | nitti | nittio |
| 100 | sata | hundre | hundra |
| 101 | satayksi | hundre og en | hundraett |
| 1000 | tuhat | tusen | tusen |

## TIME

| What time is it? | mitä kello on? | hva er klokka? | hur mycket är klockan? |
|---|---|---|---|
| It's... | kello on... | klokka er... | hon är... |
| Today | tänään | i dag | idag |
| Tomorrow | huomenna | i morgen | imorgon |
| Yesterday | eilen | igår | igår |
| In the morning | aamulla | om morgonen | om morgonen |
| In the afternoon | iltapäivällä | om eftermiddagen | om eftermiddagen |

## DAYS

| Monday | maanantai | mandag | måndag |
|---|---|---|---|
| Tuesday | tiistai | tirsdag | tisdag |
| Wednesday | keskiviikko | onsdag | onsdag |
| Thursday | torstai | torsdag | torsdag |
| Friday | perjantai | fredag | fredag |

A I

| Saturday | lauantai | lørdag | lördag |
|---|---|---|---|
| Sunday | sunnuntai | søndag | söndag |

## MONTHS

| | | | |
|---|---|---|---|
| Janaury | tammikuu | januar | januari |
| February | helmikuu | februar | februari |
| March | maaliskuu | mars | mars |
| April | huhtikuu | april | april |
| May | toukokuu | mai | maj |
| June | kesäkuu | juni | juni |
| July | heinäkuu | juli | juli |
| August | elokuu | august | augusti |
| September | syyskuu | september | september |
| October | lokakuu | oktober | oktober |
| November | marraskuu | november | november |
| December | joulukuu | desember | december |

## GETTING AROUND AND PUBLIC TRANSPORT

| | | | |
|---|---|---|---|
| I'd like... | sannko | jeg vil gjerne ha | kan jag få |
| A one-way ticket | menolipun | et enkelt billett | en enkel biljett |
| A return ticket | meno- ja luulipun | et tur-retur | en tur och retur |
| When does it leave? | milloin lähtee? | når går den/det? | när åker den/det |
| Timetable | aikataulu | tidsplan | tidtabell |
| Bus station | linja-autoasema | rutebilstasjon | busstation |
| Train station | rautatieasema | jernbanestasjon | järnvägsstation |
| Train | juna | tog | tåg |

## SIGNS

| | | | |
|---|---|---|---|
| Entrance | sisään | inngang | ingång |
| Exit | ulos | utgang | utgång |
| Gentlemen | miehet/miehille | herrer | herrar |
| Ladies | naiset/naisille | damer | damer |
| Open | avoinna | åpent | öppet |
| Closed | siljettu | stengt | stängt |
| Push | työnnä | trykk | tryck |
| Pull | vedä | trekk | drag |
| Arrival | saapuvat | ankomst | ankommende |
| Departure | Lähtevät | avgang | avgående |

## ACCOMMODATION

Single room
Finnish yhden hengen huoneen
Norwegian et enkeltrom
Swedish ett enkelrum

Double room
Finnish kahden hengen huoneen
Norwegian et dobbeltrom
Swedish ett dubbelrum

Share a dorm
Finnish makuusalin sänkypaikka
Norwegian ligge på sovesalen
Swedish bo i sovsal

# FOOD

| I am a vegetarian | Finnish *olen kasvissyöjä* |
| | Norwegian *jeg er vegetarianer* |
| | Swedish *jag är vegetarian* |
| The bill, please | Finnish *lasku, kiitos* |
| | Norwegian *regningen, takk* |
| | Swedish *notan, tack* |

## Basics

| Bread | *leipä* | *brød* | *bröd* |
|---|---|---|---|
| Butter | *voi* | *smør* | *smör* |
| Cheese | *juusto* | *ost* | *ost* |
| Salt | *suola* | *salt* | *salt* |
| Pepper | *pippuri* | *pepper* | *peppar* |
| Sugar | *sokeri* | *sukker* | *socker* |

## Fruit

| Apple | *omena* | *eple* | *äpple* |
|---|---|---|---|
| Banana | *banaani* | *banan* | *banan* |
| Orange | *appelsiini* | *appelsin* | *appelsin* |
| Pear | *päärynä* | *pære* | *päron* |

## Vegetables

| Carrot | *porkkana* | *gulrot* | *morot* |
|---|---|---|---|
| Garlic | *kynsilaukka* | *hvitløk* | *vitlök* |
| Onion | *sipuli* | *løk* | *lök* |
| Mushroom | *sieni* | *sopp* | *svamp* |
| Potato | *peruna* | *potet* | *potatis* |

## Fish

| Salmon | *lohi* | *laks* | *lax* |
|---|---|---|---|
| Arctic char | *pikkunieriä* | *røye* | *röding* |
| Herring | *silli* | *sild* | *sill* |
| Plaice | *punakampela* | *rødspætte* | *rödspätta* |
| Tuna | *tonnikala* | *tunfisk* | *tonfisk* |

## Meat

| Beef | *nauta* | *okse* | *biff* |
|---|---|---|---|
| Chicken | *kana* | *kylling* | *kyckling* |
| Pork | *porsas* | *svinekjøtt* | *fläsk* |
| Steak | *pihvi* | *stek* | *stek* |
| Reindeer | *poron* | *rein* | *ren* |
| Elk | *hirvi* | *elg* | *älg* |

## Drinks

| Beer | *olut* | *øl* | *öl* |
|---|---|---|---|
| Coffee | *kahvi* | *kaffe* | *kaffe* |
| Tea | *tee* | *te* | *te* |
| Juice | *tuoremehu* | *juice* | *juice* |
| Milk | *maito* | *melk* | *mjölk* |
| Water | *vesi* | *vann* | *vatn* |
| Wine | *viini* | *vin* | *vin* |
| Red wine | *punaviini* | *rødvin* | *rödvin* |
| White wine | *valkoviini* | *hvitvin* | *vitvin* |

AI

# Appendix 2

## GLOSSARY OF FINNISH, NORWEGIAN, SÁMI AND SWEDISH TERMS

| | |
|---|---|
| *áhpi* (Sámi) | marsh |
| *backe* (Nor, Swe) | hill |
| *berg* (Nor, Swe) | mountain |
| *boatka* (Sámi) | mountain pass |
| *bro/bru* (Nor, Swe) | bridge |
| *dal* (Nor, Swe) | valley |
| *duottar* (Sámi) | low-lying mountains |
| *fors/foss* (Nor, Swe) | waterfall |
| *järvi* (Fin) | lake |
| *jávri* (Sámi) | lake |
| *joki* (Fin) | river |
| *kåta* (Swe) | wooden teepee |
| *lávvu* (Sámi) | turf hut |
| *gákti* (Sámi) | traditional dress |
| *gieva* (Sámi) | bog |
| *øy* (Nor) | island |
| *saari* (Fin) | island |
| *sjö* (Swe) | lake |
| *skog* (Nor, Swe) | forest |
| *tunturi* (Fin) | rounded hill |
| *vaara* (Sámi) | hill |
| *vággi* (Sámi) | broad mountain valley |

Incidentally, *duottar* is the only Sámi loanword in English. Having passed via Russian into English, *duottar* is the origin of the English word 'tundra'. It is cognate with the Finnish word *tunturi*, 'rounded fell'.

**GLOSSARY OF SÁMI REINDEER TERMS** The Sámi language has hundreds of words relating to reindeer and reindeer husbandry, clearly showing the importance of the animal to the Sámi people. Some of the most enlightening are listed below.

| Sámi | English |
|---|---|
| *áldu* | reindeer in its third winter |
| *barfi* | reindeer with antlers with many branches |
| *biikasággi* | reindeer with vertical horns |
| *čaločoarvi* | reindeer with skin peeling off its antlers |
| *čearpmat* | reindeer in its first winter |
| *čora* | small reindeer herd |
| *čuoivvat* | reindeer with white muzzle or sides |

| | |
|---|---|
| *dápmat* | taming a reindeer |
| *gabba* | completely white reindeer |
| *heargi* | castrated reindeer that pulls sleighs |
| *jieva* | white reindeer |
| *luosttat* | reindeer with white flanks |
| *muzet* | black reindeer |
| *nálat* | reindeer with its antlers cut off |
| *nulpu* | reindeer without antlers |
| *ráidu* | reindeer caravan |
| *rávži* | sick reindeer |
| *rotnu* | reindeer that has failed to calf |
| *ruksesmiessi* | reindeer calf while still red |
| *ruovgat* | reindeer grunting noise |
| *sađđat* | reindeer panting noise |
| *siida* | reindeer village or mountain camp |
| *sivlá* | reindeer corral |
| *spágat* | reindeer packsaddle |
| *stáinnat* | barren female reindeer |
| *váibbat* | exhausted, worn out reindeer |
| *vuonjal* | reindeer in its second winter |

# Appendix 3

## FURTHER INFORMATION

**BOOKS** English-language books on Lapland are remarkably scant. The books listed below are the pick of a meagre crop.

Acerbi, Giuseppe *Travels through Sweden, Finland and Lapland to the North Cape in the years 1798 and 1799*, Adamant Media Corporation, 2001. A truly fabulous account of a trip to the North Cape by an intrepid Italian traveller and his encounters with the Sámi.

Beach, Hugh *A Year in Lapland*, University of Washington Press, 2001. A fascinating account of an American student living with the Sámi of Jokkmokk in the 1980s.

Bryson, Bill *Neither Here Nor There*, Black Swan, 1998. Beginning his epic journey across Europe from Lapland, Bryson sets out from Hammerfest and has some rather terse things to say about it.

Ekman, Kerstin *Under the Snow*, Vintage, 1997. The death of a teacher in a small village in Swedish Lapland polarises the community. A novel by one of Sweden's leading authors, which brings the dramatic landscapes of Lapland to life on the page.

Mann, Chris *Hitler's Arctic War: The Wehrmacht in Lapland, Norway & Finland 1940-1945*, Thomas Dunne Books, 2003. The true extent of the devastation caused by Hitler's scorched earth policy comes clear in this gripping account of World War II.

Niemi, Mikael *Popular Music*, Harper Perennial, 2004. The enchanting tale of two boys growing up in Pajala in Swedish Lapland during the 1960s and 1970s.

Ratcliffe, Derek *Lapland: a Natural History*, Poyser, 2005. A rare and wonderfully detailed account about the flora and fauna of Lapland by an author whose passion for the region shines through.

Seurujärvi, Irja *The Saami: a Cultural Encyclopaedia*, Suomalaisen Kirjallisuuden Seura, 2005. The leading authority on all aspects of Sámi life and culture. A tremendous resource and quite unique in its scope.

## Language

Ahlgren, Jennie, and Holmes, Philip *Colloquial Swedish*, Routledge, 2006. A thorough and accessible course to get your started in Swedish.

Bratveit, Kari et al. *Colloquial Norwegian*, Routledge, 1994. A good first course in Norwegian.

White, Leila *From Start to Finnish*, Finn Lectura, 2001. Undoubtedly the best beginners' course on the market. Available in Finland ISBN 951 792 105 5.

## WEBSITES
### General

**www.connex.se** Train times for Swedish Lapland

**www.eng.samer.se** Detailed information about Sweden's Sámi community

**www.hurtigruten.no** Times and prices for the Norwegian coastal ferry, Hurtigruten

**www.journey.fi** Finnish bus timetables in English

**www.laplandfinland.com** The definitive tourist site on Finnish Lapland

**www.nor-way.no** Bus times across northern Norway
**www.outdoors.fi** Masses of information about Finland's national parks
**www.santaclaus.fi** The big man's homepage including a webcam on the Arctic Circle
**www.sauna.fi** The definitive source of information on the Finnish sauna
**www.scandinavica.com/dir/webcams.htm** A list of webcams in Lapland
**www.scandinavica.com/sami** Summary about the Sámi and Lapland
**www.swedishlapland.com** Tourist information for Swedish Lapland
**www.visitnorthcape.com** Information about Finnmark and the North Cape

## Weather conditions
**www.fmi.fi/en** Finnish Meteorological Institute
**www.met.no** Norwegian Meteorological Institute
**www.smhi.se** Swedish Meteorological and Hydrological Institute

*Whale tail*

# WIN £100 CASH!
## READER QUESTIONNAIRE

**Send in your completed questionnaire for the chance to win
£100 cash in our regular draw**

All respondents may order a Bradt guide at half the UK retail price – please
complete the order form overleaf.

*(Entries may be posted or faxed to us, or scanned and emailed.)*

We are interested in getting feedback from our readers to help us plan future Bradt
guides. Please answer ALL the questions below and return the form to us in order
to qualify for an entry in our regular draw.

Have you used any other Bradt guides? If so, which titles? . . . . . . . . . . . . . . . . . .
. . . . . . . . . . . . . . . . . . . . . . . . . . . . . . . . . . . . . . . . . . . . . . . . . . . . . . . . . . . . . . . . .

What other publishers' travel guides do you use regularly? . . . . . . . . . . . . . . . . . .
. . . . . . . . . . . . . . . . . . . . . . . . . . . . . . . . . . . . . . . . . . . . . . . . . . . . . . . . . . . . . . . . .

Where did you buy this guidebook? . . . . . . . . . . . . . . . . . . . . . . . . . . . . . . . . . . . . .

What was the main purpose of your trip to Lapland (or for what other reason did
you read our guide)? eg: holiday/business/charity etc.. . . . . . . . . . . . . . . . . . . . . . .
. . . . . . . . . . . . . . . . . . . . . . . . . . . . . . . . . . . . . . . . . . . . . . . . . . . . . . . . . . . . . . . . .

What other destinations would you like to see covered by a Bradt guide?
. . . . . . . . . . . . . . . . . . . . . . . . . . . . . . . . . . . . . . . . . . . . . . . . . . . . . . . . . . . . . . . . .

Would you like to receive our catalogue/newsletters?

YES / NO (If yes, please complete details on reverse)

If yes – by post or email? . . . . . . . . . . . . . . . . . . . . . . . . . . . . . . . . . . . . . . . . . . . . .

Age (circle relevant category) 16–25     26–45     46–60     60+

Male/Female (delete as appropriate)

Home country . . . . . . . . . . . . . . . . . . . . . . . . . . . . . . . . . . . . . . . . . . . . . . . . . . . . .

Please send us any comments about our guide to Lapland or other Bradt Travel
Guides. . . . . . . . . . . . . . . . . . . . . . . . . . . . . . . . . . . . . . . . . . . . . . . . . . . . . . . . . . . .
. . . . . . . . . . . . . . . . . . . . . . . . . . . . . . . . . . . . . . . . . . . . . . . . . . . . . . . . . . . . . . . . .
. . . . . . . . . . . . . . . . . . . . . . . . . . . . . . . . . . . . . . . . . . . . . . . . . . . . . . . . . . . . . . . . .
. . . . . . . . . . . . . . . . . . . . . . . . . . . . . . . . . . . . . . . . . . . . . . . . . . . . . . . . . . . . . . . . .

## Bradt Travel Guides
23 High Street, Chalfont St Peter, Bucks SL9 9QE, UK
☎ +44 (0)1753 893444 f +44 (0)1753 892333
e info@bradtguides.com
www.bradtguides.com

# CLAIM YOUR HALF-PRICE BRADT GUIDE!

## Order Form

To order your half-price copy of a Bradt guide, and to enter our prize draw to win £100 (see overleaf), please fill in the order form below, complete the questionnaire overleaf, and send it to Bradt Travel Guides by post, fax or email.

Please send me one copy of the following guide at half the UK retail price

| Title | Retail price | Half price |
|---|---|---|
| . . . . . . . . . . . . . . . . . . . . . . . . . . . . . . . . . . . . . . . . . | . . . . . . . | . . . . . . . |

Please send the following additional guides at full UK retail price

| No | Title | Retail price | Total |
|---|---|---|---|
| . . . | . . . . . . . . . . . . . . . . . . . . . . . . . . . . . . . . . . . . . . . . . . . . . | . . . . . . . | . . . . . . . |
| . . . | . . . . . . . . . . . . . . . . . . . . . . . . . . . . . . . . . . . . . . . . . . . . . | . . . . . . . | . . . . . . . |
| . . . | . . . . . . . . . . . . . . . . . . . . . . . . . . . . . . . . . . . . . . . . . . . . . | . . . . . . . | . . . . . . . |

Sub total . . . . . . .

Post & packing . . . . . . .

(£1 per book UK; £2 per book Europe; £3 per book rest of world)

Total . . . . . . .

Name . . . . . . . . . . . . . . . . . . . . . . . . . . . . . . . . . . . . . . . . . . . . . . . .

Address . . . . . . . . . . . . . . . . . . . . . . . . . . . . . . . . . . . . . . . . . . . . . . .

Tel . . . . . . . . . . . . . . . . . . . . . . . . . . .       Email . . . . . . . . . . . . . . . . . . . . . . . . .

☐ I enclose a cheque for £ . . . . . . . . made payable to Bradt Travel Guides Ltd

☐ I would like to pay by credit card. Number: . . . . . . . . . . . . . . . . . . . . . . . .

   Expiry date: . . . / . . .       3-digit security code (on reverse of card) . . . . .

   Issue no (debit cards only) . . . . .

☐ Please add my name to your catalogue mailing list.

☐ I would be happy for you to use my name and comments in Bradt marketing material.

Send your order on this form, with the completed questionnaire, to:

**Bradt Travel Guides LAP1**
23 High Street, Chalfont St Peter, Bucks SL9 9QE
☎ +44 (0)1753 893444   f +44 (0)1753 892333
e info@bradtguides.com   www.bradtguides.com

# Bradt Travel Guides

## Africa

| | |
|---|---|
| Africa Overland | £15.99 |
| Algeria | £15.99 |
| Benin | £14.99 |
| Botswana: Okavango, Chobe, Northern Kalahari | £15.99 |
| Burkina Faso | £14.99 |
| Cape Verde Islands | £13.99 |
| Canary Islands | £13.95 |
| Cameroon | £13.95 |
| Congo | £14.99 |
| Eritrea | £15.99 |
| Ethiopia | £15.99 |
| Gabon, São Tomé, Príncipe | £13.95 |
| Gambia, The | £13.99 |
| Ghana | £15.99 |
| Johannesburg | £6.99 |
| Kenya | £14.95 |
| Madagascar | £15.99 |
| Malawi | £13.99 |
| Mali | £13.95 |
| Mauritius, Rodrigues & Réunion | £13.99 |
| Mozambique | £13.99 |
| Namibia | £15.99 |
| Niger | £14.99 |
| Nigeria | £15.99 |
| Rwanda | £14.99 |
| Seychelles | £14.99 |
| Sudan | £13.95 |
| Tanzania, Northern | £13.99 |
| Tanzania | £16.99 |
| Uganda | £15.99 |
| Zambia | £15.95 |
| Zanzibar | £12.99 |

## Britain and Europe

| | |
|---|---|
| Albania | £13.99 |
| Armenia, Nagorno Karabagh | £14.99 |
| Azores | £12.99 |
| Baltic Capitals: Tallinn, Riga, Vilnius, Kaliningrad | £12.99 |
| Belarus | £14.99 |
| Belgrade | £6.99 |
| Bosnia & Herzegovina | £13.99 |
| Bratislava | £6.99 |
| Budapest | £8.99 |
| Bulgaria | £13.99 |
| Cork | £6.99 |
| Croatia | £13.99 |
| Cyprus see North Cyprus | |

| | |
|---|---|
| Czech Republic | £13.99 |
| Dresden | £7.99 |
| Dubrovnik | £6.99 |
| Estonia | £13.99 |
| Faroe Islands | £13.95 |
| Georgia | £14.99 |
| Helsinki | £7.99 |
| Hungary | £14.99 |
| Iceland | £14.99 |
| Kiev | £7.95 |
| Kosovo | £14.99 |
| Krakow | £7.99 |
| Lapland | £13.99 |
| Latvia | £13.99 |
| Lille | £6.99 |
| Lithuania | £13.99 |
| Ljubljana | £7.99 |
| Macedonia | £14.99 |
| Montenegro | £13.99 |
| North Cyprus | £12.99 |
| Paris, Lille & Brussels | £11.95 |
| Riga | £6.95 |
| River Thames, In the Footsteps of the Famous | £10.95 |
| Serbia | £14.99 |
| Slovakia | £14.99 |
| Slovenia | £12.99 |
| Spitsbergen | £14.99 |
| Switzerland: Rail, Road, Lake | £13.99 |
| Tallinn | £6.99 |
| Ukraine | £14.99 |
| Vilnius | £6.99 |
| Zagreb | £6.99 |

## Middle East, Asia and Australasia

| | |
|---|---|
| China: Yunnan Province | £13.99 |
| Great Wall of China | £13.99 |
| Iran | £14.99 |
| Iraq | £14.95 |
| Iraq: Then & Now | £15.99 |
| Kyrgyzstan | £15.99 |
| Maldives | £13.99 |
| Mongolia | £14.95 |
| North Korea | £13.95 |
| Oman | £13.99 |
| Sri Lanka | £13.99 |
| Syria | £14.99 |
| Tibet | £13.99 |
| Turkmenistan | £14.99 |
| Yemen | £14.99 |

## The Americas and the Caribbean

| | |
|---|---|
| Amazon, The | £14.99 |
| Argentina | £15.99 |
| Bolivia | £14.99 |
| Cayman Islands | £12.95 |
| Colombia | £15.99 |
| Costa Rica | £13.99 |
| Chile | £16.95 |
| Dominica | £14.99 |
| Falkland Islands | £13.95 |
| Guyana | £14.99 |
| Panama | £13.95 |
| Peru & Bolivia: Backpacking and Trekking | £12.95 |
| St Helena | £14.99 |
| USA by Rail | £13.99 |

## Wildlife

| | |
|---|---|
| 100 Animals to See Before They Die | £16.99 |
| Antarctica: Guide to the Wildlife | £14.95 |
| Arctic: Guide to the Wildlife | £15.99 |
| Central & Eastern European Wildlife | £15.99 |
| Chinese Wildlife | £16.99 |
| East African Wildlife | £19.99 |
| Galápagos Wildlife | £15.99 |
| Madagascar Wildlife | £14.95 |
| Peruvian Wildlife | £15.99 |
| Southern African Wildlife | £18.95 |
| Sri Lankan Wildlife | £15.99 |

## Eccentric Guides

| | |
|---|---|
| Eccentric America | £13.95 |
| Eccentric Australia | £12.99 |
| Eccentric Britain | £13.99 |
| Eccentric California | £13.99 |
| Eccentric Cambridge | £6.99 |
| Eccentric Edinburgh | £5.95 |
| Eccentric France | £12.95 |
| Eccentric London | £13.99 |
| Eccentric Oxford | £5.95 |

## Others

| | |
|---|---|
| Your Child Abroad: A Travel Health Guide | £10.95 |
| Something Different for the Weekend | £12.99 |

# Index

# NOTES